# NAPOLEON

## LETTERS

# NAPOLEON'S LETTERS

*Selected, Translated and Edited by*
*J.M. Thompson,*
*Late Fellow of Magdalen College, Oxford*

This edition first published in Great Britain in 1998 by
PRION
32–34 Gordon House Road,
London NW5 1LP

A catalogue record of this book can be obtained
from the British Library.

ISBN 1-85375-269-X

Cover design by Bob Eames
Cover image courtesy of the Bridgeman Art Library
Printed and bound in Great Britain by Creative Print and Design, Ebbw
Vale, Wales

# INTRODUCTION

## I

Letters are, upon the whole, the most truthful as well as the most interesting of historical documents. Both to the spectator of life and to the student of history there is infinite value in the unconsidered confessions, the fireside confidences of public men. The orator, impressing himself upon his hearers, comes to believe what he is saying, and to fancy himself what they take him to be. The diarist, conferring with himself in a hall of mirrors, poses before his own image, and loses even that contact with reality which comes from being misunderstood. The letter-writer has an audience of one, not himself. If he is to impose his views, it must be by argument, not rhetoric; for pen and ink convey no gesture or intonation. If he is to confess, it must be (approximately, at least) the truth; for every word will be weighed by a friendly, or perhaps a hostile critic.

Not that all Napoleon's letters, or even many of them, are of a self-revealing kind. In youth he had few confidants; in middle age he had little to confide. In the stress of business and war he soon shed the idealism of the patriot, the fatalism of the revolutionary, and the romanticism of the lover. Any sense he may once have had of the beauty, the pathos, or even the humour of life was coarsened by flattery and success. He can still declare, exhort, abuse, persuade, even charm; but always in the interest of a policy, and to gain an end. He is wise, clear-sighted, eloquent, heroic; but hardly ever a human being in repose. Nevertheless, Napoleon's letters remain, beyond anything written about him, or anything else he wrote or said about himself, by far his finest portrait.

## II

When he was a young man, Napoleon wrote in the rapid and already confused hand of the relatively rare letters signed 'Buonaparte' or 'Bonaparte.' With growing age and work, his handwriting became so slovenly as to be wellnigh illegible; whilst his signature shortened from 'Napoleon' to 'Napol.', 'Nap.', 'Np.', and 'N.' Though he still wrote some private letters, and the more important military and diplomatic despatches, he habitually employed secretaries, and carried on the bulk of his correspondence by dictation.

Napoleon had three principal secretaries – Bourrienne (1797 – 1802), Méneval (1802 – 13), and Fain (1806 – 14). All of them wrote Memoirs, and there is no lack of evidence as to how their work was done. In a rather unkind conversation at St. Helena,[1] Napoleon said that Bourrienne wrote a good hand, and was active, tireless, and patriotic, but that he was a gambler, whose face lit up when his master dictated anything dealing with big figures: he was in fact dismissed for becoming involved in financial speculation. His work was done partly at the Luxembourg, and partly at the Tuileries. In his Memoirs he describes Napoleon's appearance, dress, and habits in minute detail. From breakfast at 10 to dinner at 5 every hour was taken up with reading petitions, correcting letters, giving interviews, or attending meetings. There were two tables in the study at the Tuileries – one for Napoleon near the fireplace, and another for Bourrienne near the window, through which, in summer, he could see the foliage of the chestnut trees in the garden. The chief ornament of the room was a portrait of Louis XIV, to the forehead of which some zealous Republican had fastened a tricolor cockade.

Méneval, who inherited Bourrienne's place in the Tuileries, tells us more about his workshop – Napoleon's table and chair of bronze gilt, finished with griffins' heads, and the green taffeta settee at which he does most of his work, screened from the full heat of the fire. Besides Louis XIV, there is now a bronze equestrian statuette of Frederick the Great. At Saint-Cloud, where they work in the summer, the study is a large room lined with books; the table is to Napoleon's own design, of hour-glass shape, so that two persons can easily converse across it, with space for books or papers at either end; and there are busts of Scipio, Caesar, and Hannibal, with a portrait of Charles XII of Sweden, subsequently displaced by Gustavus Adolphus. At first, Napoleon let

[1] Gourgaud, i. 565.

Méneval open his letters for him; later he did this for himself, answered some at once, put others aside to be answered later, and threw the rest on the floor; – 'he used to call *not answering* the best part of his work.' Sometimes Napoleon would work alone from 2 to 5 a.m., and begin to dictate at 7; sometimes, when there was a press of business, the secretary would be summoned at 4 or 5 a.m., and find Napoleon waiting for him in a white dressing-gown, with a Madras handkerchief round his head; striding up and down, with his hands behind his back, and now and again taking a pinch of snuff, for an hour or two he would dictate with amazing fluency and clearness, and so rapidly that it was necessary to invent a kind of short-hand, and to fill up gaps from memory or conjecture; for he hated to be interrupted, or to be asked to explain. Fortunately, Méneval, though 'a mere clerk, who could barely write correctly', had, his master admitted, a turn for imitating his style. When this early spell of dictation was over, Napoleon would call for sherbet and ices, perhaps have a hot bath, and go to bed again. After an hour's sleep, he would be ready for the real work of the day. On the first opportunity Méneval would turn his rough draft into fair copies, which Napoleon would look through, occasionally correct – but so efficient was the collaboration that out of a group of 2,000 letters scarcely 30 would need it – and add, with a flourish of an over-filled goose-quill, a signature that usually ended in a blot.

Fain's account is the same. Hour after hour he sits at the secretary's table, 'as silent as another piece of furniture, answering if the Emperor asks a question, writing if the Emperor says "write," and in the intervals addressing old letters or making fair copies of new ones: he must always be there.' Méneval had been there – almost unknown even to the Palace officials by sight – for eleven years, until he retired, worn out; Napoleon at St. Helena admitted that he had nearly killed him.[1] In Fain's time the routine was, first, to correct and sign papers dictated the previous day; then to deal with fresh correspondence; then to read Ministers' reports, the police news, the daily papers, and the contents of a red morocco case marked *Gazettes étrangères*, which really held private letters confiscated by the Post Office; and finally to

[1] Las Cases, *Mémorial*, 213.

deal with letters reserved for maturer consideration. Napoleon's dictation, says Fain, resembled a conversation, as though his correspondent were in the room; the faster he talked, the faster he walked to and fro; it was impossible to interrupt the imaginary *tête-à-tête*, or to break a thread of thought which had, from day to day, its dominant ideas, and its recurrent phrases.

When Napoleon went to the front, his secretaries went with him, and his habits of work. In the field, wherever he might be, the blue and white tent was pitched, and its two compartments arranged – one, the study, with its folding table and chairs, the other the bedroom. The papers and books were unpacked, the maps spread out; and, the moment fighting was over, dictation would begin. However far he was from Paris, the leather portfolios marked 'Despatches for the Emperor' must come and go every day, outstripping the fastest mail. Again, whether Napoleon travels in the yellow *voiture de poste*, or in the green-upholstered *berline,* Berthier is sure to be there; and as they jolt along, the Emperor goes through his order-books and muster-rolls, makes his decisions, and dictates his commands. At the first stopping-place, day or night, and the first moment of leisure, Berthier writes them out from his notes, and sends them off, with matchless method and accuracy.

Thus, in his study, in his carriage, or in his tent, Napoleon lost the *gaucherie* which prevented success as a public speaker, and became the master of a quick, vigorous, and lucid style, at once terse and rhetorical, argumentative and overbearing, which, in spite of its poverty of words and constructions, places him amongst the great letter-writers,

### III

How many letters did Napoleon write? The Committee of 1854 estimated them at 64,600, Taine at 70,000, Brotonne (in 1898) at 54,000: these figures would mean that he wrote from ten to twelve a day throughout the fifteen years of his rule. Sometimes this average was much exceeded. When Eugène became Viceroy of Italy in 1805 he received twenty-one letters – many of them long and important documents – in a single week; when, upon another occasion, Decrès incurred the Emperor's displeasure, he was punished by the arrival of five letters in one day. At other times, as when Napoleon was travelling or campaigning, the average fell off: and during the fortnight before and after his second marriage (April,1810), only eleven letters were despatched.[1]

So many documents have been destroyed (for instance, those lost or burnt during the retreat from Moscow), and so many may still be extant, but unpublished, that any estimate of the total number must be insecure. What here concerns us is that some 41,000 have been printed in the various books from which the present selection has been made.

## IV

Between 1815 and 1850 fragments of Napoleon's correspondence were published in the Memoirs to which the supporters of the Bourbon and Orleans regimes were so addicted. The establishment of the second Empire naturally brought a demand that the archives of the first should be unlocked. In 1854, Napoleon III set up a Commission 'to collect, classify, and publish the correspondence of our august predecessor, Napoleon I, concerning the various branches of public interest.' During the next ten years this Commission searched (pretty thoroughly) the French public records, secured many copies of letters preserved in foreign archives, and some few from private collections; as a result, fifteen volumes were published, containing 13,094 documents, dating from 1793 to August, 1807. But there were many omissions – duplicates of military orders, documents which the Commissioners regarded as 'devoid of interest,' and letters containing allusions that might be painful to persons or families still alive, or exaggerated expressions which (it was urged) Napoleon deliberately used to startle or to impress his correspondents, and which therefore did not fairly represent his mind.

Even so, Napoleon III was not satisfied that that correspondence, as edited by the Commission, was entirely to the credit of his 'august predecessor,' or entirely harmless to himself; and in 1864 he asked Prince Jérôme Napoleon to become chairman of a reconstituted Commission, and to supervise the remain-

---

[1] These numbers are taken from the Official Correspondence, and therefore may not be quite complete.

der of the work on more edifying lines. The Prince consented, on condition that two members of the old Commission should retire – Vaillant, because he differed from the new chairman on nearly every question, and Prosper Mérimée, because he was a sceptic and a cynic, who had (for instance) wanted to publish a letter in which Napoleon jokingly mentioned a rumour attributing to himself the paternity of Mme. \*\*\* 's baby. Saint-Beuve, another of the commissioners, was persuaded, rather unwillingly, to remain.

The principles on which publication was to proceed were soon made known. 'In general,' said the new editors, 'we have taken as our guide the simple idea that we were called to publish what the Emperor would have published, if, surveying himself, and anticipating the verdict of history, he had wanted to display his person and system to posterity.[1] 'On principle I pointed out,' wrote the Prince, 'that, as the heirs of Napoleon, we should in the first place be inspired by his own wishes, and depict him in the colours in which he himself would have desired to appear.' It was further decided that Napoleon's writings at St. Helena should be included in an additional volume, and that family and private letters should be published 'whenever they contained some characteristic point likely to bring out one of the manifold sides of the grand personality of the Emperor – so mighty and so varied in its aptitudes.'[2]

Such were the principles that ruled the publication of the thirty-two volumes of the Official Correspondence. The best commentary upon them is to be found in the work of later editors. Du Casse in 1887 and Lecestre in 1897 gleaned richly in the field abandoned by the discreet reapers. Lecestre, in particular, exposed the methods of the official editors. He showed that, out of a group of forty-two letters handed over from the Archives to Napoleon III personally in 1864, only ten had been returned; fifteen could be reconstructed from copies, but fifteen had completely disappeared, presumably in the burning of the Tuileries in 1871[3] He examined and disproved the claim of the first Commission to have printed the letters unaltered. Thus, in No.12921, Napoleon writes to his brother, Jérôme: – 'I thought you would be at Glogau. *It is the belles of Breslau who delay you, I can't*

[1] Report in Vol.16.
[2] Prince Napoleon, *Napoleon and his detractors*.
[3] Cf. J. B. Rye, 'The lost and the new letters of Napoleon' (*E.H.R.*, xiii, 473).

*help thinking'*: the editors omitted the words in italics. In
No.14764 he writes again to Jérôme, 'Cut down your extrava-
gances by half, *instead of getting money from the Treasury, on
account of the Civil List, as you have done this year'*: the itali-
cised words were omitted. In No. 15741, writing to Clarke, he
says, 'General Théodore Lameth is an abominable intriguer,
capable of causing disorder wherever he goes; dismiss him from
the army': all this was deleted. In a number of other passages,
personal reflexions were retained only by the expedient of saying that the names given by Napoleon were illegible. As for letters totally excluded by the editors, Lecestre found 165 of them
worth reprinting from the seven years covered by the first Commission: from the eight years covered by the second Commission
he took more than 1,000. In general character and interest these
documents are in no way inferior to those printed by the official
editors.

They include (1) letters to Fouché as Minister of Police,
ordering arrests or imprisonments, dealing with the censorship of
the press, and instructing him to use forged papers for propaganda
purposes, or to induce a prisoner to talk; (2) orders to generals for
the burning of villages, shooting of rebels, reprisals, and the taking of hostages; (3) some very frank letters to Napoleon's family,
especially his brother Louis; (4) some more in a similar strain to or
about the Pope; (5) suggestions of discreditable proceedings,
such as 'cooking' casualty lists and army returns, 'accidentally'
blowing up a fort evacuated under treaty, or using torture to
extract evidence from a spy – this last passage the editors had
omitted as 'illegible.'[1] These letters give a special character to
Lecestre's collection: it might be called 'The Indiscreet Letters of
Napoleon.'

Another curious collection of Addenda is supplied by
Pélissier's *Le registre de l'Ile d'Elbe*. Volume XXIX of the Official Correspondence includes 114 letters belonging to
Napoleon's residence at Elba: 33 of these, but no more, came
from a collection of 180 made by Napoleon himself, and still
available; the rest were omitted, apparently as unworthy of their
author. Yet few periods in Napoleon's career are more illuminat-

---

[1] See No.74 in the present collection.

ing than the months during which he was organising a tiny island and a skeleton navy on the scale of a world empire.

During the last thirty years the ransacking of archives, public and private, has produced some thousands more of Napoleonic letters, orders, decrees, notes, and other documents, mostly of a military origin. Some few sources, still untapped, are known or suspected to exist. But it is not likely that they will contribute anything to alter the general impression produced by the writings already published.

## V

The evidential value of Napoleon's letters has been generally recognised by historians and biographers of the period, and recent writers have followed the excellent practice of quoting them verbatim. But this has led to a danger against which English readers need to be warned. In some of these books the writers have not been over-scrupulous to preserve the original text and chronological context of their quotations; in one, at least, a translation from German into English, the quotations have apparently been re-translated from the German, with results that are sometimes quite misleading. Both sources of error may be illustrated from the English version of Emil Ludwig's *Napoleon*. On p. 39, part of a letter of 1795 is printed immediately after one of 1791, as though it belonged to the same circumstances; and on p.57 a summary of a letter is given as a quotation from it – both are common practices of the author. On p.102, Talleyrand is picturesquely described as 'reading on' from a letter dated September 19, 1797, into one dated August 16. On p. 204, the portfolio in which Méneval keeps Napoleon's papers and 'all the secret memoranda' becomes a 'map,' and makes nonsense of the passage.[1] On p. 236, – another picturesque scene – it is said that 'on his (Napoleon's) table, as he signs the letter to the Shah (dated March 30), lies a letter to George III (dated January 2).' On p.337, 'There are Popes in Hell as well as parsons,' becomes 'In the realm of shades there will be priests just as good as the Popes'; and the point is lost.[2] On p.462, one of the best things in a fine letter to Augereau is spoilt by importing a journalistic

[1] See No. 70
[2] See No. 173,

cliché, 'your seven-leagued boots.'[1] So it goes on, in one 'quotation' after another. The reader can never be sure that he has Napoleon's words, or even his meaning.

## VI

Here follows a list of the principal sources, beginning with the Official Correspondence of 1854, from which the letters in the present volume have been selected.

1854 – 69 *Correspondance de Napoléon I.* Publiée par ordre de l'Empereur Napoléon III. (32 vols. Paris.) Referred to as CORRESP.

1855 *Mémoires et Correspondance politiques et militaires du roi Joseph* (10 vols., Paris). [E.T. The confidential correspondence of Napoleon Bonaparte with his brother Joseph, 2 vols., 1855.] Referred to as JOSEPH.

1887 *Supplément à la Correspondance de Napoléon I^er.* Lettres curieuses omises par le comité de publication. Rectifications. Ed. Baron Du Casse. (Paris.) Referred to as DU CASSE.

1895 *Napoléon Inconnu.* Par F. Masson. (2 vols. Paris.) Referred to as MASSON.

1897 *Lettres inédites de Napoléon I^er*, An. VIII – 1815. Publiées par L. Lecestre. (2 vols. Paris.) [E.T. *New Letters of Napoleon I*, by Lady Mary Loyd, 1898.] Referred to as LECESTRE.

1897 *Le registre de l'île d'Elbe.* Lettres et ordres inédites de Napoléon I^er, 28 Mai, 1814 – 22 Février, 1815. Publiés par L. G. Pélissier. (Paris.) Referred to as PÉLISSIER.

1897 *Lettres, ordres et décrets de Napoléon I^er* en 1812 – 13 – 14 non inserées dans la 'Correspondance.' Recueillis et publiés par M. le vicomte de Grouchy. (Paris.)

1898 *Lettres inédites de Napoléon I^er* collationnées sur les textes et publiées par L. de Brotonne. (Paris.) Referred to as BROTONNE.i.

1903 *Dernières lettres inédites de Napoléon I^er* collationnées sur les textes et publiées par L. de Brotonne. (2 vols. Paris.) Referred to as BROTONNE ii.

1903 *Some letters of the first Napoleon.* (Fisher, English

---

[1] See No. 280

Historical Review 13/533.)

1908 *Supplément à la correspondance de Napoléon I*. L'Empereur et la Pologne. (Paris.)

1909 *Lettres de l'Empereur Napoléon* du I$^{er}$ août au 18 Octobre, 1813, non inserées dans la correspondance. Publiées par X. . . (Paris, Nancy.) Referred to as X.

1911 *En marge de la Correspondance de Napoléon I*. Pièces inédites concernant la Pologne, 1801 – 1815. Ed. A. Skalkowski. (Warsaw, Paris, Lwów.)

1911 – 12 Ordres et apostilles de Napoléon, 1799 – 1815. Ed. A. Chuquet. (4 vols. Paris.) Referred to as CHUQUET i.

1912 *Correspondance inédite de Napoléon I$^{er}$* conservée aux Archives de la Guerre. Publiée par E. Picard et L. Tuetey. (4 vols.) [E.T. *Unpublished Correspondence of Napoleon I*. 3 vols. New York.]

1913 – 19 *Inédits Napoléoniens*. Ed. A. Chuquet. (2 vols. Paris.) Referred to as CHUQUET ii.

1928 *Lettres de Napoléon à Joséphine*. Ed. L. Cerf. Referred to as CERF.

# VII

The selection of 300 documents out of 41,000 required drastic rules of rejection. Army bulletins, proclamations, orders, financial matters, and military despatches have been ruled out almost entirely. A few 'notes' have been admitted which it would have been a sin to leave out: the distinction between letter and note is in any case not absolute. With a few exceptions, letters not worth inserting in full have not been inserted at all. Where passages are omitted, there are dots: but if the dots are (as occasionally happens) Napoleon's own, this is explained in the note at the end of the letter. Generally speaking, the intention has been to pick out letters illustrating every side of Napoleon's character and career; the most important, the most interesting, and the most readable; those that a historian must have for use, and those that a general reader will like to have for pleasure. The selector can only hope that his taste is that of other admirers of Napoleon as a letter-writer.

The translator is conscious that he is not an exact French scholar, and that he may have missed the meaning of a word or phrase here and there. But he hopes that he has succeeded in catching (what is even more important) the moods which dictated Napoleon's changes of style, and some of the force and clearness of mind which he brought to his letter-writing, as to everything he touched.

The editor hopes that the short notes at the end of the letters will explain what needs to be explained, without worrying the reader with unnecessary information.

## NOTE

*The original spelling of names has been followed, except in the notes, where ordinary English usage has been adopted.*

## Napoleon Bonaparte: a chronology

**1769**    Born, son of Carlo and Letizia Buonaparte, minor nobleman and lawyer, in Ajaccio, Corsica. Corsica had long been owned by Genoa. In 1755 Paoli led an anti-Genoese rebellion, which led to Corsica being sold to France in 1769. This was at first resisted by the islanders, but in vain. Paoli left for exile in England and Buonaparte, his ardent supporter, nearly joined him, but stayed in Corsica, for the sake of his new family, and was reconciled to the gentler rule of France.

**1779**    Sent to military schools in France, to Brienne, thence to Paris, where because of his small stature, he became known as 'the little corporal.'

**1785**    Commissioned in the artillery.

**1789**    Outbreak of the French Revolution.

**1793**    War declared against Holland, Spain and Great Britain. Napoleon first comes to public attention at expulsion of British forces from Toulon. Promoted to Brigadier-General and sent to Italian front.

**1794**    Associated with the Jacobins he was briefly arrested during the Thermidorean 'reaction'. He remained out of favour.

**1795**    Placed in charge of the troops defending the Convention [parliament], he disperses the radical insurgents with 'a whiff of grapeshot', killing around 100. Given command of the army of the interior.

**1796**    In the war against the Holy Roman Empire [Austria and Germany etc.], Napoleon is sent to drive the Austrians from Italy.

**1796-7**    The Italian Campaign. Defeats the Austrians at Millesimo and Lodi, the Piedmontese at Mondovi. Marries Josephine de Beauharnais.

**1796**    Enters Milan, conquers Lombardy, sets up Lombard Republic.

**1797**    Siege of Mantua. Defeats Austrian attempts at relief at Castiglione, Bassano, Arcola and Rivoli. Mantua surrenders and Napoleon marches on Rome, signs Treaty of Tolentino with the Pope.

**1798**   Sails to Egypt with ultimate aim of destroying the British Empire by then taking India. Is accompanied by scientists and scholars. Defeats Mamelukes [rulers of Egypt] in Battle of the Pyramids but is isolated in Egypt when Royal Navy, under Nelson, destroys French fleet in Battle of the Nile. Meanwhile ruling Directory in Paris has lost Italy and is facing bankruptcy; Napoleon escapes Egypt, returns to Paris.

**1799**   French government established as consulate, with Napoleon as First Consul. Reorganises social and political administration of France under strong central control, establishes Bank of France, stabilises currency, reforms tax regime.

**1800**   Crosses Alps to regain Italy and defeats the Austrians at Marengo.

**1801-2**   Treaties with Britain and Austria end War of Second Coalition.

**1802**   Becomes First Consul for life, by popular vote.

**1804**   Crowned Emperor of the French and King of Italy.

**1804-10** The Code Napoleon established: new body of French civil law, which becomes very influential in Europe and beyond.

**1805**   Third coalition against France formed by Britain, Austria, Russia and Sweden. Defeats the Austrians at Ulm, occupies Vienna. Defeats combined Russian and Austrian forces at Austerlitz. Nelson's victory over French and Spanish fleets at Trafalgar convinces him that only economic warfare will defeat Britain and establishes the 'continental system.'

**1806**   Prussia joins the coalition, but is crushed at Jena. Napoleon enters Berlin. Dissolves the Holy Roman Empire.

**1807-8**   Defeats Prussia at Friedland. Treaty of Tilsit, Prussia becomes a vassal of France, losing half her territory. Napoleon is master of Europe. Reorganises Germany into the Confederation of the Rhine. Kingdoms of Holland, Westphalia, Italy and Naples created and handed to his family.

**1809** Austria reopens war but is defeated at Wagram. Papal States annexed to France. Pope excommunicates Napoleon, who imprisons him until he signs new Concordat.

**1810** Divorces Josephine as she bears him no son; marries Marie-Louise, daughter of Austrian Emperor, who gives birth to a son, the King of Rome.

**1812** After Tsar Alexander of Russia rejects continental system as ruinous to Russia, Napoleon forms La Grande Armée, the biggest army in European history, and invades Russia. Russian forces under Kutuzov fall back, destroying food resources. Battle of Borodino is indecisive, but expensive in lives lost. Napoleon enters Moscow which is deserted and is burnt. Retreats from Moscow, losing most of his army.

**1813** New coalition is formed of Russia, Britain, Prussia and Sweden. Napoleon forced to retreat after battle of Leipzig. Allies offer France peace if it returns to natural borders. Napoleon refuses.

**1814** Allies march on Paris and Napoleon is exiled to Elba.

**1815** Escapes and lands at Cannes. The restored monarch, Louis XVIII flees as France rallies round Napoleon, who enters Paris for the 'hundred days'. Defeated at Waterloo by allied army under the Duke of Wellington who had pushed French forces out of Spain and through France in the Peninsular War (1808-1814). Napoleon surrenders to British, hoping for asylum in England but is exiled to St. Helena where he dictates his memoirs.

**1821** Napoleon dies of cancer in exile.

**1840** Reburied at Les Invalides, Paris.

# 1

# THE BROTHERS

My Dear Uncle,

I write to inform you that my dear father passed through Brienne on his way to Paris. He was taking Mariana to Saint-Cyr, in an attempt to restore her health. He arrived here on the 21st, with Lucciano and the two young ladies whom you have seen. He left Lucciano here. He is 9 years old, and 3 feet, 4 inches, and 6 lines tall. He is in the sixth class for Latin, and is going to learn all the subjects in the curriculum. He shows plenty of talent and good intentions. It is to be hoped that he will turn out well. He is a big upstanding boy, quick and impulsive, and he is making a good start. He knows French well, and has forgotten all his Italian. He will add a message to you at the end of my letter. I shan't tell him what to say, so that you may see what he can do for himself. I hope he will write to you more often now than when he was at Autun.

I am pretty sure my brother Joseph has not written to you. How could you expect him to? He only writes two lines to my dear father, if he writes at all – though of course that's a different thing. All the same, he writes to me often enough. He is in Rhetoric, and could do better than any of us if he cared; for the Principal told my dear father that there wasn't a more talented Physicist, Rhetorician, or Philosopher in the whole school, or one who could produce a better composition. As for his future profession, he has put the Church first, as you know; and hitherto he has persisted in his resolution. Now he wants to enter the King's service. I think he is making a big mistake, for several reasons.

(1) First, as my dear father points out, he is not strong enough to face the dangers of war. His weak health doesn't allow him to bear the strain of foreign service, and so he contemplates military life merely in the form of garrison duty. Certainly my brother would make an excellent garrison officer: he is cheerful and good looking, the kind of boy who will come in for plenty of foolish flattery: in fact, he has the talent for getting on well in society. But what if it comes to fighting? – that is

what my dear father is doubtful about.

> *What warrior needs such empty gifts as these?*
> *How will they help him, if he be not brave?*
> *Were he with beauty as Adonis decked,*
> *Were he with Pindar's eloquence endowed,*
> *And yet lacked courage, he would be despised.*

(2) He has been educated for a clerical career. It is very late to change his mind. The Bishop of Autun would have presented him to a rich living, and he was certain of a bishopric. How that would have helped the family! The Bishop has done all he can to make him persevere, promising that he will never be sorry for it. It is no good: he sticks to his decision. If he has a real taste for the army – which, after all, is the best profession in the world – and if the Great Mover of human affairs gave him at birth (as he gave me) a definite turn for the military life, then I approve of his choice.

(3) He wants to go into the army. Very well, but into what branch of the service? The Marines? But he knows no mathematics; and it would take him two years to learn it. Besides, he hasn't the health for a life at sea. If it is to be the Engineers, he will need four or five years to learn what is necessary, and at the end of that time he will still be only an Engineer cadet: besides, I don't believe it is compatible with his frivolous character to spend the whole day at work. The same reason excludes the Artillery, except that he would only have to work 18 months to become a cadet, and another 18 to get his commission. No! that's not the sort of thing for him either. No doubt, then, he would like to enter the Infantry. Very good: I understand. He wants to do nothing all day but parade the town. Besides, what is a smart young infantry officer up to, three quarters of his time, except misconducting himself? And that is something that neither my dear father, nor you, nor my mother, nor my dear uncle the Archdeacon, can ever allow, especially as he has already shown some signs of extravagance and frivolity. We shall therefore make a last effort to get him to stick to the clerical career; and failing that, my dear father will take him back to Corsica with him, and keep an eye on him, and try to turn him into a lawyer.

I end by begging you to continue your kindness towards me. It will be my first duty and my earnest endeavour to make myself worthy of it.

I am, with profound respect,
Your very humble and very obedient servant and nephew,
NAPOLÉONE DI BUONAPARTE.


P. S. – Tear up this letter, my dear Uncle; but it is to be
hoped that, with his talents, and with the good feelings his education should have imparted to him, Joseph will take the right
course, and become the mainstay of our family. Do what you
can to make him see the advantages of this.

[MASSON, i, 79. Napoleon, aged 15, has been five years at the Military
School at Brienne. Lucciano is his younger brother Lucien; Mariana is his
younger sister Maria-Anna; the two young ladies are cousins, also bound for
Saint-Cyr; his dear uncle, the Archdeacon, is his father's uncle Lucien,
Archdeacon of Ajaccio.]


# 2

# HIS FATHER'S DEATH

## TO HIS MOTHER

PARIS, *MARCH* 28, 1785.

My Dear Mother,
Today, when time has somewhat calmed the first transports
of my grief, I hasten to assure you of the gratitude that all your
goodness to us inspires. Comfort yourself, mother dear; the situation requires it. We shall be doubly grateful and attentive to
you, and feel happy, if by our obedience we can recompense
you a little for the incalculable loss of your beloved husband. I
end, my dear mother – my grief prevents my saying more – by
begging you to calm your sorrow. My health is perfect, and it is
my daily prayer that Heaven may grant you the like. Present my
respects to Zia Gertrude, Minana Saveria, Minana Fesch, etc.
P.S. – On March 27th, at 7 p.m., the Queen of France gave
birth to a prince, named the Duke of Normandy.
Your very affectionate son,
NAPOLÉON DI BONAPARTE.

[MASSON, i, 121. Zia Gertrude is his mother's sister-in-law, Minana Fesch
her half-sister, and Minana Saveria a servant of the Bonaparte family.]

## 3

# THE CORSICAN PATRIOT

## TO GENERAL PAOLI

AUXONNE EN BOURGOGNE, *JUNE* 12, 1789.

General,

I was born when my country was dying. Thirty thousand Frenchmen disgorged upon our shores, and drowning the throne of Liberty in a sea of blood – such was the hateful spectacle that offended my infant eyes.

My cradle was surrounded, from the very day of my birth, by the cries of the dying, the groans of oppression, and the tears of despair.

You left our isle, and took with you every hope of happiness. To submit was to be enslaved. Our compatriots, weighed down by the triple chain of soldier, lawyer, and tax-collector, live despised – despised by those who wield the power of government. Is there crueller torment a man of sensibility can endure? Did the unhappy Peruvian, perishing by the sword of some greedy Spaniard, ever feel such agony as this?

Traitors to the country, vile souls corrupted by the love of base gain, have tried to justify themselves by scattering charges against the national government, and against yourself. Writers take these charges for the truth, and hand them down to posterity.

As I read them I am fired with zeal, and am resolved to scatter these mists, the offspring of ignorance. A study begun in France long ago, constant observations, and memories drawn from the portfolios of patriots, encourage me to hope for some success. I want to compare your government with that of the present day. I want to blacken with the pencil of infamy those who have betrayed our common cause. I want to call our rulers before the court of public opinion, to give chapter and verse for their oppression, to trace the secret history of their intrigues, and, if possible, to interest the virtuous minister who governs the State in the deplorable lot under which Corsica suffers so cruelly.

If I possessed the means to live in Paris, I should doubtless have found other ways of making our grievances heard; but the obligations of military service confine me to the sole resource of publicity. Private appeals would never reach their objective, or would be stifled by the clamours of vested interests, and end only in the ruin of their author.

I am still young, and may be rash to undertake this: but I shall be upheld by my love of truth, of my country, and of my compatriots, and by the enthusiasm I never cease to derive from the prospect of an improvement in our state. If you, General, condescend to approve of a work which bears so much upon yourself, and to encourage the efforts of a young man whose birth you witnessed, and whose family were always on the right side, I dare to predict a favourable issue.

I shall hope some time to be able to come to London, to express sentiments which owe their origin to you, and to converse with you about our country's misfortunes; but the distance is an obstacle. Perhaps a day will come when I shall be in a position to make the journey.

Whether my book is successful or not, I am aware that it will raise up against me the whole battalion of French officials who govern our island, and whom I am attacking. But what matter, if it is in my country's cause? I shall hear the thunder of ill-will; and if the bolt falls, I shall take refuge in my conscience, recall the rightness of my motives, and be encouraged to face the storm.

Allow me, General, to offer you the respects of my family, and – why should I not say it? – of my fellow-citizens. They remember with tears the time when they had hopes of freedom. My mother, Mme Letizia, asks me to recall to your memory the old days at Corte.

I am, General, with respect,

Your very humble and very obedient servant,

NAPOLÉON BUONAPARTE.

[MASSON, ii, 64. Pasquale Paoli, soldier and patriot, headed the rebellion which freed Corsica from the Genoese in 1755. Defeated by the French, who purchased the island in 1769, he had now been in exile for twenty years. Napoleon, after a year and three-quarters' holiday in Corsica, had rejoined the La Fère artillery regiment at Auxonne in May, 1788. Corte, forty miles north-east of Ajaccio in Corsica, had been the headquarters of the Paolist party during the French invasion, and Napoleon's father had attended the university there.]

# 4

# HISTORY OF CORSICA

## TO THE ABBÉ RAYNAL

1789 (?)

A friend of free men, you are interested in the fate of your beloved Corsica. The character of its people destined it for liberty: its central position, its many harbours, and its fertile soil pointed to a great commercial career. Why has it never had liberty or trade? Some inexplicable fate has always armed its neighbours against it. It has been the prey of their ambition, and the victim both of their policy and of their prejudices. You have seen Corsica in arms, shaking off the atrocious Government of Genoa, and recovering its independence: for a moment it is alive and happy, but it falls again, pursued by this resistless fate into unbearable degradation. Such are the scenes that succeed one another, without break, for 2,400 years; the same vicissitudes, the same misfortunes; but also the same resolution, the same audacity, the same courage. The Romans could annex the island only by making it their ally. Swarms of barbarians landed there: they overran the fields, they burned the houses; the Corsicans ceased to be land-owners, but they never ceased to be men; they became vagrants to preserve their freedom. Corsica trembled before the hydra of feudalism, but only to study it, and to destroy. If in slavery it hugged the chains of Rome, it soon broke them in the name of Nature. If at last it bowed its head beneath the Genoese nobles, if for 20 years sheer force kept it subject to the tyranny of Versailles, yet 40 years of stubborn warfare astonished Europe, and confounded its foes: and you, who prophesied the fall of Holland, and the regeneration of France, promised Corsica that its Government should be restored, and the unjust domination of France come to an end. When this intrepid people awoke from its slumber, and reminded itself that, whilst death is but a state of the soul, slavery is its very degradation, your prediction was fulfilled. Yes, fulfilled. In a moment – needless to ask why – all was changed. From the heart of a nation that had known no rulers but foreign tyrants, flashed the electric spark: an enlightened, generous, and powerful people remembered its old rights and its old strength: it willed to be free, and allowed us to share its freedom. It opened its bosom to us: we have now the same interests, the same cares: nothing separates us but the sea.

Amongst the paradoxes of the French Revolution, this is not the least. Those who once put us to death as rebels are now our protectors, and our feelings animate their minds. O Man, Man! how despicable in slavery! how great when fired with the love of freedom! Thy prejudices fade away, thy soul is uplifted, thy reason resumes its rule! Regenerate, thou art indeed the King of Nature!

How many vicissitudes, Sir, the nations undergo! Is it blind chance, or is it the foresight of a higher intelligence that directs their lot? Forgive me, God! But tyranny, oppression, and injustice devastate the world, and the world is thy work. Suffering and anxiety are the lot of the righteous, and the righteous is made in thine image!!! These thoughts are written upon every page of Corsican history; for it is the story of a constant struggle between a small people that wishes to be free and its neighbours who wish to oppress it. The former defends itself with an energy inspired by justice and the love of independence: the latter attack it by methods perfected by science and centuries of experience. Those have their mountains as a last resort: these their ships. Masters of the sea, they intercept the Corsican communications, retiring, returning, and varying their attacks at will. Thus the sea, which for all other nations has been the chief source of wealth and power; the sea, which gave rise to Tyre, Carthage, and Athens; the sea, which still supports England, Holland, and France at their climax of splendour and power – the sea was a source of misfortune to my country. Alas, that mankind is not more limited in the sublime capacity of perfection! It would not then, in its restless thirst for knowledge, and its constant use of observation, have chained to its fancy the fire, the ocean, and the air: it would have respected the barriers of nature: it would have wondered at the sheer physical size of these great arms of the ocean, without ever an idea that they might be crossed. Corsica would never have known there was a continent. O happy, happy ignorance!!

What a picture modern history presents! People killing each other for family quarrels, or murdering one another in the name of the Prime Mover of the universe; greedy and dishonest priests misleading them by the potent means of fear, imagination, and love of miracles! What can an enlightened reader find to interest him in this confused scene of affliction? But then a William Tell appears, and our hopes are centred in this avenger of the nations. The picture of America ravished by brigands, and by the power of the sword, inspires a detestation of the human race; but we share the labours of a Washington, we enjoy his triumphs, we follow his 2,000 leagues' march; for his cause is that of the human race. Very well: the history of Corsica too presents a series of truths of this kind. If these islanders did not lack swords, they lacked a fleet to profit by their victory, and to secure themselves against a second attack. Thus the years could not but pass in fighting. On one side a people strong in its steadfastness and sobriety: on the other powerful nations, enriched by the commerce of Europe – such are the actors who dispute the history of our island....

[MASSON, ii, I 27. The Abbé Raynal had been banished by Louis XV's government for writing his *Histoire philosophique et politique des...Européens dans les deux Indes*. He lived to protest against the work of the National Assembly in 1791.]

# 5

# BROTHER LOUIS

## TO JOSEPH BUONAPARTE

AUXONNE, *EASTER DAY, APRIL* 24, 1791.

. . . Louis has written 5 or 6 letters: Heaven only knows what nonsense he makes of them.

He is working hard, learning to write French. I am teaching him mathematics and geography. He is also reading history. He will do very well. All the women in the place are in love with him. He has caught the French manner in miniature: he is correct and easy in society: he comes into the room, bows gracefully, and makes conventional small-talk with the seriousness and poise of a man of thirty. It is not difficult to see that he will turn out the best of us four. True, none of us will have had such a good education.

Perhaps you won't find he makes very rapid progress in writing; but you must remember that hitherto his master has only taught him how to cut his pens, and write in capitals. You will be better pleased with his spelling. He is a delightful pupil, who takes a pleasure as well as a pride in his work, and is full of feeling. He has the application and the judgment of a man of forty. All he needs is knowledge. It's a pity, but I'm afraid there is to be no examination. In that case he will have to return to Corsica, and his education will be utterly *ruined*. . . .

[MASSON, ii, 203. At the end of another visit to Corsica (February, 1791) Napoleon had brought his brother Louis (aged 13) back with him to Auxonne.]

# 6

## THE YOUNG JACOBIN

### TO M. NAUDIN

VALENCE, *JULY* 27, 1791.

Happy about the future of my country, and the honour of my friend, I have no anxieties left but for the motherland. What moments are left me during the day, I would devote to conversing with you on that subject. To go to sleep with one's head full of great public questions, and one's heart stirred by companions whom one respects, and from whom one is sincerely sorry to have parted, is such pleasure as only great Epicureans can enjoy.

Will there be war? The question has been asked for months past. I have always said, no. Tell me what you think of my reasons.

Europe is divided between those sovereigns who rule over men, and those who rule over cattle or horses. The former thoroughly understand the Revolution. They are terrified of it. They would willingly make pecuniary sacrifices to destroy it. But they will never dare raise the mask, for fear the flame may set their own houses on fire. That is the history of England, Holland, etc.

As for the sovereigns who rule over horses, they cannot grasp the Constitution: they despise it. They think this chaos of incoherent ideas spells the ruin of France. Judging from what they say, you would suppose our brave patriots are going to cut each other's throats, purge the earth with their blood from the crimes committed against kings, and end by bowing their heads lower than ever beneath the mitred despot, the cloistered *fakir,* and (above all) the brigand whose weapon is a deed-box. Such sovereigns will make no move. They are waiting for the outbreak of civil war, which, according to themselves and their dull ministers, is sure to come.

This part of the country is full of zeal and enthusiasm. A fortnight ago a meeting consisting of 22 societies from the three Departments drew up a petition asking for the King to be brought to trial.

Give my kind regards to Mme Renaud and to M. and Mme Goy. At the dinner on July 14 I proposed the health of the patriots of Auxonne. This regiment is thoroughly sound – the men, the sergeants, and half the officers. There are vacancies for two captains. . . .

P.S. – The southern blood in my veins runs as swiftly as the Rhone. So forgive me, if you find my scrawling hand hard to read.

[MASSON, ii, 208. Napoleon was with his regiment at Valence during the summer and autumn of 1791. On June 21 the King fled from Paris, and was arrested at Varennes. On July 17 a petition for his deposition, and for the setting up of a new form of government, was presented for public signature on the Champ de Mars, and the petitioners were fired on by the National Guard. Naudin was war *commissaire* at Auxonne. The 'friend' in line 2 is Paoli.]

# 7

# PARIS IN REVOLUTION
## (I)

### TO JOSEPH BUONAPARTE

PARIS, *MAY* 29, 1792.

I reached Paris yesterday. At present I am staying at the same hotel as Pozzo di Borgo, Leonetti, and Peraldi, viz. Hôtel des Patriotes Hollandais, rue Royale. But it is too expensive there, so that I shall move to-day or tomorrow. I have only seen Pozzo di Borgo for a moment so far: we were formal, but friendly.

Paris is in a state of great commotion. It is crowded with foreigners, and there is a great deal of discontent. For the last three nights people have kept their lights burning. They have doubled the National Guard left at the Tuileries to protect the King. The troops of the royal Household are said to be of very bad material, and will be disbanded.

The news from the frontiers is the same as before. We shall

probably retire, and make it a defensive campaign. There is an enormous amount of desertion among the officers. The position is critical in every respect.

It is not true that the National Guardsmen who receive pay are to wear red facings: they are to wear white like the rest. I have seen more than twenty different battalions, and they all have white facings. . . .

Keep on close terms with General Paoli. He is everything, and can do everything. He will be all-important in a future that no one in the world can predict . . . .

I am going to the Assembly to-day for the first time. This Assembly doesn't enjoy the same reputation as the Constituent. It needs to, badly. . . .

[MASSON, ii, 387. Pozzo di Borgo (later in the Russian diplomatic service), Leonetti, and Peraldi are the Corsican deputies to the Legislative Assembly, which is within three months of its end. The dots represent the omission of personal messages only.]

## (2)

### TO JOSEPH BUONAPARTE

PARIS, *June 22,* 1792.

M. de Lafayette has written to the Assembly, attacking the Jacobins. It is a strong letter, and many people think it a forgery. M. de Lafayette, most of the officers in the army, all sound people, the ministers, and the Paris Department are on one side: the majority in the Assembly, the Jacobins, and the populace are on the other. The Jacobin attacks on Lafayette have passed all bounds: they describe him as a rascal, an assassin, and an object of pity. The Jacobins are lunatics, and have no common sense. The day before yesterday seven or eight thousand men armed with pikes, hatchets, swords, muskets, spits, and pointed stakes, marched to the Assembly to present a petition. From there they went on to the King's palace. The Tuileries Garden was closed, and protected by 15,000 National Guards. The mob battered down the doors, forced an entrance into the palace, mounted cannon against the King's apartments, rased four gates to the ground, and presented the King with two cockades – one white, and the other red, white and blue. They gave him the choice. 'Make up your mind,' they said, 'whether you will reign here, or at Coblentz.' The King showed up well.

He put on the *bonnet rouge*: so did the Queen and the Prince Royal. They gave the King a drink. They stayed in the palace four hours. This event has provided plenty of material for aristocratic harangues at the Feuillants' Club. None the less, it is unconstitutional, and sets a very dangerous precedent. It is certainly hard to guess what will become of the country under the present stress of affairs. ...

[MASSON, ii, 392. On June 16, Lafayette wrote from the front to the Assembly, attacking the Jacobins. On June 20 the people 'visited' the Tuileries, to force the King to withdraw his veto on two government measures. This is the scene Napoleon describes.]

# (3)

## TO LUCIEN BUONAPARTE

PARIS, *JULY 3*, 1792.

I am sending you the proposals of the Committee for Public Education: nothing has been decided yet, and the Assembly is not likely to deal with the question at such an inflammatory moment. Read it attentively, my dear Lucien, and profit by it: it is not a masterpiece, but it is a sound bit of work.

Sensible men think Lafayette's *démarche* necessary, yet a serious menace to public liberty. In times of revolution precedents become law; and the General has set a very dangerous one. The people, that is to say the lowest classes, are irritated, and there will undoubtedly be an outbreak – an outbreak of a kind likely to hasten the ruin of the Constitution.

The men at the head of affairs are a poor lot. One must admit, upon closer acquaintance, that the people are hardly worth all the trouble that is taken to merit their support. You know the history of Ajaccio. That of Paris is exactly the same, though perhaps people here are pettier, viler, more abusive, and more censorious. You have to look closely before you realize that enthusiasm is still enthusiasm, and that the French are an ancient and independent people. . . . Every individual is out for his own interests, and will forward them, if he can, by insult and outrage: intrigue is as underhand as ever. All this discourages ambition. Such is the complaint of those who are unhappy enough to hold important positions, especially when they could afford to refuse them. A quiet life, spent in the enjoyment of one's own tastes and of the affection of one's family – that, my dear friend, is the happiest choice, especially if one has an income of 4 – 5000 livres, and is between the ages of 25 and 40, when imagination torments one no longer, but is at rest. I send you my love, and advise moderation in all things. In short, if you want to live happily, you must agree with your neighbours.

[MASSON, ii, 396. Condorcet's Education Bill was presented on April 20 – 21. Lafayette followed up his letter of June 16 by a visit to the Jacobin Club on June 28. On August 10 the people invaded the Tuileries and the King was deposed. The dots represent a defective phrase in the text.]

# 8

# HEROICS

## TO MADAME PERMON (AND SALICETI)

PARIS, *JUNE 18,* 1795.

I have never let myself be thought a dupe; and you would think me so, if I did not tell you that I know Saliceti has been hidden in your house now for more than three weeks. Remember what I said to you. As long ago as the 1st prairial I was morally certain of it; now I am quite sure. You see, Saliceti, I could have returned evil for the evil you did me, and could have had my revenge; whereas the harm you did me was entirely unprovoked. Which of us is playing the hero now – you, or I? Yes, I might have had my revenge, but I chose not to. Perhaps you will say you are protected by your kind friend, Madame Permon. That is indeed a strong argument with me. But had you been isolated, unarmed, and proscribed, even so I should have held your life sacred. Go, then, and seek undisturbed for a refuge in which you can recover a more patriotic state of mind. I shall not say a word about you, now or ever. Repent, and (above all) appreciate my motives as they deserve; for they are noble and generous.

Madame Permon, my good wishes follow you and your child. You are both weak and unprotected. May Providence and the prayers of a friend accompany you! Be very careful, and never stay in large towns. In all friendship, goodbye!

[CORRESP., i, 40. In August 1794 Napoleon, involved in the fall of the Robespierrists, was imprisoned for a short time near Antibes. Saliceti, who played some part in his imprisonment, afterwards found himself proscribed, and took refuge with Mme Permon, a widow with two children, to whom Napoleon had made an unsuccessful offer of marriage.]

# 9

# BROTHER JOSEPH

## TO JOSEPH BUONAPARTE

PARIS *JUNE* 24, 1795.

I will do all I can to carry out your wife's commissions. Désirée is asking for a portrait of me: I will have one made. If she still wants it, let her have it; if not, keep it yourself. I needn't tell you, my dear friend, that, however fortune treats you, you have no better friend than myself, and none who is fonder of you, or who more sincerely desires your happiness. Life is an unsubstantial dream that soon fades away. If you are leaving home, and it is likely to be for some time, send me your portrait. We have lived so many years together, and in such close comradeship, that our two hearts have become one: you know better than anyone how devoted I am to you. I experience as I write these lines an emotion that has not often found a place in my life. I have a feeling that we shall not meet for a long time. I cannot go on. Goodbye, my dear friend, goodbye.

[CORRESP., i, 42. Julie and Désirée Clary were daughters of a rich silk merchant of Marseilles. Joseph married Julie in 1794. Napoleon and Désirée grew fond of one another, but nothing came of it. In 1798 she married Bernadotte, and in 1818 became Queen of Sweden.]

# 10

# PARIS LIFE

## TO JOSEPH BUONAPARTE

PARIS, *JULY* 12, 1795.

... Here in Paris, luxury, enjoyment, and the arts are resuming their sway in surprising fashion. Yesterday 'Phèdre' was put on at the Opera – a benefit performance for a retired actress. Though the seats cost three times as much as usual, the house was crowded out as early as 2 o'clock. Smart carriages and fashionably dressed people are seen about again: they have the air of waking up after a long dream, and forgetting that they ever ceased to display themselves. The book-shops are open again. There is a succession of lectures on history, chemistry, botany, astronomy, and so forth. The place is crammed with everything that can distract, and make life agreeable. No one is given time to think. Anyhow, who could be a pessimist in this mental workshop, this whirlwind of activity? Women are every-where – applauding the plays, reading in the book-shops, walk-ing in the Park. The lovely creatures even penetrate to the pro-fessor's study. Paris is the only place in the world where they deserve to steer the ship of state: the men are mad about them, think of nothing else, only live by them and for them. Give a woman six months in Paris, and she knows where her empire is, and what is her due.

[CORRESP., i, 44.]

# 11

# FATALISM

## TO JOSEPH BUONAPARTE

PARIS, *AUGUST* 12, 1795.

. . . Fesch seems to want to return to Corsica as soon as peace is declared. He is just what he always was – building cas-tles in the air, and writing me 6-page letters on some meticulous point of speculation: the present means no more to him than the past: the future is all in all.

Personally, I hardly care what happens to me. I watch life almost indifferently. My permanent state of mind is that of a soldier on the eve of battle: I have come to the conclusion that, since a chance meeting with death may end it all at any minute, it is stupid to worry about anything. Everything disposes me to face my destiny without flinching. At this rate, my friend, I shall end by not stepping out of the way of a passing carriage. As a reasonable man I am sometimes astonished at this attitude; but it is a natural tendency produced in me by the moral state of the country, and by the habit of running risks. . . .

[JOSEPH, i, 141. Joseph Fesch was Napoleon's mother's half-brother, by her mother's second marriage with Francis Fesch.]

## 12

## 'WHIFF OF GRAPE-SHOT'

### TO JOSEPH BUONAPARTE

PARIS, *OCTOBER* 6, 1795, 2 A.M.

At last it is all over. My first thought is to give you news of myself. The royalists, organised in Sections, were becoming more aggressive every day. The Convention gave orders that the Lepelletier Section should be disarmed. The troops sent to do this were repulsed. Menou, it was said, was a traitor. He was at once dismissed. The Convention appointed Barras to command the armed forces of the Government: the Committees chose me as second in command. We disposed our troops. The enemy attacked us at the Tuileries. We killed a large number of them. They killed 30 of our men, and wounded 60. We have disarmed the Sections, and all is quiet. As usual, I haven't had a scratch.

[CORRESP., i, 72. In the troubles culminating on the '13th vendémiaire' the Le Pelletier Section led the attack on the Convention and the 'Two-thirds Decree.' Paul Barras, afterwards the Director, was one of the Defence Committee of the Convention.]

## 13

## FIRST NIGHT

### TO JOSÉPHINE DE BEAUHARNAIS

PARIS, *DECEMBER,* 1795.

I awake all filled with you. Your image, and the intoxicating pleasures of last night, allow my senses no rest. Sweet and matchless Joséphine, how strangely you work upon my heart! Are you angry with me? are you unhappy? are you upset?. . . my soul is broken with grief, and my love for you forbids repose. But how can I rest any more, when I yield to the feeling that masters my inmost self, when I quaff from your lips and from your heart a scorching flame? Yes! One night has taught me how far your portrait falls short of yourself!

You start at midday: in three hours I shall see you again.

Till then, a thousand kisses, *mio dolce amor*: but give me none back, for they set my blood on fire.

[CERF, i. Joséphine Tascher de la Pagerie was left a widow with two children, Eugène and Hortense, by the execution of her husband, Alexandre de
Beauharnais, in 1794. Napoleon met her at Paris in 1795. They were married
on March 9, 1796.]

# 14

## JOSÉPHINE – SEPARATION

### TO CITIZENESS BONAPARTE

NICE, *MARCH.* 31, 1796.

Not a day passes without my loving you, not a night but I
hold you in my arms. I cannot drink a cup of tea without cursing the martial ambition that separates me from the soul of my
life. Whether I am buried in business, or leading my troops, or
inspecting the camps, my adorable Joséphine fills my mind,
takes up all my thoughts, and reigns alone in my heart. If I am
torn from you with the swiftness of the rushing Rhone, it is that
I may see you again the sooner. If I rise to work at midnight, it
is to put forward by a few days my darling's arrival. And yet, in
your letter of the 23rd, and again of the 26th ventôse, you call
me *vous! Vous* yourself! Wretch! How could you ever write
such a letter? How cold it is! And then, from the 23rd to the
26th, four days without a word. What were you doing, not to
write to your husband? . . . Yes, my dear, that *vous*, and those
four days, make me regret my previous complaisance. Curses
on whoever was the cause of it! May he suffer every pain that I
should, had I evidence and proof such as his. There are no such
torments in Hell! – neither Furies, nor serpents! *Vous! Vous*
indeed! what will it be in a fortnight's time? . . .My soul is sad;
my heart is in chains, and I imagine things that terrify me.... You
do not love me as you did; you will console yourself elsewhere.
One day you will love me no more; tell me so, then I shall at
least know how to deserve the misfortune . . . Good-bye, my
wife, my tormentor, my happiness, the hope and soul of my life,
whom I love, whom I fear, the source of feelings which make
me as gentle as Nature herself, and of impulses under which I
am as catastrophic as a thunderbolt. I do not ask you to love me
for ever, or to be faithful to me, but simply . . . to tell me the
truth, to be entirely frank with me. The day on which you say
to me 'I love you less,' will be the last of my love, or of my life.
Had I a heart so base as to love without return, I would tear it to
pieces with my teeth. Joséphine! Joséphine! Do you remember

what I have sometimes said to you – that Nature has made my soul resolute and strong, whilst yours she has constructed of lace and gauze? Do you love me no more? Forgive me, soul of my life. My mind is intent upon vast plans. My heart, utterly engrossed with you, has fears that make me miserable . . . . I am bored, because I cannot be saying 'Joséphine.' I am waiting for you to write.

Good-bye! Ah! If you love me less, it must be that you never loved me at all. Then were I indeed to be pitied.

BONAPARTE.

P.S. – The war, this year, is utterly different from what it was. I have given the army meat, bread, and forage. My armed cavalry will soon be on the march. I cannot tell you how the men trust me. You are my one anxiety, my only pleasure in life, and my only torment. I send a kiss to your children. You never mention them. Begad! if you did, your letters would be half as long again, and your early morning visitors would lose the pleasure of your company! O woman!!!

[CERF, 5. They have been parted less than three weeks. Napoleon is on his way to the Italian front. The dots are his own: nothing has been left out.]

# 15
# JOSÉPHINE, IN ABSENCE
## TO CITIZENESS BONAPARTE

PORT-MAURICE, April 3, 1796.

I have had all your letters, but none has affected me like the last. Darling, do you think what you are doing, when you write to me in such terms? Do you suppose my position is not so painful already, that you must pile regret upon regret, and reduce my soul to distraction? The way you write! The feelings you describe! They are flames that scorch my poor heart. Away from you, my one and only Joséphine, there is no pleasure in life: away from you, the world is a desert in which I am all alone, without even the solace of expressing my feelings. You have robbed me of more than my heart: all my thoughts are about you alone. Whenever I am bored and worried with business, whenever I am troubled as to how things will turn out, whenever I am disappointed with mankind, and feel inclined to curse the day I was born, I put my hand to my heart: there throbs your likeness; I have but to look at it, and my love is perfect happiness, and there is pleasure in every prospect but that of long absence from my beloved.

What art did you learn to captivate all my faculties, to absorb all my character into yourself? It is a devotion, dearest, which will end only with my life. 'He lived for Joséphine': there is my epitaph. I strive to be near you: I am nearly dead with desire for your presence. It is madness! I cannot realize that I am getting further and further away from you. So many regions and countries part us asunder! How long it will be before you read these characters, these imperfect utterances of a troubled heart of which you are queen! Ah! wife that I adore. I cannot tell what lot awaits me; only, that, if it keeps me any longer away from you, it will be insupportable, beyond what bravery can bear. There was a time when I prided myself on my courage; and sometimes, at the sight of misfortunes that fate might have in store for me, I would face in imagination unheard-of ills, without a frown, without a feeling of surprise. But nowadays the mere thought that my Joséphine may be unwell, or that she might be taken ill – above all the cruel possibility that she may not love me as she did, wounds my heart, arrests my blood, and makes me so sad and despondent that I am robbed even of the courage of anger and despair.

Once I would tell myself that to die without regret is to be safe from any harm the world can inflict; but now the thought of dying without the certainty of your love is like the torments of Hell, the very image of utter annihilation. I experience all the feelings of a drowning man.

My perfect comrade, whom fate has allotted to make life's painful journey at my side! The day when I lose your heart, Nature will lose for me all her warmth and vegetation. . . .I cannot go on, dearest: my soul is so sad, my mind over-burdened, my body tired out. Men bore me. I could hate them all; for they separate me from my love.

I am at Port-Maurice, near Oneille. I shall be at Albenga tomorrow. Both armies are on the move: we are trying to out-wit one another. May the cleverer man win. I like Beaulieu: he manoeuvres well: he is a better soldier than his predecessor. I shall beat him, I hope, and in the grand manner. Don't be worried about me. Love me as you love your eyes. No, that is not enough: love me as you love yourself – and not yourself only, but your thoughts, your mind, your life, your all. Darling, I'm raving, forgive me. Nature is a poor recompense for such feelings as mine, or for the man you love.

BONAPARTE.

Remember me very kindly to Barras, Sucy, and Mme Tallien: give Mme Château-Renard my kind regards. My love to Eugène and Hortense. Good-bye, good-bye. I am going to bed – alone: I shall sleep – without you by my side. Please let me go to sleep. Night after night I feel you in my arms: it is such a happy dream: but alas, it is not yourself!

[CERF, 7. Beaulieu is the Austrian General whom Napoleon defeated at Dego a week later. 'It is a devotion. . .' – the last word is illegible.]

## 16

## DEATH

### TO CITIZENESS BONAPARTE

ALBENGA, APRIL 5, 1796.

It is an hour after midnight. They bring me a letter. It is a sad one, and my soul is touched: for Chauvet is dead. He was our Q.M.G. You met him once or twice at Barras' house. I feel the need of some one to comfort me, dearest. My only consolation is in writing to you: the thought of you is the lode-star of my moral ideas: you are the confidant of all my troubles. What is the future? What is the past? What enchanted medium surrounds us, and hides from us the things we are most concerned to know? We live and move and die encompassed by miracles. Is it surprising that priests, astrologers, and charlatans have traded on this tendency, this strange weakness of ours, to parade our fancies, and to make them subservient to their own passions?

Chauvet is dead. He was fond of me. He rendered all-important services to the country. His last message was that he was starting to join me. And it is true. I can see his shade before me: it wanders among the combatants; it whistles through the air; his soul is in the battle-smoke – it is an omen of my destiny.

But it is foolish of me to mourn for a mere friend. Who knows but that I may have tears to shed for a loss that is irreparable? Write to me, soul of my life, by every post. I could not live otherwise.

I am very busy here. Beaulieu's army is on the move. We are in touch with one another. I am rather tired. I am on horseback every day.

Good-bye, good-bye, good-bye. I am going to bed, for I find comfort in sleep. It puts you by my side; I clasp you in my arms: but when I wake, alas! I find myself so far away from you.

Remember me to Barras, Tallien, and his wife.

[CERF, 10.]


# 17

## DIFFICULTIES OF A GENERAL
### TO DIRECTOR CARNOT

CAIRO, *APRIL* 16, 1796.

I enclose a letter which I have just received, and which will show you that there is no more hope of my getting that light artillery. If the company you assigned me had been allowed to start – it had passed Montargis a month ago – I shouldn't be in such a fix as I am. But that's the sort of thing that happens, under government by clerks. I can't see how it is possible for a company that I urgently asked for, and that you ordered to march, to be turned to the right – about, except by malice aforethought. No department could be more out of touch with its troops than the Artillery: it reckons upon regiments which simply do not exist.

Another request, my dear Director. Please order General Châteauneuf-Randon not to hold back the troops assigned to this army. The enemy are a good deal stronger than we thought; they fight very well, and have much more cavalry and artillery than I have. In spite of this, I am hoping to account for some of them to-day: I am making a feint march, with the intention of surrounding a body of 6,000 men, which seems to have become isolated from their main army.

What with dead, wounded, and prisoners, the enemy has lost, to date, over 12,000 men. You can't imagine my despair, not to say exasperation, at not having a single good officer of engineers, upon whose eye for the ground I can rely; nor one of those 5 or 6 artillery officers whom you ordered to join me; and at finding myself without light guns at the very moment when I am in open country.

[CORRESP., i, 176. Cairo is the Italian village Cairo-Montenotte, north of Savona.]

# 18

# THE DIRECTORY

## TO THE EXECUTIVE DIRECTORY

HEADQUARTERS, TORTONA, MAY 6, 1796.

I write on the return of the first messenger I sent you. I beg you to express to the Legislative Body the gratitude of the army for the complimentary decree which it has just passed. It is the pleasantest reward that the army could derive from its success. Speaking for myself, it is long since anything could increase the esteem and devotion that I intend to show upon every occasion towards the Government and the Constitution. I saw that Government set up amidst a welter of delorable passions, whose common issue could only be the destruction of France and the French Republic: indeed, I myself was enabled, in my zeal, and by the turn of events, to be of some service to its early career. My motto will always be to die, if need be, in its defence.

[CORRESP., i, 338. Written shortly after the Sardinian surrender at Cherasco.]

# 19

# DIVIDED COMMAND

## TO CITIZEN CARNOT

HEADQUARTERS, LODI, MAY 14, 1796.

. . .I am writing to the Directory about this idea of dividing the command. I assure you that my only thought in the matter is for the country. Whatever happens, you will always find me playing the game. I am prepared to sacrifice to the Republic every idea in my head. If they try to misrepresent me to you, my reply is in my heart and in my conscience.

As it is possible that my letter to the Directory may be misinterpreted; and, as you have shown signs of friendship towards me, I am taking the step of writing to you, and would ask you to make such use of this letter as your prudence and your attachment to me may suggest.

Kellermann would command the army quite as well as I do; for I am certain that our victories are due to the bravery and daring of the men. But I am convinced that to combine Kellermann and myself in Italy would be to court disaster. I cannot willingly serve alongside a man who considers himself the best general in Europe. In any case, I am certain that one bad general is better than two good ones. Fighting is like governing; it needs tact.

I can be of no use to you unless you show me the same confidence that you did in Paris. It is no matter to me, whether I fight here or elsewhere. My whole ambition is to serve my country, to give the Government proof of my devoted attachment, and to deserve, in years to come, a page in our national histories. But it would go to my heart to sacrifice in a week two months' fatigue, pain, and danger, and to find myself at a dead end. I have won some glory at the start: I want to go on being worthy of you. But be assured that, whatever happens, nothing will alter the respect you inspire in all who know you.

[CORRESP., i, 421. Soon after his victory at Lodi (May 10) Napoleon heard from the Government that Kellermann, the victor of Valmy, was to be sent out to share his command.]

# 20

# PATRON OF LEARNING

## TO CITIZEN ORIANI, THE ASTRONOMER

MILAN, *MAY* 24, 1796.

Science which dignifies the mind of men, and Art, which beautifies life, and transmits its great achievements to posterity, ought to be specially honoured by every free government. Every man of genius, every office-holder in the Republic of letters, in whatever country he may have been born, is a French citizen.

Learned men in Milan used not to enjoy the consideration they deserved. Hidden in their laboratories, they thought themselves happy if kings and priests did them no harm. It is not so to-day. In Italy thought has become free. There is no more inquisition, no more intolerance, no more tyranny. I invite all learned men to meet together, and to tell me what methods should be adopted, or what needs supplied, in order to give the sciences and the fine arts a new life and a new existence. Any of them who care to visit France will meet with a distinguished reception by the Government. The French people sets a higher value upon the acquisition of a learned mathematician, a famous painter, or the distinguished exponent of any branch of study, than upon that of the richest and most populous city in the world.

Pray express these sentiments for me to the distinguished men of learning resident at Milan.

[CORRESP., i, 491. Barnabé Oriani of Milan (1752 – 1832) was a writer of books on astronomical subjects.]

21

## REVOLT OF PAVIA

### TO THE EXECUTIVE DIRECTORY

HEADQUARTERS, PESCHIERA, *JUNE* 1, 1796.
. . . When quiet had been restored at Milan, I resumed my march on Pavia. Lannes, in command of the light troops, attacked Binasco, where 7 or 800 armed peasants appeared to be putting up a defence. He charged them, killed a hundred or so, and scattered the rest. I had the village set on fire immediately. The step was necessary, but the sight was none the less distressing, and I was painfully affected by it. But I foresaw that an even worse fate still threatened the town of Pavia. I therefore summoned the Archbishop of Milan, and sent him to convey to the insensate populace, on my behalf, the following proclamation.

*'Proclamation to the inhabitants of Lombardy.*

*MILAN, MAY* 25, 1796.
'A misguided mob, without any real means of resistance, is committing the wildest excesses, refusing to recognise the Republic, and defying an army which has conquered a succession of kings. Such incredible folly deserves pity: these poor people are being misled by men who wish to destroy them. In accordance with the principles of the French nation, which makes no war on the common people, the General in command

is anxious to leave open a door of repentance: but those who, within 24 hours, have not laid down their arms, and taken a fresh oath of obedience to the Republic, will be treated as rebels, and their villages will be burnt to the ground. Take warning by the terrible example of Binasco! Such will be the fate of every town and village that persists in the revolt.

Bonaparte.'

But it was in vain. I reached Pavia at day-break. The rebels' outposts were overwhelmed. The town seemed to be full of people, and in a state of defence. The castle had been taken, and our men were prisoners. I ordered up the artillery, and after firing a few rounds, summoned the wretched inhabitants to rely upon French generosity, and to lay down their arms. They replied that they would never surrender, so long as Pavia had walls standing. General Dommartin accordingly drew up the 6th battalion of grenadiers in close order, axes in hand, and headed by two 8-pounders. The gates were broken down, and the mob scattered in all directions, taking refuge in the cellars or on the roofs, and trying in vain, by throwing down tiles, to prevent our entry into the streets. Three times I was upon the point of giving orders to set the whole place on fire. At that moment I saw the castle garrison appear – they had broken their fetters, and came with eager cries to embrace their deliverers. I called over the names, and there was not a man missing. If the blood of a single Frenchman had been shed, I should have set up on the ruins of the place a column with the inscription – 'Here stood the town of Pavia.' As it was, I had the Town Council shot, arrested two hundred people, and sent them to France as hostages. Today all is absolutely quiet, and I have no doubt that this lesson will be an example to the people of Italy.

[CORRESP., i, 493, 536. Napoleon does not add that his troops 'massacred all the armed men for some hours, and glutted their lust and rapacity.' (Rose, 'Life of Napoleon,' i, 98.)]

## 22
# MAKING WAR PAY
## TO THE EXECUTIVE DIRECTORY

HEADQUARTERS, PISTOIA, *June* 26, 1796.

I enclose the terms of the armistice with the Pope. M. d'Azara, the actual negotiator, had the impudence to offer us 5 millions in cash and 3 in kind. I stood out for 40 millions, including 10 in kind. Seeing that I would not come down, he went to the Government Commissioners, and managed to worm out of them our weak point, namely our inability to march on Rome. After that I could only get 20 millions out of him, in spite of a night march on Ravenna. I had made it a condition all along that he should hand over the treasures of Our Lady of Loretto, and I thought he had agreed to it: but he had now changed his tune to such effect that I had to put up with a million under this head. This three-sided method of negotiation is fatal to the interests of the Republic: a clever man can go behind the back of one negotiator, and get what he wants from another. Quite apart from the Republic's loss of 10 millions on this transaction, the whole affair has been disagreeable for me, since I have almost lost my opportunity of advancing on Bologna. I am consoled, however, by the knowledge that the results still surpass your estimates. In addition to the rich districts which we still occupy, I find that we have derived from the Papal States the following sums: –

|  |  |
|---|---|
| *In Cash* | |
| 15,500,000 | livres under the treaty. |
| 2,000,000 ' | Bologna indemnity. |
| 1,200,000 ' | from the Bologna banks. |
| 800,000 ' | from the Bologna pawnshops. |
| 2,500,000 ' | the Ferrara indemnity. |
| 500,000 ' | found in the Ferrara banks. |
| 2,000,000 | found at Faenza, and the Ravenna Legation. |
| *In Kind* | |
| 5,500,000 | livres under the treaty. |
| 2,000,000 ' | Bologna. |
| 1,500,000 ' | Ferrara. |
| <u>1,200,000</u> ' | Faenza and the Ravenna Legation. |

Total 10,200,000 in kind
   <u>24,500,000</u> in cash
Grand total  <u>34,700,000</u>

[CORRESP., i, 685. After driving the Austrians back on Mantua, Napoleon turned south, occupied Bologna, and forced an armstice on the Papal States.]

## 23

# GENERALS' CHARACTERS

## TO THE EXECUTIVE DIRECTORY

HEADQUARTERS, BRESCIA, *August* 14, 1796.

I think it worth while to give you my opinion of the generals serving with this army. You will see that very few of them are of any use to me.

*Berthier:* ability, energy, courage, character; everything in his favour.

*Augereau:* plenty of character, courage, firmness, energy; is accustomed to war, popular with his men, lucky in the field.

*Masséna:* active, tireless, enterprising, grasps a situation and makes up his mind quickly.

*Serurier:* fights like a soldier; dislikes responsibility; firm, has too poor an opinion of his men; an invalid.

*Despinoy:* dull, slack, unenterprising; doesn't understand war, is unpopular with his men, doesn't use his head; in other ways a man of high character, intelligence, and sound political principles; good for a home command.

*Sauret:* good, an excellent soldier; not enough education for a general; unlucky.

*Abbatucci:* not fit to command fifty men.

*Garnier, Meunier, Casabianca:* incapable; unfit to command a battalion on such an active and serious campaign.

*Macquart:* a good fellow; no ability; lively.

*Gaultier:* all right for a clerical job; has never seen a shot fired.

*Vaubois* and *Sahuguet* were on garrison duty, and have only just been listed for active service: I will try to form an opinion of them. They have done very well in the duties so far assigned them: but the example of General Despinoy, who did very well at Milan, and very badly at the head of his division, compels me to judge men by their actual performance.

[CORRESP., i, 890.]

## 24

# WAR COMMISSIONERS

## TO THE EXECUTIVE DIRECTORY

MILAN, *August* 26, 1796.

. . . Salva, the war commissioner, leaves the army. His mind is affected. He sees enemies everywhere. He crosses the Po, and infects everyone he meets with the fears that distract him. He thinks the Uhlans are at his heels. He posts away two days and nights; but nothing can restore his confidence. He writes round to everyone '*Sauve qui peut*,' whilst he is within two leagues of Genoa. Finally he dies, after 24 hours' violent fever; believing himself wounded, in his fits of delirium, by a hundred sword-cuts, and for ever haunted by those terrible Uhlans. Such cowardice is only equalled by the courage of our soldiers. And plenty of war commissioners have been no braver than he was.

Such are the disadvantages of the law which insists that war commissioners shall be civilians, whereas they really need even more courage and military experience than officers. The courage they need is moral courage, which can only be acquired by the habit of facing danger. This incident has convinced me how essential it is to appoint as war commissioners only men who have served several campaigns with the troops, and have given proof of their courage. No man ought to belong to the French army who values his life more highly than the glory of the nation, and the good opinion of his comrades. It is revolting to hear, as one does every day, members of the administrative department admitting that they are afraid, and even boasting of it. . . .

[CORRESP., i, 925. Civil *commissaires* had been attached to the armies by a decree of the Convention, April 9 1793.]

## 25

# CORRECTING A CARDINAL

## TO CARDINAL MATTEI

HEADQUARTERS, MILAN, *September* 26, 1796.

Your character, which is a cause of congratulation to all who know you, induces me to allow your return to Ferrara, and to throw a veil of oblivion over your behaviour during the last month.

I am glad to think that you did no more than forget a principle of whose truth your native intelligence and your knowledge of the Gospel must have convinced you – that any priest who interferes in politics ceases to deserve the regard due to his character.

Go back to your diocese: put into practice the virtues that everyone agrees you possess: but never again meddle in State affairs. And be assured that the clergy, and all who are in the service of the church, will be under the special protection of the French Republic.

[CORRESP., ii, 1036. Cardinal Mattei had opposed the anti-Papal revolt which enabled Napoleon to include Ferrara in the Cispadane Republic. He represented the Pope in the negotiations at Tolentino in February, 1797.]

# 26

# ITALIA FARA DA SE

## TO THE CITIZEN PRESIDENT OF THE CISPADANE CONGRESS

MILAN, *JANUARY* 1, 1797.

I learn with the liveliest interest, from your letter of December 30, that the Cispadane Republics have united into a single state, that their emblem is a quiver, and that they are convinced their strength lies in unity and indivisibility. Unhappy Italy was long ago erased from the list of European powers. If Italians of today are fit to regain their rights, and to give themselves a free government, their country will some day play a famous part amongst the powers of the world. But do not forget that, without force, law is of no avail. Your first care ought to be for your military organisation. Nature has given you all you need. After the remarkable unanimity and prudence of your various deliberations, nothing is needed to attain your end, but battalions hardened to war, and fired with the sacred flame of patriotism.

You are in a more fortunate position than the French people. You can achieve liberty without the Revolution and its crimes. You will never experience the ills which afflicted France before the establishment of the Constitution. The unity which binds together the different parts of the Cispadane Republic will be a permanent inspiration for the union of all classes of its citizens; and from this agreement of principles and feelings, courageously defended, will flow liberty, prosperity, and a republic.

[CORRESP., ii, 1349. The Cispadane Republic was formed of Modena, Bologna, and Ferrara.]

# 27
# THE ARMY IN ITALY
## TO THE EXECUTIVE DIRECTORY

MILAN, *JANUARY* 6, 1797.

The more I probe, in my leisure moments, the irremediable wounds of the Italian army administration, the more I am convinced of the need of a quick and certain cure.

In the paymaster's department the books are in a shocking state of disorder. Nothing is properly accounted for. The paymaster himself – there is good reason to think – is a rascal. His staff are fools. Everyone has his price. The army costs five times as much as it need, for the storekeepers are in league with the war commissioners, and make false returns.

The leading actresses in Italy are kept by employés of the French army. Luxury, embezzlement, and malversation are rampant. The laws cannot deal with all this. There is only one remedy, and it is one suggested alike by experience, history, and the character of republican government – namely a *syndicature,* or court consisting of one or three persons, whose authority should not last more than 3 or 5 days, and who should have authority, during that short space of time, to shoot any one member of the administrative staff.

If this court were sent to the armies every two years, the result would be that everyone would have regard for public opinion, and preserve a certain decency, not only in morals and expenditure, but also in the duties of every day.

Marshal Berwick had a Quartermaster hung because his food supply gave out: and here are we, in the middle of Italy, where there is abundance of everything, spending every month five times as much as we should, and yet constantly going short.

But don't think I'm doing nothing about it, or that I'm letting the country down in this all-important part of my functions. Every day I have officials arrested. I go through their papers, examine their accounts. The trouble is nobody backs me up, and the laws don't give the general in command enough authority to put the fear of God into this horde of scoundrels. However, the evil is lessening, and what with cursing, punishing, and worrying, I hope things will be done a little more decently. But, as I said before, do think over my idea of a *syndicature*. . . .

[CORRESP., ii, 1363. Marshal Berwick, a natural son of James II, served with the French at the battle of the Boyne, defeated the English and Portuguese at Almanza in 1707, and was killed at Philippsburg in 1734.]

# 28

# VENICE

## TO THE MOST SERENE,
## THE DOGE OF THE REPUBLIC OF VENICE

HEADQUARTERS, JUDENBURG, *April* 9, 1797.

All the territory of the Most Serene Republic of Venice on the mainland is up in arms. On every side the rallying cry of the peasants you have armed is 'Death to the French!' Many hundreds of soldiers of the Italian army have already lost their lives. It is useless for you to disown gatherings that you have authorised. Do you imagine that, because I am at the moment in the heart of Germany, I am not strong enough to enforce respect for the greatest nation in the world? Do you suppose that the legions of Italy will tolerate the massacre you are instigating? No, the blood of my comrades in arms will be avenged, and there is not a French battalion but will feel its courage redoubled, and its means thrice what they were, when entrusted with the noble mission of revenge. The Venetian Senate has repaid our constant generosity with the blackest treachery.

I send this letter by the hand of my senior aide-de-camp. It is war or peace. Unless you take immediate steps to disperse these gatherings, unless you at once arrest and hand over to me the perpetrators of the recent assassinations, we are at war. There are no Turks on your frontiers; you are not threatened by any foe; you have merely invented excuses to justify the mass-ing of troops against my army. They must be disbanded within 24 hours. We are not living in the times of Charles VIII. If you force me, contrary to the express wish of the French government, to declare war, do not suppose that the French troops will ravage the lands of the innocent and unfortunate people of the mainland, as your armed forces have done. I shall protect them, and they will live to be grateful even for the crimes which obliged the French army to rescue them from your tyrannous rule.

[CORRESP., ii, 1712. Hearing of anti-French risings at Bergamo and Brescia, Napoleon sent Junot with orders to read this message to the Venetian Senate. Charles VIII of France invaded Italy in 1494.]

# 29

# LIGURIAN REPUBLIC

## TO THE PROVISIONAL GOVERNMENT OF GENOA

MOMBELLO, *JUNE* 16, 1797.

I have received your letter from citizen Emmanuel Balbi. The first steps your Government has taken justify the confidence reposed in it by the people of Genoa.

Provincial governments are in a difficult situation, and ought to consider nothing but the public safety, and the interests of the country.

The Republic of Genoa cannot exist without commerce, and commerce cannot exist without credit. Under a weak government, or in a country divided by factions, credit is impossible.

The government must be weak, the state cannot but be torn by factions, so long as some hundreds of the citizens organise an assembly of their own, take part in all the debates, and enjoy popularity, whilst all the time their motive is exaggeration, and their only aim is to destroy.

During your provisional government, a commission ought to be chosen to draw up your Constitution, and the organic laws of your Republic. Your chief duty is to silence political passion, to see that the legislative does its work undisturbed, and thus to ensure that you are not given trumped up laws and an ephemeral Constitution.

Prudence and moderation are found in all countries and in every age, for both are based upon our physical nature: but they are vitally necessary to small states and commercial cities.

Throughout the period of your provisional government, and up to the moment when you have laws and a stable constitution, act as though you were in a vessel buffeted by the waves: insist that every citizen goes about his own work, and that no one tries to compete with the Government.

As you do not know what your Constitution will allow or disallow, prohibit for the present any kind of association among the citizens.

Your National Guard is large and sound. If, under your government, the Republic loses any of its commerce or of its happiness, the responsibility will rest entirely upon yourselves. . . .

[CORRESP., iii, 1933. In October, 1796, Genoa had been forced to sign a treaty admitting a French garrison, closing its ports against British ships, and paying a heavy indemnity. A rising in May, 1797, was followed by an ultimatum, and the imposition of a further treaty (June 6) transforming Genoa into the Ligurian Republic.]

## 30

# THE ARMY AND PARIS
## TO THE EXECUTIVE DIRECTORY

HEADQUARTERS, MILAN, *JULY* 15, 1797.

I enclose a copy of a letter I have received from General Clarke: you will see from it that negotiations are still dragging on. There can be no doubt that the Emperor wants to see how events go in France, and that foreign influence counts for more than is generally supposed in all these machinations.

A great many Paris papers reach the army – especially the worst of them; but the result is quite contrary to what they intend. Indignation is rampant in the army. The men are asking angrily whether the only reward they are to expect, on their return home, for all their labours, and for their six years at the front, is the assassination which threatens every patriot. The situation gets worse every day, and I think that you, Citizen Directors, will soon have to take it in hand.

. . .There is not a man here who would not sooner die sword in hand than be assassinated in some dark corner of Paris.

For my own part, I am used to sacrificing all my private interests; yet I cannot be insensible to the outrageous slanders circulated every day, and upon every opportunity, by some 80 journals, whilst there is not one that gives them the lie. I cannot be insensible to the treachery and the accumulation of outrages suggested in the motion printed by order of the Council of the Five Hundred. I see that the Clichy Club would like to march over my body in order to destroy the Republic. Are there no Republicans left in France? After conquering Europe, are we to be reduced to searching for some corner of the earth in which to end our unhappy days?

One stroke, and you can save the Republic – save 200,000 lives, perhaps, which stand or fall with it, and make peace within 24 hours. Arrest the *émigrés*. Destroy the influence of foreigners. If this needs force, summon the armies. Break up the presses of the papers which are in English pay – they are more sanguinary than any Marat.

To return to myself: I cannot go on living in this clash of loyalties; if no remedy can be found to cure the country's ills, and to put an end to the rule of murder and to the influence of Louis XVIII, I must ask to be relieved of my command.

I enclose the stiletto found on the Verona assassins.

But, whatever may happen, I shall never forget the proofs you have constantly given of your complete confidence in me.

[CORRESP., iii, 2014. Negotiations for peace with Austria began after the arrangement of an armistice in April: the Peace of Campoformio was not signed till October 17. General Clarke assisted Napoleon in the negotiations. The Clichy Club was a royalist organisation working for the restoration of the Bourbons. There were troubles at Verona preceding the fall of Venice in May.]

# 31

# MUSIC AND MORALS

## TO THE INSPECTORS OF THE CONSERVATOIRE DE MUSIQUE AT PARIS

HEADQUARTERS, MILAN, *JULY* 26, 1797.

I have received your letter of the 16th messidor, with the accompanying memorandum. There are persons busy, at this very moment, in the different cities of Italy, copying and arranging all the music you ask for.

Let me assure you that I shall take the greatest trouble to see that your intentions are fulfilled, and that the Conservatoire is enriched with any musical treasures it may lack.

Of all the Fine Arts, music is that which most influences the passions, and that, therefore, which a legislator should do most to encourage. A few bars of moral music, composed by a master hand, cannot fail to affect the feelings, and have much more influence than a well-written book about morality, which convinces our reason without altering our habits.

[CORRESP, iii, 2042.]

# 32

## OCCUPATION OF CORFU

### TO THE EXECUTIVE DIRECTORY

HEADQUARTERS, MILAN, *August* 1, 1797.

After a successful fortnight's voyage, the fleet which left Venice (composed of a number of ships of the line and a few frigates under the command of Captain Bourdé, and carrying landing forces under General Gentili) anchored in the roads at Corfu. Four Venetian warships, which happened to be there, joined forces with our fleet.

On the 10th messidor our troops disembarked, and occupied the Corfu ports, in which they found 600 pieces of artillery, mostly of bronze. A huge crowd gathered on the shore to greet our troops with such cries of eagerness and enthusiasm as animate people who are recovering their freedom.

At the head of the crowd was the 'pope,' or religious chief of the district, an educated man of great age. He advanced towards General Gentili, and said: 'Frenchmen! you will find in this island a people ignorant of those arts and sciences which distinguish other nations. But do not despise them on that account: they can still become again what they once were. Read this book, and learn to appreciate them.' The general opened with curiosity the book which the 'pope' presented to him, and was not a little surprised to find that it was the 'Odyssey' of Homer.

The islands of Zante, Cephalonia, and Santa Maura have the same aspirations, and express the same wish and feeling for freedom. Every village has its tree of liberty. Every commune is ruled by a municipal body; and these people hope that, under the protection of the Great Nation, they will recover the sciences, the arts, and the commerce that they have lost under the tyranny of the oligarchs.

According to Homer, the island of Corcyra was the country of the Princess Nausicaa. Citizen Arnauld, who enjoys a deserved reputation in *belles lettres,* tells me that he went ashore to plant the tricolor on the ruins of Ulysses' palace.

The chief of the Maniotes, a people who trace a genuine descent from the Spartiatae, and who occupy the peninsula on which Cape Matapan is situated, has sent one of his principal men to express to me his wish to see French vessels in his port, and to be of some service to the Great Nation.

[CORRESP., iii, 2061. The occupation of Corfu, Cephalonia, and Zante (Zakynthos) followed the fall of Venice. A. V. Arnauld, the dramatist, met Napoleon at Mombello, and was sent to organise the government of the Ionian islands. Nausicaa (Homer, *Odyssey,* vi) was the daughter of Alcinous, King of the Phaeacians. The Spartiatae were the ruling class in Sparta.]

## 33

# ADRIATIC POLICY
## TO THE EXECUTIVE DIRECTORY

HEADQUARTERS, MILAN, *AUGUST* 16, 1797.

. . .The islands of Corfu, Zante, and Cephalonia matter more to us than all the rest of Italy put together. I believe that, if we had to choose, it would be better to restore Italy to the Emperor, and to keep the four islands. They are vital to the wealth and prosperity of our commerce. The Turkish Empire is breaking up every day. If we had these islands we should be in a position either to bolster it up as long as possible, or to take what part of it we want. It will not be long before we realise that, if we are effectively to destroy England, we must get hold of Egypt. The huge Ottoman Empire, perishing day by day, forces us to anticipate events, and to take early steps for the preservation of our commerce in the Levant....

[CORRESP., iii, 2103.]

## 34

# AUSTRIAN NEGOTIATORS

TO THE MINISTER FOR FOREIGN AFFAIRS

HEADQUARTERS, PASSARIANO, *SEPTEMBER* 6, 1797.

You will be astonished when you read the minutes of the meetings of September 3 and 4, and the declaration of the Emperor's plenipotentiaries to the effect that they have no instructions as to the Imperial Congress. Usually, when one mentions German affairs to them, these gentry say it is no business of theirs. They conceal very unskilfully their desire to deprive us of the Italian fortresses, so that they may proceed to do what they like in the German business.

It would be impossible to carry on important negotiations with a set of men less courageous, less logical, and with less backing from their government.

*Gallo.* He's a foreigner, and though he's supported by the Empress, he dare not oppose Thugut's policy.

*Merveldt.* Colonel of a regiment of Light Horse: brave enough personally, but just like the rest – without a blush for all the nonsense they have to talk, and the plain inconsistency of their proposals. When they have said, 'Those are our instructions,' they have nothing more to say. It has become such a farce, that I have retorted, 'If your instructions told you that day was night, I suppose you would go on saying so!'

*Degelmann.* A man of no weight or decision; a hypochondriac.

They all have very little to say, few resources, and no power of reasoning. We are constantly forcing them to admit that their words entirely disagree with their actions; but they always quote Thugut, and their instructions. Privately, and after looking both ways to see that no one is listening, they will tell you in a whisper that Thugut is a rascal, and deserves to be hanged. But Thugut is the real King of Vienna. . . .

In private conversation, when these gentry asked me whether I still thought their army formidable, I replied that I would give them my own view in confidence, because they knew better than anyone I was no Gascon, and because of their confidential admission that morning that the Emperor wished to have himself crowned King of Rome; and I assured them that within a fortnight of the opening of the campaign I should be outside Vienna, and that at my approach the people, who on a previous occasion had broken M. Thugut's windows, would certainly seize this opportunity to hang him. . . .

[CORRESP., iii, 2153. Written towards the end of the Campoformio peace negotiations, which Napoleon transferred to Passariano on August 27. Baron von Thugut was the Austrian Foreign Minister.]

# 35

## APOSTOLIC SUCCESSION

### TO CITIZEN THE ARCHBISHOP OF GENOA

HEADQUARTERS, PASSARIANO, *SEPTEMBER* 10, 1797.

I have this moment received your Pastoral Letter of September 5. 1 could believe myself listening to one of the Twelve Apostles. St. Paul himself might have written it. How one respects religion when it has ministers like you! A true preacher of the Gospel, you inspire respect; you compel your enemies to value and admire you; you turn even the sceptic into a believer.

Why should a church with such a leader as yourself have these wretched subalterns, unenlightened either by charity or peace? Their sermons breathe none of that moving unction which is the essential utterance of the Gospel. Jesus Christ died rather than defeat his enemies by other means than faith. But these wild-eyed reprobate priests preach rebellion, murder, and bloodshed. They live on rich men's gold: they have sold the poor for thirty pieces of silver. Drive them out of your Church. Cast upon them the anathema and curse of Heaven. Liberty, and the sovereignty of the people, are the political code of the Gospel.

I hope soon to be at Genoa: one of my greatest pleasures will be to see you there. A prelate like Fénelon, or the Archbishop of Milan, or of Ravenna, makes men love religion by practising all the virtues it enjoins. Heaven has no greater gift for a government, or for a great city.

Pray be assured of my high esteem and consideration.

[CORRESP., iii, 2182. For the situation at Genoa, *v.* No.29.]

## 36
# CONSTITUTION-MAKING

### TO THE MINISTER FOR FOREIGN AFFAIRS

HEADQUARTERS, PASSARIANO, *SEPTEMBER* 19, 1797.

I have received your 'confidential' letter of the 22nd fructi-
dor about the mission you wish Sieyès to carry out in Italy. I
certainly think, as you do, that his presence will be as necessary
at Milan as it probably was in Holland, and is now in Paris.

For all our pride, our thousand-and-one pamphlets, and our
blustering airy orations, we are extremely ignorant of the science of political conduct. We have never yet defined what is
meant by the executive, legislative, and judicial powers. Mon-
tesquieu defined them wrongly: not because that famous man
was incompetent to do otherwise, but because – as he admitted
– his work was only a kind of description of conditions which
had once existed, or still existed in his day – a summary of
notes made during his travels or his reading. His gaze was fixed
on the government of England: he defined, in general terms, the
executive, legislature, and judiciary of that country.

But why, in point of fact, should it be thought a function of
the legislative power to declare war and peace, or to regulate
the amount and character of the taxes? The English constitution
has reasonably enough entrusted the second of these functions
to the House of Commons; and it is a good arrangement,
because the English constitution is nothing but a charter of priv-
ilege – a black picture, framed in gold. Since the House of
Commons is the only body which, for better or worse, represents the nation, it is proper that it should have sole power to
impose taxation: it is the only defence they have been able to
devise against the insolent tyranny of the court party. But why,
in a government whose whole authority emanates from the
nation; why, where the sovereign is the people, should one
include among the functions of the legislative power things
which are foreign to it? There is only one thing, so far as I can
see, that we have really defined during the last fifty years, and
that is the sovereignty of the people. We have been no happier
in settling what is or is not constitutional, than in allocating the
different powers in the state. The French people is organised
only in outline.

The governmental power, taken in the wide sense that I

would give it, ought to be regarded as the real representative of the nation, governing in virtue of the constitutional charter and the organic laws. It falls naturally, it seems to me, into two quite distinct authorities. One of these is supervisory, but not executive: to this body what we nowadays call the Executive Power would be obliged to submit every important measure: it would be, if I may call it so, the legislative side of the executive. This great body would be in a real sense the National Council: it would control all that part of the administration and of the executive which our present constitution entrusts to the Legislative Power.

Thus the governmental power would consist of two authorities, both nominated by the people; and one would be a very large body, containing only such persons as had already occupied some of the posts that give men experience in the business of government. The legislative power would enact all the organic laws in the first instance, and would have power to alter them, but not at a few days' notice, as can be done now; for, once an organic law is placed upon the statute book, I think there should be no power to change it without four or five months' debate.

This Legislative Power, carrying no rank in the Republic, closed to outside influence, hearing and seeing nothing of what goes on around it, would have no ambitions, and would not inundate us with thousands of ephemeral measures, whose very absurdity defeats their own ends, and which have turned us into a nation with 300 law books in folio, and not a single law.

There you have, I think, a complete system of government, and one that finds its excuse in the present situation. It would really be disastrous if a nation of 30 million people, in this 18th century, were unable to save the country except by recourse to arms. Violent remedies discredit the legislator. He who gives men a constitution ought to consider beforehand how it will affect them.

If you see Sieyès, please show him this letter. I am sure he will write to tell me I am wrong. But I can assure you that I shall be delighted if you can do anything to send to Italy one whose talents I so much admire, and whose friendship I hold particularly dear. I will help him in every way I can; and my hope is that, by our united efforts, we may give Italy a constitution more in conformity with the character of its people, its local conditions, and perhaps the principles of political science, than

that which was given it before. It was difficult then to act otherwise. We did not want to try experiments at a moment when war
and passion ran riot.

To sum up: it is not only my private desire that Sieyès
should come to Italy, but my official belief also that, unless we
give Genoa and the Cisalpine Republic a suitable constitution,
France will get nothing out of them. Their legislative bodies,
bribed by foreign gold, will be at the beck and call of Austria
and Rome. It will be the story of Holland over again.

This letter is neither a field – order nor a plan of campaign.
Keep it to yourself and Sieyès. But you can make use, at your
discretion, of what I have said about the unsuitability of the present Italian constitution. . . .

[CORRESP., iii, 2223. Napoleon is writing to Talleyrand. The Abbé Sieyès,
Revolutionist Director, and maker of constitutions, was associated with them
both two years later, in the *coup d'état* of Brumaire, and in the Constitution
of the Year VIII.]

# 37

# FRANCE AND ITALY

## TO THE MINISTER FOR FOREIGN AFFAIRS

HEADQUARTERS, PASSARIANO, *OCTOBER* 7, 1797.
I enclose the confidential proposals submitted to me by
Count Cobenzl. I have expressed to him all the indignation that
you will feel when you read them. I enclose my answer. It will
all be settled – war or peace – in three or four days. I need hardly tell you that I shall do all I can to secure peace, considering
how late in the year it is, and how little hope there is of our
doing anything big now.

You don't know the Italians. They are not worth the lives of
40,000 Frenchmen. Your letters show that all your ideas are
based on a false assumption. You imagine that liberty can make
heroes out of people as soft as they are superstitious, and as
cowardly as they are contemptible. You expect me to work miracles, and I can't. I haven't a single Italian in my army, unless
you count some 1,500 degenerates, raked out of the gutter in
various Italian towns, and good for nothing but looting. Don't
be imposed upon by a handful of Italian adventurers at Paris,
and perhaps a Minister or two, if they tell you there are 80,000

Italians under arms. For all I can hear, and from what I see in the papers, public opinion in France has gone sadly astray, for some time past, about the Italians. It needs some dexterity and tact, all my prestige, and a severe lesson now and again, to make these people respect us, and to give them the slightest interest in the cause for which we are fighting.

I should like you to send for the various Cisalpine ministers who are in Paris, and to ask them, pretty brusquely, to let you have there and then in writing the number of soldiers of the Cisalpine Republic serving with the army in Italy. If they tell you that I have more than 1,500 with the army, and perhaps another 2,000 at Milan, policing that district, they are imposing on you, and will deserve anything you like to say to them. Misstatements of that kind are good enough for coffee-house talk, or tub-thumping, but not for Government use. They give people wrong ideas, and may lead to the adoption of an unsuitable policy, productive of incalculable ills.

I have the honour to repeat it: the Cisalpine Republicans will gradually become keen for liberty; gradually they will organise themselves; perhaps in 4 or 5 years – especially if they recruit among the Swiss – they will have 30,000 passable soldiers: I say 'perhaps,' because it needs a clever statesman to teach them a taste for arms; as a nation they are thoroughly enervated, and very cowardly.

If the negotiations don't take a turn for the better, France will always be sorry for the tone it has adopted towards the King of Sardinia. That prince, with one of his infantry battalions, and one of his squadrons of cavalry, could beat the whole Cisalpine army. If I have never told the Government this in so many words, it is because I never imagined you would form such an opinion about the Italians as I find in your letters. I do all I can to kindle a warlike spirit in them, but I barely succeed in keeping them well-disposed. Never once, since I arrived in Italy, have I been able to count, except in the feeblest degree, on a national love of liberty and equality. The good discipline of our army; the great respect we have all shown for religion – a respect carried, in the case of the priests, to the point of flattery; our justice; and above all the activity and promptness with which we have suppressed those who were ill disposed, and punished those who declared against us – these have been the real auxiliaries of our army. Such are the plain facts: all that it is worth saying in proclamations, or in reported speeches, is romantic fiction.

As I am hoping for a satisfactory end to the negotiations, I won't go into more detail, much as I should like to clear up a number of points that seem to be little understood. It needs prudence, wisdom, and a fair share of dexterity, to surmount every obstacle, and to achieve great ends. There is no other road to success. It is only a step from victory to disaster. My experience is that, in a crisis, some detail always decides the issue.

If we had followed the same foreign policy as in '93, we should have failed as completely as we have succeeded under the present contrary system: and remember that the resources of man-power, the methods of recruiting, and the outburst of enthusiasm upon which we then relied will never occur again.

It is a French characteristic to take prosperity much too lightly. Could we but base all our operations on a sound policy – by which I mean simply calculating *what* is likely to happen, and *when*, we might remain for a long time the greatest nation, and the arbiter of Europe. Nay more; we already hold the scales of power, and can incline them which way we will; indeed, I see nothing to prevent our reaching, in a few years' time, if fate wills it so, results which only burning enthusiasm can envisage, and only a man of cool and reasoned constancy can attain.

I beg you to read nothing into this letter, except my desire to contribute every talent I have to the success of my country. I write as I think: I cannot better express my high regard for you.

[CORRESP., iii, 2292. Count Ludwig Cobenzl was an Austrian diplomatist employed by Thugut in the final negotiations at Udine (September 26) that issued in the peace of Campoformio on October 17.]

# 38

# VENICE AGAIN

## TO CITIZEN VILLETARD

HEADQUARTERS, TREVISO, OCTOBER 26, 1797.

I have received your letter of 3 brumaire. I don't understand a word of it. I can't have explained myself clearly.

There is no treaty between the French Republic and the municipality of Venice which obliges us to sacrifice our interests and advantages to those of the Committee of Public Safety, or of anyone else there. The French Republic has never made it a matter of principle to fight for other nations. I should like to know of any philosophical or moral obligation to sacrifice 40,000 Frenchmen, against the express wishes of the nation, and the evident interests of the Republic. No doubt it comes easily enough to a few gas-bags, who only deserve the name of fools, to call for a universal Republic. I should like to see these gentry on a winter campaign. In any case, there is no such thing as a Venetian nation. Effeminate, corrupt, split up into as many divisions as there are towns, and as false as they are cowardly, the Italians are quite unfit for freedom. The Venetians are worse. If they really value liberty, and have the qualities necessary to win it – very well, they have never had a better opportunity to prove this. Let them defend it! But they have never had the courage to win their freedom, even from a few wretched oligarchs. At Zara they could not even put up a few days' defence. It is likely enough that, if the army had entered Germany, we should have had a recurrence, if not of the scenes at Verona, at least of wholesale assassinations, which have an equally sinister effect upon the troops.

Finally, the French Republic is not in a position, as people seem to think, to make a gift of the Venetian states. There is no real doubt that these states belong to France by right of conquest; but it is contrary to our principles to dispose of any people in this way. Until, therefore, the French army evacuates Italy, the various governments are free to take whatever steps they think to the advantage of their own countries.

The reason why I commissioned you to consult with the Committee of Public Safety about the possible evacuation of the French army is that they may be ready to take the necessary steps, both for the country as a whole, and for such individuals as may wish to remove into the districts annexed to the Cisalpine Republic, and placed under the protection of France. You should also have informed the Committee that persons who wished to follow the French army would be given time to sell their property, whatever the final fate of the country, and even if I knew it was the intention of the Cisalpine Republic to grant them titular citizenship. There your mission ends. In everything else they can do as they please. You have told them enough to show that all was not lost; that everything that happened was part of a vast plan; and that, if the Republican armies had continued to be successful against a power stimulated and financed by the whole Coalition, Venice might perhaps have been annexed to the Cisalpine Republic. But I can see that they are cowards. They understand nothing but running away. Well, let them run! I don't want them. . . .

[CORRESP., iii, 2318. Napoleon's treatment of Venice, culminating in the humiliating surrender of May 16, and its cession to Austria at Campoformio, had been attacked by Dumolard and other 'gas-bags' at Paris.]

# 39

# FERSEN

## TO THE MINISTER FOR FOREIGN AFFAIRS

RASTADT, *NOVEMBER* 30, 1797.

. . .All the members of the Congress have arrived, and they have visited me. The King of Sweden has sent, as his ambassador, the Baron de Fersen. . . . When the Baron came to see me he displayed all the fatuous mannerisms of Versailles. After the usual compliments, to which neither of us listened, I asked him who was the King of Sweden's Minister in Paris. At the moment, he replied, there was none; but this was due to one of those petty misunderstandings which are easily settled, and the small point of difference between the two powers had already been set right. Upon that, I spoke to him in these terms: –

'The French nation and the House of Sweden have been allies for some hundreds of years: they helped one another to wreck the ambitions of that proud dynasty which in past ages aimed, not without some hope of success, at universal empire. But there is another country, nearer to Sweden, and therefore more dangerous, which is a geographical link between the interests of the two powers, and the consideration of which should no less vitally suggest a certain attitude towards the French Republic. How is one, then, to explain the conduct of the Swedish court, which seems to go out of its way to send – whether to Paris, or to meet the French plenipotentiaries – agents, ministers, or ambassadors, who are on personal grounds entirely unacceptable to every French citizen? One cannot suppose that the King of Sweden would remain indifferent to the presence of a minister who had incited rebellion among the people of Stockholm. No, Sir, the French Republic will not suffer it that men who are only too well known for their relations with the late French court, men whose names may still be on the list of *émigrés*, should come and outface the ministers of the greatest people on earth. The French nation puts its self-respect even before its political interests.'

During this speech the Baron de Fersen frequently changed colour. At the end he fell back on his character as a courtier, replied that His Majesty would take into consideration all that I had said, and retired. I saw him out, naturally, with all the usual ceremonial. He was accompanied by the Swedish Minister at Ratisbon, who seemed to realise well enough that the Swedish court would have to take my words to heart.

[CORRESP., iii, 2382. A Congress was held at Rastadt, in accordance with an article of the Treaty of Campoformio, to conclude peace between France and the German States. The King of Sweden, as Duke of Pomerania, was represented by Count Axel Fersen, the friend (and, as Napoleon believed, the lover) of Marie Antoinette; he had played a large part in the Flight to Varennes in 1791, and had carried on a 'treasonable' correspondence with her during 1792. The 'proud dynasty' is the Hapsburgs; 'another country' is Prussia.]

# 40

# INVASION OF ENGLAND

## TO THE EXECUTIVE DIRECTORY

PARIS, *February* 23, 1798.

Whatever efforts we make, it will still be many years before we achieve supremacy at sea. To carry out an invasion of England without command of the sea is as difficult and daring a project as has ever been undertaken. It could only be done by a surprise crossing – either by eluding the fleet that is blockading Brest and the Texel, or by landing in small boats, during the night, after a 7 or 8 hours' passage, at some point in the counties of Kent or Sussex. This operation requires long nights, and therefore wintertime. It can't be attempted later than April. Any such invasion by means of sloops during a calm spell in the summer is impracticable: the enemy would offer insuperable obstacles to our embarkation, and still more to our passage. Our fleet is no further advanced than it was when we mobilised the army of invasion, four months ago. . . . The English expedition therefore seems to me impossible until next year; and then it is likely to be prevented by fresh embarrassments on the continent. The real moment for preparing this invasion has passed, perhaps for ever. . . .

We should therefore give up any real attempt to invade
England, and content ourselves with the appearance of it, whilst
devoting all our attention and resources to the Rhine, so as to
deprive England of Hanover and Hamburg. It is admitted that,
if we are to achieve both aims, we must not keep a large army
at a distance from Germany.

Or we might well make an expedition into the Levant, and
threaten the commerce of India.

If none of these three operations is feasible, I see no alternative but to make peace with England. I am confident that the
terms Malmesbury refused would be acceptable to them today.
In that case we should secure greater advantages for our negotiations at Rastadt. If peace were made with England during the
Congress, we should naturally be in a position to make many
fresh demands on the German Empire.

[CORRESP., iii, 2419. On October 27, 1797, Napoleon had been given the
command of an army to invade England. During the winter he studied the
question: this letter was the result of his investigations. Lord Malmesbury had
represented Pitt in peace overtures in 1796 and 1797.]

# 41

# NAVAL STRATEGY

## TO VICE-ADMIRAL BRUEYS

PARIS, *April* 22, 1798.

You must fit out the fleet for sea immediately. Citizen Ganteaume, Divisional Commander, will act as Chief of Staff. Citizen Casabianca will be your Flag-Commander. You are to distribute the other Divisional Commanders and officers among
the various ships.

Our 13 ships will be divided into 3 squadrons. The right
and left squadrons will consist of 4 ships each, the centre of 5.
There will be 1 frigate and 1 corvette to each squadron. Rear-
Admirals Blanquet du Chayla and Villeneuve will each be in
command of a squadron.

General Decrès will command the convoy, and will have
under his orders, in that capacity, the 2 vessels and 7 brigades
that he is convoying. He will have below him a Divisional
Commander, or an experienced naval captain, who will be on
board the 'Dubois.' General Decrès will also have under his

direct orders 3 armed frigates and a number of fast-sailing brigs to be chosen by yourself. With these vessels he will scout ahead of the fleet, and everything will be ready for him to take command of any light squadron that you might decide to form by detaching vessels from the force. But the moment the enemy is sighted, and the fleet forms for battle, the only concern of General Decrès and of his frigates must be to look to the safety of the convoy, and to carry out whatever orders you have given him.

It seems to me, therefore, that the duties confided to this general are extremely important. Whilst on the march, he is going on ahead, personally verifying the reports made by his scouts, and transmitting accurate information to you. This function in itself is so important that, at sea, as on land, the general himself ought to be the first to observe the enemy. But at sea the admiral cannot leave his forces, because once he has done so he cannot rejoin them.

As soon as the enemy is sighted, you will consider it the moment to reinforce the frigates with 2 or 3 war-ships: then the light squadron is constituted on recognised lines, and the General is in command. Finally, if the battle is fought in line formation, the General's responsibilities are by no means lightened: he has to secure from any danger of disaster a convoy immensely precious to the Republic; and, that done, he and his frigates may still be of some use to the fleet.

This plan of mine is perhaps contrary to that generally adopted, but the benefits I see in it are so great that I am sure it will be to our advantage. It will get us out of the habit the navy has of entrusting the command of the advance guard to the captain of a mere frigate, whereas in fact all subsequent events turn upon the first view of the enemy, and the first reports.

I am starting tomorrow night, and I hope to find the fleet ready when I arrive.

[CORRESP., iv, 2540. Napoleon left Paris on May 4, and the fleet (of nearly 400 ships) sailed from Toulon for Egypt on the 19th. The mixture of military and naval terms belongs to the original.]

## 42
# MISANTHROPY
### TO JOSEPH

CAIRO, *JULY* 25, 1798.

The papers will tell you about the result of the fighting, and the conquest of Egypt. There was enough resistance to add a glorious page to the military annals of the army. Egypt is the richest country in the world for corn, rice, meat, and vegetables. It is as barbarous as it can be. There is no money, not even enough to pay the troops. I may be in France again in two months. Please look after my interests. There is plenty to worry me at home. . . . Your friendship means a lot to me: were I to lose it, and to see you betraying me, I should become a complete misanthrope. It is a melancholy business, when all the affections of one's heart are wrapped up in a single person.

I want you to arrange to have a country place ready for me when I return, either in Burgundy or near Paris. I am counting on spending the winter there, and seeing no one. I am sick of society. I need solitude, isolation. My feelings are dried up, and I am bored with public display. I am tired of glory at 29; it has lost its charm; and there is nothing left for me but complete egotism. I mean to keep my Paris house – I shall never give that up to anyone. I have no other resources.

Good-bye, my one and only friend. I have never treated you unfairly, have I? You must give me credit for that, much as I should have liked to do so. You know what I mean. My love to your wife and Jérôme.

[JOSEPH, i, 188. Napoleon had captured Alexandria on July 2, won the Battle of the Pyramids on the 21st, and entered Cairo on the 24th. But he had heard that Josephine, left behind in Paris, was being unfaithful to him. He soon consoled himself with Pauline Fourès, the wife of a lieutenant in the *Chasseurs*. The dots are in the original.)

## 43
# A LETTER OF CONDOLENCE
### TO MADAME BRUEYS

HEADQUARTERS, CAIRO, *AUGUST* 19, 1798.

Your husband was killed by a cannon-ball whilst fighting

on board his ship. He died honourably, and without suffering, as every soldier would wish to die.

Your sorrow touches me to the quick. It is a dreadful moment when we are parted from one we love. It shuts us off from the world. The body is convulsed with pain, and the faculties of the mind so overwhelmed that all its contacts with reality are cut off by a distorting dream. Things are such that, if there were no reason for living, it were better to die. But when second thoughts supervene, and you press your children to your heart, your nature is revived by tears and tenderness, and you live for the sake of your offspring. Yes, Madame, you will weep with them, you will nurture their infancy, you will educate their youth; you will speak to them of their father and of your grief, of their loss and of the Republic's. And when you have linked your soul to the world again through the mutual affection of mother and child, I want you to count as of some value my friendship, and the lively interest that I shall always take in the wife of my friend. Be assured that there *are* men – a minority – who can turn grief into hope, because they feel so intimately the troubles of the heart.

[CORRESP., iv, 3046. Admiral Brueys was in command of the French fleet destroyed by Nelson at Aboukir Bay on the night of August 1, and is generally supposed to have been blown up on board his flagship, the 'Orient.']

# 44

# CAIRO REBELS

## TO GENERAL BERTHIER

HEADQUARTERS, CAIRO, OCTOBER 23, 1798.

Instruct the officer in command of the place to decapitate all prisoners taken with arms in their hands. They are to be taken tonight to the bank of the Nile between Boulâq and Old Cairo; and their headless bodies are to be thrown into the river.

[CORRESP., v, 3527. A revolt against the French broke out in Cairo on October 16.]

## 45

# SYRIAN CAMPAIGN

### TO GENERAL DESAIX, AT QOUS

HEADQUARTERS, GAZA, *FEBRUARY* 27, 1799.

I have had no letters from you for more than a month, though I have heard of you indirectly from the commandants of Cairo and Beny-Soueyf. At the present moment we are, I suppose, nearly 300 leagues apart.

You will have heard from the Staff of the military situation here. We have crossed 70 leagues of desert – a very tiring business. Brackish water, often none at all. We have eaten dogs, donkeys, and camels. The last three days here there has been a terrible wind, with torrents of rain. The sky is overcast; the climate might be that of Paris. The lemon-bushes, olive-groves and broken ground are just like the scenery of Languedoc: you might think yourself somewhere near Béziers In the fort at Gaza we found more than 30 *milliers* of powder, and a great quantity of cannon-balls of every calibre, cases and all. We are starting tomorrow on our march to Jaffa. The Mamelukes and Ibrahim Bey have fled into the mountains of Naplouse. . . .

[CORRESP., v. 4000. Turkey had declared war on France in September, 1798. Napoleon left Cairo for Syria on February 10, and occupied Gaza on the 24th. On May 20 he began his retreat from Acre, and reached Cairo again on June 14.]

## 46

# SLAVE-TRADE

### TO THE SULTAN OF DARFOUR

HEADQUARTERS, CAIRO, *JUNE* 30, 1799.

In the name of God the Clement and Merciful!

There is no other god but God, and Mahomet is his prophet!

To the Sultan of Darfour, Abd-el-Rahmân, Servitor of the two Holy Cities, Caliph of the glorious Prophet of God, Master of the Worlds.

I have received your letter; I have understood its contents.

I was absent when your caravan arrived, having been in Syria to punish and destroy our enemies. I beg you to send, by the first caravan, 2,000 black slaves over sixteen years of age, strong and vigorous: I will purchase them on my own account.

Order your caravan to come at once and not to stop on the way. I am giving instructions for its safe conduct throughout the journey.

[CORRESP., v, 4235. Darfur is a district in the Sudan, south-west of Khartum.]

## 47

# ISLAM IN EGYPT

### TO THE DIVAN OF CAIRO

HEADQUARTERS, EL-RAHMÂNYEH, *July* 21, 1799.

There is no other god but God, and Mahomet is his prophet!

To the Divan of Cairo, Chosen amongst the Wisest, the most Instructed, and the most Enlightened! May the Salutation of the Prophet be upon them!

I am writing you this letter to let you know that, after occupying the Natroun lakes, and passing through Bahyreh, to punish my enemies and to restore tranquillity to that unhappy people, we have betaken ourselves to El Rahmânyeh. We have granted a general pardon to the province, which is now in a state of perfect tranquillity.

Eighty vessels, large and small, threatened to attack Alexandria. Though received with bombs and cannon-balls, they anchored at Aboukir, and are beginning to disembark. I am letting them do so, because my intention is to attack them when they have landed, to kill all who will not surrender, and to spare the lives of the rest, in order to bring them back as prisoners: it will be a fine spectacle for the city of Cairo. This fleet came here in the hope of co-operating with the Arabs and Mamelukes in looting and devastating Egypt. There are Russians on board, who abominate those who believe in the unity of God, because they accept the lie that there are three gods. But they will soon see that it is not the number of their gods that gives them strength, and that there is only One God, the Father of Victory, Clement and Merciful, Who fights always for the good, and confounds the plans of the wicked, and Who, in His wisdom, ordained that I should come to Egypt, to change the face of the country, and to substitute for a destructive rule one of order and justice. He grants thereby a sign of His Omnipotence; for what the believers in three gods have never been able to do, has been done by us, who believe that One God alone governs nature and the universe.

If there are any Moslems among them, they are damned, because they have allied themselves, contrary to the command of the Prophet, with infidel and idolatrous powers. They have forfeited the protection that would otherwise have been accorded them, and they will perish in their sins. A Mussulman who is on board a ship flying the cross, and who hears daily blasphemies against the One God, is worse than an infidel. I would have you make these things known to the different Divans of Egypt, that the various villages may not be troubled by persons of ill intent; for they shall perish like Dumanhour and many others whose evil conduct had merited my revenge.

May the salutation of peace be upon all members of the Divan!

[CORRESP., v. 4296. Napoleon defeated the Turkish expeditionary force at El-Ramanieh on July 25. The Divans were administrative Councils that he had set up in Cairo and the provinces.]

# 48

# ALLOCATIONS

## TO GENERAL SONGIS, O.C. ARTILLERY

HEADQUARTERS, CAIRO, *August* 16, 1799.

You should know beforehand that, in yesterday's orders, the Commander-in-chief has put down the grant for army uniforms at double the amount actually issued. This is for public consumption to make them think in Europe that our effectives are twice what they really are. Warn the battalions concerned not to count upon more than half their allocations.

[CORRESP., v, 4361.]

# 49

# KLÉBER'S COMMAND

## TO GENERAL KLÉBER

HEADQUARTERS, ALEXANDRIA, *AUGUST* 22, 1799.

I enclose an order appointing you Commander-in-chief of the army. Fearing that the English cruiser may reappear at any moment, I am putting forward the date of my departure by two or three days.

I am taking with me Generals Berthier, Lannes, Murat, Andréossy, and Marmont, as well as Messrs. Monge and Berthollet.

I enclose the English and Frankfort papers up to June 10. You will see there that we have lost Italy, and that Mantua, Turin, and Tortona are besieged. I have reason to expect that Mantua will hold out till the end of November, and I am hoping to arrive in Europe before the beginning of October. I enclose a cypher for corresponding with the Government, and another for corresponding with me. . . .

The arrival of our Brest fleet at Toulon and of the Spanish fleet at Cartagena puts it beyond doubt that we can transport to Egypt the muskets, sabres, pistols, and cast-iron fittings that you need – I have an accurate list of them; with recruits enough to make good the losses of two campaigns. The government itself will then inform you of its intentions; and I will take steps, both in my public and private capacity, to keep you frequently informed of what is happening

Supposing that, owing to events we cannot foresee, all our attempts are fruitless, so that by May you have received no reinforcements, and no news from France; and if this year, in spite of all precautions, the plague reaches Egypt, and you lose more than 1,500 men – a serious loss, when added to the daily war casualties; under such circumstances I think you ought not to risk another season's campaign, and you are authorised to conclude peace with the Ottoman Porte, even though the evacuation of Egypt is made a *sine qua non*. The best plan would be to postpone the carrying out of this condition, if possible, until a general peace is signed.

You can appreciate as well as anyone how important to France is the possession of Egypt. The Turkish Empire is in ruins all round us, and is daily crumbling away. A French evacuation of

Egypt would be a disaster all the greater because we shall live to see this fine province in the hands of another European power.

Your plans should also be strongly influenced by the news you receive of the success or failure of the Republic in Europe. If, before you get news of me from France, the Porte answers the offers of peace that I have made it, you should reply that you have all the powers I had, start negotiations, reiterate my declaration that it was never the intention of France to take away Egypt from the Porte and ask the Porte to abandon the Coalition, and to give us trading-rights in the Black Sea, and a six months' armistice, during which ratifications can be exchanged.

Supposing the circumstances are such that you think you ought to conclude this treaty with the Porte, you must insist that it cannot be executed before it is ratified; and it is in accordance with international usage that there should always be an armistice during the interval between the signature of a treaty and its ratification.

You know my views about the government of Egypt. Whatever you do, the Christians will always be our friends. But they must not be allowed to become too insolent, lest the Turks become as fanatical against us as against them, and thus irreconcilable. Fanaticism must be put to sleep until it can be destroyed. Win the good opinion of the sheiks at Cairo, and you have that of all Egypt, and of any leaders the people are likely to possess. The sheiks are, for our purposes, the least dangerous of all, for they are timid, unwarlike, and, like all priests, inspire fanaticism without being fanatics themselves. . . .

I have already repeatedly asked for a troupe of actors, and I shall take special trouble to send you one. This is very important for the army, and will be a first step towards changing the customs of the country.

The important post you occupy as Commander-in-chief will enable you to use the talents nature has given you. Everything that happens here in Egypt is intensely interesting, and will have far-reaching results on commerce and civilisation. Great revolutions will date from this epoch.

I am wont to find a reward for the troubles and travails of this life in the opinion of posterity. I therefore abandon Egypt with the deepest regret. Nothing less than the interests and honour of my country, a feeling of duty, and the extraordinary happenings at home, could decide me to risk my way through hostile fleets to reach Europe. My heart and mind will be with you; your success will be as dear to me as any won in my own presence; and I shall consider any day in my life ill-employed on which I do nothing to help the army I leave in your charge, or to consolidate the magnificent edifice whose foundations have already been laid.

The men I entrust to you are like children to me: they have always shown me, even in times of the greatest hardship, proofs of their affection. Carry on this tradition: it is due both to my special regard and affection for you, and to the genuine attachment I feel toward themselves.

[CORRESP., v, 4374. Napoleon had long been talking of returning to France. On August 2, he received through Sir Sidney Smith copies of the *Gazette de Frankfurt* and the *Courrier français de Londres* with news of the defeat of Schérer in Italy, and of Jourdan in the Rhine valley. He at once determined to return, and sailed on August 23.]

# 50

# BRUMAIRE

## TO CITIZEN BEYTZ

PARIS, *NOVEMBER* 24, 1799.

I have received your letter of 27 brumaire. Why do you feel distressed about a day whose results are so much to the advantage of order, liberty, and enlightenment?

But by this time first impressions have passed, and no doubt you are anxious to resume the part befitting a distinguished savant, which should be as alien to any spirit of partisanship as patriotism itself.

I remember reading an excellent report you wrote on the ratification of the treaty of Campoformio, which fixed for ever the destinies of your own country, Belgium. No sensible man can suppose that the peace which Europe still demands can be reached by way of factions, and the disorder to which they lead.

I want you all to rally the mass of the people. The simple title of French citizen is worth far more than that of Royalist, Clichien, Jacobin, Feuillant, or any of those thousand-and-one denominations which have sprung, during the past ten years, from the spirit of faction, and which are hurling the nation into an abyss from which the time has at last come to rescue it, once and for all.

That is the aim of all my efforts. It is that upon which is centred, from this moment, the regard of all thoughtful men, the esteem of the people, and the hope of glory.

[CORRESP., vi, 4398. Napoleon landed at Fréjus on October 9, and reached Paris on the 16th. The *coup d'état* of 18th Brumaire (November 9 – 11) placed him in power. J. F. Baron de Beytz was a distinguished Belgian suspected of opposing Napoleon's rise to power.]

# 51

# LOCAL GOVERNMENT

## NOTE DICTATED TO LUCIEN BONAPARTE, MINISTER FOR HOME AFFAIRS

PARIS, *DECEMBER* 25, 1799.

If I had not to go to war, I should initiate the prosperity of France through the local authorities. If one is to regenerate a nation it is much simpler to deal with its inhabitants a thousand at a time than to pursue the romantic ideal of individual welfare. Each local body in France represents 1,000 inhabitants. If you work for the prosperity of 36 thousand communities you will be working for that of 36 million inhabitants, whilst simplifying the issue, and reducing the difficulties arising out of the difference in scale between thousands and millions. That was what Henri IV had in mind when he talked about providing everyone with a fowl for his stock-pot: it would have been a stupid remark otherwise.

The Minister for Home Affairs should pay special attention to the following ideas:

Before the Revolution every village belonged to its landlord, and to its priest. The tenant and the parishioner had no roads to travel by; there were no byres where their cows or sheep could shelter, no meadows where they could go to grass. But since 1790, when this common right of moving and grazing cattle was suddenly and quite properly taken out of the hands of the feudal landlord, each municipality has become a real *person*, under the protection of common law, with the right of possessing, acquiring, and buying property, and of performing, for the benefit of the municipal family, every act contemplated in our codes. Thanks to this great national conception, France found herself suddenly divided into 36 thousand personalities, each of which was faced with the responsibilities of *ownership* – anxious to extend its property, improve its produce, increase its income, and so forth.

In that change lay the germ of French prosperity. Why has further development been impossible? Because, whilst an individual owner, with a personal interest in his property, is always wide awake, and brings his plans to fruition, communal interest is inherently sleepy and unproductive; because individual enterprise is a matter of instinct, and communal enterprise a matter of public spirit – and that is rare.

Consequently, since 1790, the 36 thousand local bodies have been like 36 thousand orphan girls. Heiresses to the old feudal rights, they have been neglected or defrauded for the past ten years by the municipal trustees of the Convention or of the Directory. A new set of mayors, assessors, or municipal councillors has generally meant nothing more than a fresh form of robbery: they have stolen the by-road, stolen the foot-path, stolen the timber, robbed the church, and filched the property of the *commune*; and this looting is still going on under the slack municipal system of the Year VIII.

If this system were to last another ten years, what would become of the local bodies? They would inherit nothing but debts, and be so bankrupt that they would be asking charity of the inhabitants, instead of giving them the help and protection that is their due. Like the family prodigal, they would have sold or pawned their last stick of furniture, and be unable to borrow a penny to live on. No one would venture to settle down in a community so heavily in debt that he would have nothing to look forward to but fees and taxes of all kinds – charitable contributions, donations, subscriptions, special collections, and so forth. The existence of a local authority ought to attract population: under these conditions it would repel it.

It is the first duty of a Home Secretary to arrest a disease which would carry infection into the 36 thousand limbs of the great body of society. And the first thing to do, towards this end, is to form a clear notion of the seriousness of the disease, and of its symptoms. The Minister will therefore begin by having a general inventory made of the 36 thousand *communes* – this has always been wanting. . . . Local bodies will be divided into three classes: those which are in debt, those which just pay their way, and those which show a surplus. The second and third classes are in a minority, and there need be no hurry to deal with them. The point is to restore solvency to those which are in debt. . . . Once this inventory is drawn up, the Prefects and Sub-prefects will be warned to bring the whole force of the administration to bear upon the insolvent municipalities, and to get rid at once of any mayors or assessors who do not see eye to eye with them as to local improvement and regeneration. It will be the duty of the Prefect to visit these bodies at least twice a year, and of the Sub-prefect four times a year, under penalty of dismissal. He will make a monthly report to the Minister about each municipality, stating the results of what he has tried to do, and what still remains to be done.

I should like proposals for a prize for those mayors who have got their municipalities out of debt within 2 years: whereas, in the case of any municipality which is not solvent at the end of 5 years, the Government will nominate a special commission to take over its administration. (This will involve the drafting of a law.)

Thus at the end of 5 years France will have only two classes of local bodies left – those that are working at a profit, and those which make both ends meet. We shall have expunged from the map of France the insolvent municipalities, whose property is falling to pieces, and becoming a burden on the inhabitants.

This first levelling-up accomplished, the efforts of the Minister and of the municipalities will be devoted to securing that, by the end of a further period, the solvent *communes* rise into the class of those which show a surplus; so that, in 10 years' time, this may be the only class left.

When this is done, the movement towards national prosperity initiated by the efforts of 36 million individuals will be multiplied by the regenerative power of 36 thousand communal personalities, all working, under the supreme direction of the Government, towards the goal of progressive perfectibility.

Every year the 50 mayors who have done most to rid their community of debt, or to manage it at a profit, will be summoned to Paris at the expense of the State, and formally presented to the three Consuls.

A column put up at the expense of the Government, at the main entrance of the village or town, will perpetuate the name of its mayor; and posterity will read these words: – 'To the

Guardian of the Community; from his grateful Country.'

[CORRESP., vi, 4474. The eighty-eight *départements* of France proper in 1799 contained about 36,000 *communes* or *municipalités*, grouped in 400 *arrondissements.*]

## 52

# PEACE PROPOSALS

## TO H.M. THE KING OF GREAT BRITAIN AND IRELAND

PARIS, *DECEMBER* 25, 1799.

Called by the will of the French people to hold the highest office in the Republic, I think it proper, upon assuming my functions, to inform Your Majesty of the fact by my own hand.

Is there to be no end to the war which, for the past eight years, has desolated every quarter of the globe? Is there no means by which we can come to an understanding? How is it that the two most enlightened nations in Europe, both stronger and more powerful than their safety and independence require, consent to sacrifice their commercial success, their internal prosperity, and the happiness of their homes, to dreams of imaginary greatness? How is it that they do not envisage peace as their greatest glory as well as their greatest need?

Such sentiments cannot be strange to Your Majesty's heart, for you rule a free nation for the sole end of making it happy.

I beg Your Majesty to believe that, in broaching this subject, it is my sincere desire to make a practical contribution, for the second time, towards the establishment of a general peace. I do so by a *démarche* that is prompt, confidential, and freed from those formalities which may be necessary to save the face of a weak state, but which between great powers become a mask of mutual trickery.

If France and England abuse their power, they can, for a long time yet, stave off exhaustion; but it would be an international disaster; and I make bold to say that the fate of every civilised nation depends upon the ending of a war which is embroiling the whole world.

[CORRESP., vi, 4445. The Constitution of the Year VIII, under which Napoleon became First Consul, was promulgated on December 15 .]

## 53

# NATIONAL GOVERNMENT

TO CITIZEN D'ANDIGNÉ

PARIS, *DECEMBER* 30, 1799.

I have been pleased at reading the letter from the most remarkable citizens of the western Departments. They show a disposition which does them honour, and which will, I am confident, be useful to the country.

Only too much French blood has flowed during the last ten years; yet there are enlightened men, in whom the sentiment of honour still burns, who fail to use all their influence on behalf of a government solely concerned to re-establish order, justice, and true freedom – a government which will soon be surrounded by the trust and respect of all Europe, and which will soon have the glory of proclaiming, for a second time, that peace for which the whole world is crying out.

Be sure, then, to tell your fellow-citizens that never again shall revolutionary laws devastate the fair soil of France, that the Revolution is over, that consciences will be utterly and absolutely free, that protection will be given equally to all citizens, and relieved from any taint of prejudice, and that, for myself, I shall appreciate and know how to reward any services rendered on behalf of peace and quietness. . . .

[CORRESP., vi, 4488. On December 27, following an armistice of November 24, d'Andigné, the Chouan leader, came to Paris, and discussed terms of pacification with Napoleon. On December 28 an amnesty was offered to all rebels who would lay down arms.]

## 54

# STATUARY

TO CITIZEN LUCIEN BONAPARTE, MINISTER FOR

HOME AFFAIRS

PARIS, *FEBRUARY* 7, 1800.

The First Consul instructs me to request you on his behalf to give the necessary orders for erecting, in the Great Gallery of the Tuileries, statues of Demosthenes, Alexander, Hannibal, Scipio, Brutus, Cicero, Cato, Caesar, Gustavus Adolphus,

Turenne, the great Condé, Duguay-Trouin, Marlborough, Prince Eugène, Marshal Saxe, Washington, Frederick the Great, Mirabeau, Dugommier, Dampierre, Marceau, and Joubert.

You are to take suitable steps to provide such of these statues as are no longer in existence, or are not at present available.

[CORRESP., vi, 4572.]

## 55

# THE DE STAËLS

## TO CITIZEN JOSEPH BONAPARTE

PARIS, *MARCH* 19, 1800.

M. de Staël is destitute: his wife is giving dinners and dances. If you are still seeing her, couldn't you induce the woman to make her husband an allowance of 1,000 or 1,200 francs a month? Or have we really reached a point when people can ride rough-shod, not merely over every-day morality, but over the most sacred of family duties, and be thought none the worse by decent society? They may, indeed, judge Mme de Staël's conduct as though she were a man: but if a man had inherited M. de Necker's fortune, had enjoyed for years the advantages of a famous name, and had then let his wife starve, while he himself lived on the fat of the land, he would be cut by all his friends.

[LECESTRE, i, 20. Germaine Necker, daughter of the Genevan banker and French minister, married Baron de Staël-Holstein in 1786, and was separated from him in 1798. He died in 1802.]

## 56

# CENSORSHIP AND POLICE

## TO CITIZEN FOUCHÉ, MINISTER OF POLICE

PARIS, *APRIL* 5, 1800.

The Consuls of the Republic intend that *Le Bien Informé, Hommes Libres*, and *Défenseurs de la Patrie* shall cease publication, unless the proprietors procure editors of good character and of incorruptible patriotism. You must insist that every issue of these journals is signed by a recognised editor.

You are to instruct the Prefect of Police to take whatever steps are necessary:

(1) To prevent any bill-posting on the walls of Paris, or any crying of papers or pamphlets without a police licence;

(2) To prevent the print-dealers displaying for sale anything contrary to sound morals, or to the policy of the Government.

The Prefect of Police is to forbid the public announcement of any play, unless the director of the theatre has a permit from the Minister for Home Affairs.

The Consuls wish you to send them, within ten days, a report,

(1) On the best way of ridding Paris of the great number of Italian and other foreign refugees who live here without any means of subsistence;

(2) On the most appropriate measures for removing from the territory of the Republic those *émigrés* who have returned into the Seine Department, whether or not they are under supervision, provided that they did not claim to be removed from the proscription list before 4 nivôse last;

(3) On the names and addresses of some 50 persons, who habitually make their living out of revolutions, and are constantly agitating public opinion; and on the means of ridding Paris of these men, many of whom are in foreign pay, command some sort of following, and are at the disposal of anyone who will bribe them to disturb the public peace.

Lastly, you are to inform M. Payne that the police have information as to his suspicious behaviour, and that on the first complaint he will be sent back to America, the country to which he belongs.

[CORRESP., vi, 4707. Joseph Fouché, ex-Oratorian and Terrorist, became Napoleon's Minister of Police in 1799. 'Tom' Paine had been in prison under the Terror, and was released in November, 1794. He returned to America in 1802, and died at New York in 1809.]

## 57

# AFTER MARENGO

## TO H.M. THE EMPEROR AND KING

MARENGO, *JUNE* 16, 1800.

I have the honour of writing to Your Majesty to inform you of the desire of the French people to put an end to the war which desolates our countries.

English cunning has prevented my frank and simple *démarche* producing its natural effect upon Your Majesty's heart.

There has been war between us. Thousands of Frenchmen and Austrians are no more. . . . Thousands of bereaved families are praying that fathers, husbands, and sons may return! . . . The evil is irremediable: may it at least teach us to avoid anything that might prolong hostilities! The prospect so affects my heart that I refuse to accept the failure of my previous advances, and take it upon myself to write again to Your Majesty, to entreat you to put an end to the misfortunes of Europe.

On the battle-field of Marengo, surrounded by sufferers, and in the midst of 15,000 dead bodies, I implore Your Majesty to hear the cry of humanity, and not to allow the offspring of two brave and powerful nations to slaughter one another for the sake of interests of which they know nothing.

It is for me to urge Your Majesty, because I am nearer to the scene of war, and your heart cannot be so keenly affected as mine.

Your Majesty's arms have won glory enough. You govern a vast number of states. What reasons, then, can they allege, who, in Your Majesty's study, counsel the continuance of the war?

The interests of religion, and of the Church?

Then why do they not advise Your Majesty to make war on the English, the Muscovites, or the Prussians? They are further from the Church than we are.

The character of the French Government, which is not hereditary, but simply elective?

But the Government of the Empire is elective too. Besides, Your Majesty is well aware how powerless the whole world would be to change one jot of the French determination, derived from Nature herself, to govern themselves as they will. Why is not Your Majesty advised to insist that the King of England shall suppress the Houses of Parliament, or the United States of America destroy their Congress?

The interests of the German Confederation?

But Your Majesty yielded us Mayence, which a series of campaigns had not put in our power, and which could have sustained several months of siege; the German Confederation calls loudly for peace – nothing else can save it from utter ruin; whilst the majority of that Confederation, even the states of the King of England, the sole author of the war, are at peace with the Republic.

An extension of Your Majesty's territory in Italy?

But the treaty of Campoformio has given Your Majesty the constant object of your ancestral ambitions.

The balance of power in Europe?

The recent campaign is sufficient proof that it is not France which threatens the balance of power. Every day shows that it is England – England, who has so monopolised world-commerce and the empire of the seas that she can withstand single-handed the united fleets of Russia, Denmark, Sweden, France, Spain, and Holland. Yet Your Majesty, now a great commercial power, is interested in the independence and freedom of the seas.

The destruction of revolutionary principles?

If Your Majesty considers its results, you will see that the war itself is likely to revolutionise Europe, by increasing popular discontent, and swelling the national debt in every country.

If you force the French people to make war, you force it to think of nothing and live for nothing but war; and the French legions are many and brave.

If Your Majesty wishes for peace, it is as good as made: we have only to carry out on both sides the terms of Campoformio, and to remedy what seems to have been the chief cause of the rupture by an additional clause guaranteeing the lesser powers.

Let us give peace and repose to the present generation. If future generations are so foolish as to fight – well, after a few years of war they will learn wisdom, and live at peace with one another.

I could have captured the whole of Your Majesty's army. I contented myself with an armistice, in the hope that this would be a first step towards a world-peace. That is an aim which I cherish all the more, as it might be supposed that one nurtured and brought up on war would be more hardened than I am to the evils it involves. At the same time Your Majesty will realise that, unless this armistice leads to peace, it is useless, and inimical to French interests.

The proposals that I think it right to make to Your Majesty are therefore these: –

(1) That the armistice be extended to all the armies.

(2) That negotiators be sent by both sides, either secretly or publicly, as Your Majesty prefers, to some place between the Mincio and the Chiese, to agree upon means of guaranteeing the lesser powers, and to elucidate those articles of the treaty of Campoformio which experience has shown to be ambiguous.

If Your Majesty rejects these proposals, hostilities will recommence, and – you must permit me to speak frankly – you alone, in the eyes of the world, will be responsible for the war.

I beg Your Majesty to read this letter with the feelings which prompted me to write it, and to believe that, next to the happiness and interests of the French people, nothing concerns me more than the prosperity of that nation of soldiers whose courage and military prowess I have admired for the last six years.

[CORRESP., vi, 4914. Napoleon had defeated the Austrians at Marengo two days before. The dots are in the text.]

# 58

# THE BOURBONS

## TO THE COUNT DE PROVENCE

PARIS, *SEPTEMBER* 7, 1800.

I have received your letter. I thank you for your kind remarks about myself. You must give up any hope of returning to France: you would have to pass over 100,000 dead bodies. Sacrifice your private interests to the peace and happiness of France. . . . History will not forget. I am not untouched by the misfortunes of your family. . . I will gladly do what I can to render your retirement pleasant and undisturbed.

[CORRESP., vi, 5090. The Comte de Provence, the elder of Louis XVI's surviving brothers, afterwards Louis XVIII, was at this time a refugee in Russia. The dots are in the text.]

## 59

# HANOVER & EGYPT

## TO THE EMPEROR OF RUSSIA

PARIS, *FEBRUARY* 27, 1801.

. . .The Marquis de Lucchesini has communicated to me a note from the King of Prussia, from which it appears that this prince has at last done what was expected of him by Your Majesty and all Europe in closing the Elbe and Weser to English shipping. Would not Your Majesty think it well, whilst occupying Hanover until the conclusion of a general peace, to send M. de Sprengporten's troops there? They might be joined by a French division; in which case I would undertake to supply them with whatever military equipment they might need.

If Your Majesty sees to it that the English carry on no trade with the northern powers, and if M. de Sprengporten's troops move into Hanover, and guarantee the closing of the Elbe and Weser, whilst the army of reconnaissance that I have despatched to Bordeaux compels Portugal to shut her ports against England, and if those of Naples and Sicily are similarly closed, then the English will be completely cut off from Europe. . ..

The English are attempting to land in Egypt. It is to the interests of all the Mediterranean powers, as well as of the power which controls the Black Sea, that Egypt should remain in French hands. The course of the Suez canal, which would join the Mediterranean and the Indian Ocean, has already been laid out. The work would be easy, and would not take long; and it might result in incalculable benefits to Russian commerce. If Your Majesty is still of the opinion, so often expressed before, that part of your northern trade should travel by way of the south, you could associate yourself with this great enterprise, which will so deeply affect the future situation in Europe, by intervening at the Porte in the affairs of Egypt.

Your Majesty will see that in the peace treaty concluded between France and Austria everything has been done to meet Your Majesty's wishes. . . .

[CORRESP., vii, 5417. Napoleon, having won the support of the Emperor Paul I by the generous return of 6,000 Russian prisoners of war, hoped for his support against England. General Sprengporten, the Russian envoy, visited Paris, and on December 16 – 18 the Second Armed Neutrality was formed by the Baltic powers against England. In January the Tsar offered to help Napoleon. On March 23 he was assassinated.]

## 60

# BOYS' SCHOOLS

### TO CITIZEN CHAPTAL, MINISTER FOR HOME AFFAIRS

PARIS, *JUNE* 11, 1801.

The Consuls have considered the general regulations that you propose to adopt for the schools affiliated to the *Prytanée*. Some of the provisions made by these regulations seem to them inadequate, and in other respects capable of improvement. Their wish is that their comments should be submitted to you, not as notifying changes which must be made, but as suggesting points which you will doubtless appreciate, and, if they commend themselves to you, adopt. . . .

### *Police.*

The Consuls consider the Section headed 'Police' quite inadequate. They think that, in order to complete it, you would do well to study the regulations made for the Military School by the Minister of War: most of their provisions are appropriate to the establishments you are organising. These rules were drawn up to meet every contingency, and have worked well in practice.

Articles 22 and 30 of the Section headed 'Police' give the cadet officers the ranks of captain, lieutenant, and sub-lieutenant. It would be more suitable to substitute 'sergeant' and 'corporal.' The cadets would wear the badges of these ranks.

### *Education.*

The Section on Education is inadequate. I have the honour to inform you of certain views which the Consuls have expressed on this subject.

The education given ought to fall into two main parts: the first, for boys under 12; the second, for boys above that age.

The lower part of the school should have the same kind of education throughout. It should be divided into classes of 25 pupils each – a first, a second, a third, and if necessary a fourth class. In the first class they should learn reading, writing, arithmetic, and the elements of grammar; in the second, the four rules, spelling, and the principles of Latin; in the third, fractions, higher mathematics, and those parts of education which cannot be done in a year, drawing, dancing, and the use of arms. In addition all three classes would take, up to their capacity, and in order to train their memory, lessons in natural history, geography, stories in French and Latin, the elements of ancient history, and a collection of virtuous and heroic deeds calculated to inspire them with patriotic and moral ideals.

The higher part of the school, consisting of boys over 12, would naturally fall into two classes – those destined for a civil and those for a military career. Into which class each boy is put, would be determined by the Inspector-general, at an inspection specially held for this purpose, and after hearing statements from the teachers, and any wishes that might be expressed by the boys' parents.

The pupils destined for a civil career would learn ancient languages, primarily Latin, and go through the full course of rhetoric and philosophy. They would also be taught the first volume of the course in mathematics.

The pupils destined for a military career would make a special study of all four volumes of the mathematical course; and they would learn a little astronomy, drawing, fortification, planning, etc. The most advanced pupils would be taught the principles of physics and chemistry, how to serve a gun, and so on.

The pupils composing each of these divisions would be divided into 3 or 4 classes, according to their progress. It would be settled every year to which class each of them should belong: they could then either be kept in the same class as before, or allowed to skip a class, if they knew too much or too little to be moved into the next above them.

The regulations must prescribe exactly what subjects are to be taught in each class.

It is recognised that each school must have a library of its own; probably 2,000 volumes would be more than enough. Each library ought to have a catalogue printed in accordance with the regulations.

### After-career of pupils.

This important heading is barely hinted at in Article 54. After paying for the education and keep of the pupils for a number of years, the Republic cannot abandon them at the most critical moment of all. It must guarantee them employment in their chosen career.

If they are destined for a civil career, and devote themselves to administration, they will be placed on the administrative side of the War Office, or of the Navy, or in the offices of ministers, prefects, etc., or in the School of Mines, or in the Department of Roads and Bridges. If they take up law or medicine, they will be given studentships created for this purpose in schools that specialise in these subjects.

If they are destined for a military career, they will be commissioned as sub-lieutenants in the infantry, or be allowed to sit for examinations for employment in the navy, artillery, or engineers.

It will be possible to create every year 8 or 9 scholarships of 200 francs each, to be distributed among the different schools, and given to those pupils who most distinguish themselves.

[CORRESP., vii, 5,602. Starting from the 'Prytanée,' i.e., the old College of Louis le Grand, Napoleon planned to reorganise secondary education on more classical, military, and utilitarian lines., A Report by Lucien Bonaparte in 1800 was followed by another by Chaptal in 1801. It is the latter he is here criticising. The first section, on 'Management,' and the last, on 'Saint-Cyr College,' have been omitted.]

# 61

## PUBLIC OPINION

### TO CITIZEN RIPAULT

PARIS, *JULY* 23, 1801.

Citizen Ripault is to see that he is supplied every day with all the papers that come out, except the 11 political papers. He will read them carefully, make an abstract of everything they contain likely to affect the public point of view, especially with regard to religion, philosophy, and political opinion. He will send me this abstract between 5 and 6 o'clock every day.

Once every ten days he will send me an analysis of all the books or pamphlets which have appeared during that period, calling attention to any passages that might bear on moral questions, or interest me in a political or moral connexion.

He will take pains to procure copies of all the plays which are produced and to analyse them for me, with observations of the same character as those above mentioned. This analysis must be made, at latest, within 48 hours of the production of the plays.

He is to send me every 1st and 6th day, between 5 and 6

o'clock, a list of all the bills, posters, advertisements, etc., which deserve attention as well as anything that has come to his knowledge, and anything that has been done or said in the various Institutes, literary meetings, sermons, new educational establishments, or fashionable trials, that might be of interest from a political and moral point of view.

In consideration of these new duties imposed upon citizen Ripault, I am instructing the Minister for Home Affairs to pay him 500 francs a month, and I am ordering Pfister to give him a like amount.

[CORRESP., vii, 5647. Ripault was Napoleon's librarian till 1807.]

## 62
## JÉRÔME GOES TO SEA

TO JÉRÔME BONAPARTE

PARIS, *AUGUST* 16, 1801.

I'm glad to hear you are getting used to the life of a sailor. There's no better career in which to win a name for yourself. Go up aloft, get to know every part of the ship; and when you come back from your voyage, I hope to hear that you are as active as any powder-monkey. Don't let anyone dictate your profession to you. Make up your mind that you are going to be a sailor. I hope you have already learnt to keep your watch, and box the compass.

[LECESTRE, i, 49 bis. Napoleon paid for Jerome's education, and sent him to sea at 17.]

## 63
## THE POPE'S DEVOTED SON

TO HIS HOLINESS THE POPE

PARIS, *AUGUST* 28, 1802.

Holy Father, I have read with the greatest attention the letter that Your Holiness was good enough to write me, dated the 18th of August. I cannot but express my approval of Your Holiness' intention to nominate one of my subjects to the Grand

Mastership of Malta.

I observe with some anxiety that Your Holiness does not think it proper to agree to a *concordat* with the Italian Republic. If your mind is made up on this point, I beg you to empower the Cardinal-Legate to regulate with me, by separate briefs, the various religious questions in the Italian Republic, so that matters may not go from bad to worse, but that everything may proceed in such a way as to satisfy Your Holiness' desires.

The Cardinals I would propose to Your Holiness are the Archbishops of Paris and Lyon, and the Bishops of Troyes and Autun. The Archbishop of Paris is known to Your Holiness: he is full of virtue, and though he is 93, he still retains his memory and his physical powers. The Archbishop of Lyon is a young man with fewer claims, but he is marked out by his high moral character, and by my special regard for him, as a near relation of my own. The Bishop of Autun is a worthy old man of 84: he suffered much under the Revolution, spending a long time in prison. His virtues have enabled him to triumph over all changes of fortune. It was the Bishop of Troyes who played the most decisive part in inducing the bishops in London to obey Your Holiness' orders. He too is a very old man. He has been a great success in his diocese. In learning and knowledge he is one of the most distinguished men the Gallican church has ever had.

Your Holiness will see that I have not put forward the Bishop of Orleans. I will say quite frankly that I should like you to tell him that you will nominate him on the first opportunity but I do not think it in the best interests of religion to give a cardinal's hat at this moment to a man who has indeed been of great service to us, but who, in those unhappy times, took too prominent a part in the civil war. The government would derive more embarrassment than benefit, at the present moment, from his promotion. As, however, I gave him a sort of promise that I would some day ask Your Holiness to give him this appointment, you will be able to nominate him to the first vacancy; and it cannot be long coming, since three out of the four candidates I have put forward are over 80 years old.

I hear from indirect sources that Your Holiness has experienced considerable difficulty in your relations with Russia. I think that in dealing with this power, you should play for time as much as possible. The Emperor really pays no attention to requests that come to him through his Cabinet; so that, if Your

Holiness has to answer him, it is better that you should do so yourself, by a brief addressed to the Emperor personally, than by a note from one Cabinet to the other. The Emperor Alexander is fair-minded, honest and peaceable; his Cabinet is unprincipled, quarrelsome, and presumptuous. This, as Your Holiness will realise, is for your ears alone.

I must inform Your Holiness that I have just induced the Bey of Algiers to release a large number of Christians, many of whom are Your Holiness' subjects: it was part of the satisfaction demanded from the Bey for an insult to the French flag.

I have placed the Holy Sepulchre and the Syrian Christians once more under French protection, as used to be the case with all the churches in Constantinople. I have received a series of appeals from the Armenian bishops and the persecuted Christians of Wallachia. I have written about them to Sultan Selim, with whom I correspond personally, and who seems to me anxious to do the right thing.

I should like to rouse the China Missions to fresh activity; and I will not conceal it from Your Holiness that, quite apart from the general interests of religion, I am prompted by a desire to deprive the English of the management of these missions, which they are beginning to claim for themselves.

The Elector of Bavaria asks me to help him in his ecclesiastical difficulties. I beg Your Holiness to tell me how far you are ready to go, and what you are willing to do for this prince. You can rest assured that I shall make use of what you tell me only in the cause of peace, and for the good of the Church.

I remain, with filial respect, Your Holiness' devoted son.

[CORRESP., viii, 6273. Pius VII had become Pope in March, 1800. After long negotiations, Napoleon signed a Concordat with him on July 1, 1801; it was publicly announced along with the Peace of Amiens on April 18, 1802. The Archbishop of Lyon was Napoleon's uncle, Joseph Fesch, *v.* No.11.]

## 64

## SEBASTIANI'S MISSION

PARIS, *SEPTEMBER* 5, 1802.

Citizen Sebastiani will sail to Tripoli in Barbary on the frigate assigned him by the Minister of Marine.

(1) He will get the Bey to recognise the Italian Republic; for this purpose he will take with him specimens of Italian flags.

(2) If the blockade is still in force he will offer to mediate an agreement between the Bey and the powers with whom he is at war, but without using pressure, or showing too much interest in these powers.

(3) He is then to go to Alexandria, and to observe what vessels are in port and whether there are any warships; what troops the English and Turks have there, and what is the condition of the defences, and of the forts. He is to find out all that has happened, since our departure, both at Alexandria and in Egypt. He is to discover the present condition of the Egyptians, take notes of his conversations with the Sheik El-Messiry, and the English and Turkish commandants, and send a fast brig home with information on all these points.

(4) If Gyzeh is in the hands of the English, he must go there under English escort, break his journey frequently, and talk to the natives at El-Rahmânyeh, Terrâneh, and other places, taking notes of everything. On arrival at Gyzeh, he will write to the Pasha; travel, with his leave, to Great Cairo; interview the great Sheiks El-Messiry, El-Cherqâouy, El-Fayoumy, etc.; take notes of their conversation, and of the condition of the Cairo citadel and the surrounding fortifications; and give everyone in the place pleasant impressions of myself, without compromising me in any way – he may say 'that I love the people of Egypt, that I often talk of them and hope for their happiness.'

(5) He should carry a letter from Talleyrand to the Pasha of Cairo, acquainting him of my desire to send a commissioner to Cairo as soon as possible, and to know whether all is quiet there: saying also that I take an interest in the happiness of Egypt, and asking whether I can contribute towards it by mediating with the Beys. If the Pasha suggests his going into Upper Egypt to interview the Beys, he should go; otherwise, he should stay 8 or 10 days at Cairo, and when he has seen everything, and talked to everybody, return. He will ask for any Frenchmen still in hospital, or in the Mamelukes' hands, and bring them back with him, if they wish to return. He must in any case ask for Elias, the interpreter, and bring him back.

He is to give notice of the arrival of a commissioner of foreign affairs at Cairo; and to recommend Mount Sinai to the care of the Pasha.

(6) He will go to Jaffa; view the state of the walls, and of Palestine; discover who is in command at Jaffa, Gaza and Jerusalem; recommend to their care the monasteries at Jaffa,

and find out from the monks all that has been happening in Palestine; discover what has become of the Motoualys, and how Djezzar's position has changed; and recommend the Christians of Nazareth to Turkish protection.

(7) He will go to Saint-Jean d'Acre, recommend to Djezzar's care the monastery at Nazareth, warn him of the arrival of the republican agent at Acre, and find out about the fortifications he has built there, visiting them personally, if it can be done without danger. If he hears that the Motoualys are at Tyre, he must go ashore there, and convey to them my desire for their happiness.

Wherever he goes, he must say all the good he can about the Porte, but never utter a word that might compromise his own position.

[CORRESP., viii, 6308. General Sebastiani's mission and the publication of his report in the *Moniteur*, on January 30, 1803 (during the Peace of Amiens), was much resented in England, and contributed to the resumption of war the following May.]

# 65

# SWITZERLAND

## TO CITIZEN TALLEYRAND,
## MINISTER FOR FOREIGN AFFAIRS

SAINT-CLOUD, *September* 23, 1802.

Please send for Colonel Mullinen. Tell him that his letter has reached me and that I have read it with close attention; that none of the Swiss moves has escaped me; and that there could be no greater outrage against French honour than the Soleure and Berne proclamations, which are not the acts and words of level-headed men, but of lunatics who exaggerate their selfish passions.

Tell him that the 200 families in Berne claim sovereign rights, and that, whatever they may say, I have too good an opinion of the Swiss to suppose them willing to subject themselves again to family government.

Tell him that, in any case, France has guaranteed equal rights in Switzerland, and that it is a country in which counter-revolution might indeed be attempted, but could never be carried through. What he says about the will of the people is all nonsense: – you don't express the will of the people by bribing a handful of armed men to raise a riot. Besides, my calculations are not based simply upon what the Swiss people would like, but upon what is to the advantage of 40 million Frenchmen. . .

Tell him that I am now convinced of the necessity of definite action, and that, unless the provisions of my proclamation are carried out within the next few days, 30,000 men under General Ney will cross the frontier. If they force me to this step, it is all up with Switzerland.

Tell him that my primary need is for a frontier to cover the Franche-Comté. The first desideratum is a firm and settled government friendly to France. If this cannot be secured, my course will be dictated by the interests of France. Every word in my proclamation speaks volumes: there is not a syllable of rhetoric in it: it expresses exactly what I mean. My policy is honest and above-board, for it springs from long meditation backed by force.

Tell him that he is useless at Paris, where he can only mislead those he represents as to my intentions. He had better be off within twelve hours, reach Berne as quickly as he can, and report all you have said to him: for if a single French flag enters Switzerland, it will be a bad business for them. Tell him that I take sides in none of their quarrels; that I have no favourites; and that I have constantly complained of Dolder and Reding, neither of whom has followed my advice.

If my intervention is accepted, and no French troops enter Switzerland, I consider that the end of the voyage is reached. It will be useless to talk of modifications, or loopholes: I shan't listen to a word. Colonel Mullinen can tell his compatriots that for the last two years this has been a regular game, which it is now time to end; and that I can see no half-way house between *a Swiss Government firmly organised and friendly to France*, and *no Switerland at all*.

Whatever you do, insist upon his leaving Paris. There is nothing for him to do there: Berne is now the only place where he can help his fellow-countrymen.

[CORRESP., viii, 6339. In May, 1801, Napoleon imposed upon Switzerland the Constitution of Malmaison. During the troubles that followed, Reding was made *Landammann* (Premier) by malcontents at Berne. After a conference with representatives of the rival parties, Napoleon, by the Act of Settlement (February, 1803), gave the country a fresh Constitution, one condition of which was that the Swiss Confederation should supply him with troops. Dolder was a Moderate member of the Directory of 1800.]

## 66

# ADVICE TO AN ARCHBISHOP

## TO THE ARCHBISHOP OF LYON

ROUEN, *NOVEMBER* 2, 1802.

I arrived at Rouen three days ago. I am very pleased with the people in this Department, and have reason to be satisfied with the character of the clergy, and especially of the Archbishop.

It is time that you were starting for your diocese, without further delay. You should take with you a respectable but not luxurious number of servants, modelling your household on the best at Lyon – those of the Prefect and the General commanding that district. Be careful what you do, but appoint as many constitutional priests as possible, and make certain of support from this party. You must face the fact that whilst this controversy about constitutionals and non-constitutionals is for most of the priests a matter of religion, their leaders regard it purely as a political question. In addition you must show great consideration and respect for the Pope, and for the virtues and (as he is your superior authority) the views of the Archbishop of Paris.

I wish you to send me your episcopal charge before it is published and printed. The fact is, if you offend the constitutional clergy, you will excessively annoy me, and do the state great harm. I would much rather that you alienated some fanatic than that you broke with the constitutionals.

Do not forget that, upon the stage you are going to occupy, everybody will see what you do. Be austere in your private life, keep up a proper state in public, and give all your time to the duties of your office. Profess not to meddle in politics: if they present you petitions for me, reply that you are a Minister of religion, and of that alone. Don't give too much rein to your enthusiasm, even for the management of alms-houses, or the care of the poor.

Your first business, and one that will occupy you for some months, is to administer the sacraments in your diocese, to conciliate and to get to know your priests, and to organise your church. Lyon was once a great industrial centre, and contains a large number of priests formerly attached to a party in opposition to the state. Don't employ these men; or if you cannot see how to avoid employing some of them, let me know what the trouble is, and I will have them moved elsewhere, on my own

initiative. Lastly, it may be a serious error, in your delicate position, to underact your part; but it is the worst mistake of all to
overact it. Beware of your natural liveliness, and your readiness
to take sides, and to put yourself forward.

The Bishop of Chambéry had not the necessary qualities
for such a post. What I should really like, as your first move,
would be for you to give your hand to one of the most consistent members of the refractory party – provided he is not too
much of an extremist – and also to one of the most consistent
members of the constitutional party, and to bless them and
embrace them both at once, telling them that union and broth-
erhood are the foundation of all religion. Some striking gesture
of this kind would have good results for religion, and benefit
the state.

As for the mere talkers, who will always be telling you that
there is going to be a schism between the constitutionals and the
non-constitutionals, you should reply that 'the things that
belong to your ministry do not belong to theirs,' that any
movement or expression of opinion likely to produce pride
would be a sin that it is your duty to denounce, and that trying
to humiliate one's neighbour means raking up memories of the
time when he was an enemy, and thereby violating the first
principle of the law. The Archbishops and Bishops of 1802 are
not the Archbishops and Bishops of 1789: they are those who
come nearest to the Early Church. You know enough, and you
have sufficient acquaintance with the doctrines and precepts of
Christianity, to extract rules and maxims of conduct from religion itself, without talking about the good of the state.

Take what I have written to heart. It is the only way to be
of service to religion or to the state, to win the respect and confidence of all parties, and to be acceptable to myself.

The Pope has informed me that you are to be made a Cardinal immediately.

[CORRESP., viii, 6408. The new Archbishop of Lyon was Fesch; *v.* No.
63. The 'constitutional' clergy were those who had accepted the oath required
of them under the Republic; the 'non-constitutional' or 'refractory' clergy
were those who had refused it.]

## 67
## JOAN OF ARC
### TO CITIZEN CHAPTAL, MINISTER FOR HOME AFFAIRS

PARIS, *FEBRUARY* 9, 1803.

Please write to citizen Crignon-Désormeaux, mayor of Orleans, to say that I approve of the resolution. The illustrious career of Joan of Arc proves that there is no miracle French genius cannot perform in face of a threat against national freedom. The French nation has never known defeat. But our frank and loyal nature has been taken advantage of by clever and calculating neighbours. Time after time they have sown dissension among us. Hence the calamities of past history, and of our own generation.

[LECESTRE, i, 58. The 'resolution' was a proposal by the Municipal Council of Orleans to put up a statue to Joan of Arc.]

## 68
## REWARDS FOR CLERGY
### TO CITIZEN PORTALIS, STATE COUNCILLOR, IN CHARGE OF ALL MATTERS OF PUBLIC WORSHIP

SAINT-CLOUD, *MAY* 12, 1803.

Please inform the Prefect of La Vendée and the Bishop of La Rochelle that I wish them to distribute 150 francs to the 60 vicars or curates-in-charge who are best educated, and best behaved, and who show the greatest attachment to the Concordat, to religion, and to the government. You are to make these payments to them up to 9,000 francs, the total of the grants, from the list of names supplied to you by the Bishop, and approved by the Prefect.

Write in the same sense to the Bishop of Le Morbihan, asking him to send you a list of the 100 vicars or curates-in-charge who have most intelligence, and most attachment to the Concordat and to the government: I intend to give each of them a bonus of 150 francs. When he sends you the list, you can send him the money.

[Corresp., viii, 6738.]

## 69

# THEORY OF HEAT

TO THE COUNT DE RUMFORD, FOREIGN ASSOCIATE OF
THE NATIONAL INSTITUTE

PARIS, *September* 29, 1803.

I have received your Memoir of September 15, and have
read it with care. The roughnesses of unpolished bodies are like
mountains by comparison with the excessively tenuous molecules of the calorie. Their total surface being much greater than
that of the same body when polished, and the area of the surface
serving as a measure for the number of caloric molecules given
off or taken in, it follows that this number must be greater, and
the changes of temperature correspondingly more rapid, in an
unpolished than in a polished body. Such were the ideas that I
had formed for myself, and that your Memoir has confirmed. It
is only by a large number of experiments, carefully made, with
the talent that you have brought to yours, and with a view to
discovering the truth, that advances are made little by little, and
theories arrived at which are not only simple, but also useful at
every turn of life.

Please believe that it is my wish, whatever the circumstances, to give proof of the special respect I have for you.

[CORRESP., ix, 7141. Sir Benjamin Thompson, Count von Rumford,
F.R.S. (1753 – 1814) was an American who made a name in various countries
for chemical, culinary, and philanthropic experiments. Cf. No. 239.]

## 70

# SECRETARIAT
*Note*

SAINT-CLOUD, *November* 1, 1803.

Bonaparte hardly ever writes. He dictates, walking up and
down his study to a young man of 20, named Méneval, who is
the only person to enter, not merely the study, but also the three
rooms on either side of it. This young man succeeded Bourrienne, whom the First Consul had known from childhood, but
whom he dismissed for allowing himself to get mixed up in
monetary transactions. Méneval is the sort of man of whom
much is expected. Besides, he would not care to be dishonest,

because, if anything went wrong in the study suspicion would
at once fall upon him. Notes dealing with matters of high policy
the First Consul does not dictate: he writes them himself. He has
on his table a large portfolio divided into compartments – one
for each Ministry. This portfolio, which is strongly made, is
locked up by the First Consul alone. He keeps the only key to
it. Every time he leaves the study it is Méneval's duty to put this
portfolio away in a safe with sliding doors screwed to the floor
under his desk. The portfolio could be removed, but there is no
place where a thief could hide himself. Suspicion could fall on
no one but Méneval, or the study attendant, who is the only person to light the fire and tidy the room; and his disappearance
would at once be noticed. This portfolio must by now contain
all that the First Consul has written for some years past; for it is
the only one that always travels with him, and constantly
accompanies him from Paris to Malmaison and Saint-Cloud.
All the secret notes on his military operations are to be found
there; and, as the only way to destroy his authority would be to
confuse his plans, there can be no question that the theft of this
portfolio would throw them all into confusion.

[CORRESP., ix, 7241. Méneval succeeded Bourrienne as Napoleon's secretary in 1802, and remained until 1813, when his place was taken by Fain. v.
Introduction.]


# 71

# PAULINE

## TO PAULINE, PRINCESS BORGHESE

BOULOGNE, *NOVEMBER* 11,, 1803.

I shall not be back for some days yet. But the season for
travelling is nearly past, and the Alps will soon be icebound. So
set off for Rome. Make yourself remarked for your gentleness,
your politeness to everyone, and an extreme regard for the
ladies who are friends or relations of your mother's side of the
family. More is expected of you than of anyone. Above all, conform to the customs of the country; never run down anything;
find everything splendid; and don't say, 'We do this better in
Paris.' Show great attachment and respect for the Holy Father,
of whom I am very fond, and whose simple manners make him
worthy of the post he holds. Whatever I am told about you,

nothing will please me more than to hear that you are good-tempered. The only foreigners you must never receive at your house, as long as we are at war with them, are the English – indeed, you must never allow them to be in your company. Love your husband, make your household happy, and above all don't be frivolous or capricious. You are 24 and it is time you were mature and sensible. I love you, and shall always be pleased to hear that you are happy.

[BROTONNE, ii, 2107. Pauline Bonaparte had accompanied her first husband, General Leclerc, on a military expedition to St. Domingo, where he died of fever on November 2, 1802. She returned to France with his body; and a year later married Prince Borghese. For the sequel, *v.* No. 75.]

# 72

# ENGLISH INVASION

(1)

## TO CONSUL CAMBACÉRÈS

BOULOGNE, *November* 16, 1803.

The Minister of Marine arrived two days ago. I have spent the last three days in the camps and the port. Everything here is beginning to get into shape, and to move in the right direction.

From the heights of Ambleteuse I have seen the English coast as clearly as one can see the Calvary from the Tuileries. One could pick out the houses, and see people moving about. The Channel is a mere ditch, and will be crossed as soon as someone has the courage to attempt it.

The Seine must be very high at Paris; it has never stopped raining here. We have more than 200 vessels, between Saint-Malo and this place, either at anchor or sailing to join us. I am expecting the arrival of a division today.

[CORRESP., ix, 7279. Ambleteuse is on the French coast, a few miles north of Boulogne.]

## (2)

### TO CITIZEN CHAPTAL, MINISTER FOR HOME AFFAIRS

PARIS, *NOVEMBER* 29, 1803.

I want you to get a song written, to go to the tune of the *Chant du départ*, for the invasion of England. While you are about it, have a number of songs written on the same subject, to go to different tunes. Plenty of topical plays, I know, have been produced. Make a selection of them, so that they may be put on at various Paris theatres – still better, at Boulogne, Bruges, and other places where the army is encamped.

[CORRESP., ix, 7333.]

## 73

# IRISH INVASION

### TO GENERAL BERTHIER, MINISTER OF WAR

PARIS, *JANUARY* 13, 1804.

Send for Messrs. Emmet, Thompson, and the other Irish leaders, and inform them:

(1) That I have read the enclosed memorandum with the closest attention; that I cannot issue any proclamation before actually landing on Irish territory; but that the general in command of the expedition will be provided with sealed letters declaring my refusal to make peace with England unless the terms include the independence of Ireland – always upon condition that the invading army is joined by a considerable corps of United Irishmen; and that Ireland will be treated exactly as America was in the last war;

(2) That every Irishman sailing with the French army, and taking part in the expedition, will be given a French commission: if he is captured, and treated otherwise than as a prisoner of war, reprisals will be practised on English prisoners;

(3) That every corps formed in the name of the United Irishmen will be regarded as forming part of the French army; that, if the expedition were to fail, France would support a certain number of Irish brigades, and grant pensions to individual Irishmen who had taken part in the government or administration of their country – such pensions to conform to those given

in France, under similar conditions, to persons out of employment; that I should like to have a committee of United Irishmen formed, and that I see no reason why they should not issue manifestoes, and instruct their fellow countrymen as to the situation. These manifestos could be published in the *Argus,* and other European papers, in order to enlighten the Irish as to the hopes they may conceive, and the part they will have to play.

If the Committee cared to draw up an account of all the tyrannies practised in Ireland, it would be put into the *Moniteur*.

[CORRESP., ix, 7475. This Irish invasion, in which Ganteaume was to command the fleet, and Augereau the army, never matured. Emmet is not Robert Emmet, who had been executed after an abortive rising the year before, but his brother Thomas, at this time in Holland. For the sequel, *v*. No. 225.]

# 74

## CADOUDAL PLOT

### TO GENERAL SOULT

LA MALMAISON, *February* 13, 1804, 8 *P.M.*

For the last week we have been pursuing 40 brigands – Georges and his party – who landed at three different times between Tréport and Dieppe. A third party, 20 strong, is still expected to land. We have arrested all those who might signal to them, and Savary is waiting for them at Biville. All the same, you must double the sentries along the coast, so that, if the wind prevents their landing at the points where we are waiting for them (though I don't think this likely), they may not come ashore on the flank of your army.

See to the immediate arrest of the skipper and crew of the fishing-boat which communicated with the English. I blame myself for neglecting to have them arrested at the time. [You must make the skipper speak. You have my authority to promise him pardon if he gives information; and, if he should seem to hesitate, you can go so far as to follow the usual practice with men suspected of spying, and squeeze his thumbs under the hammer of a musket.]

Arrest the agent whom——sent to Boulogne on his own initiative.

Have a confidential talk with the mayor and others, and

arrest at once anyone whom they conscientiously believe to be in communication with the English.

More than 13 of this first body of brigands have been arrested. One party is in the forests of Gournay, Eu, Forges, and Lyons. Then there is that rascal Pichegru, who came to Paris with Georges and his brigands: we know where they slept on Sunday. Some even of the most prominent generals of the moment are implicated by the evidence of men we have arrested. If the evidence is confirmed, I shall punish them as they deserve. I thought it right to let you know at once of my earliest suspicions, so that this may put you onto the scent of any plot that is afoot in your army.

I haven't time to write to Davout. Pass on this information to him.

You will gather from the obscurity which prevails in one part of my despatch that I am not yet in a position to say anything for certain about the latest developments.

The police encourage me to hope that they will lay their hands on Lajolais, Pichegru, and Georges tonight.

[CORRESP., ix, 7541, and LECESTRE, i, 66. Georges Cadoudal plotted the assassination of Napoleon, and royalist risings in Brittany and La Vendée. One of his supporters, under sentence of death, revealed that Cadoudal and Pichegru were in Paris, and that a Bourbon prince was expected to land at Biville, near Dieppe. Pichegru was arrested on February 28, and Cadoudal on March 19. The passage within square brackets was omitted as 'illegible' by the editors of the official Correspondence.]

## 75

## PAULINE AGAIN

### TO CARDINAL FESCH

LA MALMAISON, *April* 10, 1804.

I am sending you a letter for Madame Paulette. I don't believe half what you say in your letter; all the same it annoys me to think that Madame Borghese doesn't realise how much her happiness depends upon behaving as the Romans behave, and finding compensation in the good port of that great city – compensation such as should be pleasant to so aristocratic a soul. In any case, I am telling her my intentions as simply and precisely as possible, and I hope she will fall in with them.

Besides, she will benefit by the arrival of her mother, who is the natural person to advise her. Tell her therefore, from me, that she is no longer as pretty as she was, and that in a few years' time she will be much less so; whereas she can be good and respected all her life. Further, it is only fair that her husband should take advantage of his habit of living in Paris, and of the liberty it gives him – a liberty to which wives in this country are well accustomed. She ought to make a point of being polite to her husband's family, and to the important people in Rome, and cultivate a social poise worthy of her rank, instead of her present ill manners, which would be considered bad form even in the most disreputable circles of Paris.

[CORRESP., ix, 7678. Cf. No. 71.]

# 76

# NAVAL PROGRAMME

## TO REAR-ADMIRAL DECRÈS

SAINT-CLOUD, APRIL 28, 1804.

I am signing a decree today about naval construction. I will listen to no objections. Go through all the orders you have given twice a week, and see that they are carried out. If special measures are needed, let me know. I shall not regard any excuse as valid. Under proper management I could build 30 ships of the line in a year, if I needed them. A country like France ought to produce everything we want. You will understand that my idea is to lay down a number of ships, but not at Brest, where I want no more built. My intention is to have 26 warships launched before vendémiaire, Year XIV (September, 1805); it being understood that their launching must primarily depend upon whether or not the war comes to an end between now and then. Work on all the 74-gun ships at Antwerp ought to begin at once. Antwerp must be our biggest dockyard. It is the only place where the French fleet can be reconstructed in a few years.

By the Year XV (September, 1806) we ought to have 100 warships.

[CORRESP., ix, 7731. Decrès was Minister for the Navy and Colonies.]

## 77

# NIGHT-PIECE

### TO THE EMPRESS JOSÉPHINE

PONT-DE-BRIQUES, *JULY* 21, 1804.

Madame, and dear wife: during the four days that I have been away from you I have been on horseback and on the move all the time, without any bad effect on my health.

M. Maret has told me of your plan to leave on Monday: if you travel in short stages, you will have time to reach the watering-place without tiring yourself.

Last night the wind freshened, and one of our gun-boats in the roads dragged her anchor, and ran on the rocks off Boulogne. I was afraid she would be a total loss, both men and gear; but we succeeded in saving them all. It was a magnificent spectacle: the reports of alarm-guns, watch-fires all along the shore, the sea raging and roaring, and all night long the anxiety as to whether the poor fellows could be rescued, or would perish before our eyes! The soul was surrounded by the ocean, darkness, and Eternity! At five in the morning everything could be seen clearly, the crew had all been saved; and I went to bed with the impression of a romantic and epic dream. I was in a mood when I might have brooded on my loneliness. But I was exhausted, and soaked to the skin, and there was no desire left me but for sleep.

[CORRESP., ix, 7861.]

## 78

# BARÈRE

### TO M. FOUCHÉ

AIX-LA-CHAPELLE, *SEPTEMBER* 9, 1804.

. . . I see that Barère has written a 'Letter to the Army.' I haven't read it; but I am sure there is no need to talk to the Army: it doesn't read the idle gossip of pamphleteers; one word in the Orders of the Day would do more than a hundred volumes of Cicero and Demosthenes. One can encourage the troops against England without talking to them; and nothing could be more absurd than to write them a pamphlet. It suggests distrust and intrigue, and the army needs none of it. Tell Barère, whose rhetoric and sophistry ill accord with his big reputation, not to do any more writing of this kind. He is always thinking the mob must be roused to excitement: on the contrary, the right way is to guide them without their knowing it. In short, he is a man of little ability. If it is not too late, stop the circulation of his pamphlet, and don't let it be sent to the army. The army is not an administrative body. The only legal means of communication with it is an Order of the Day. Everything else is factiousness and intrigue. I haven't read the pamphlet. But if it is a good piece of work, the contents, not addressed to anyone in particular, might be inoffensive, and have a good effect.

[CORRESP., ix, 8001. Barère de Vieuzac, Conventional, Jacobin, and one of the most prominent members of the Committee of Public Safety, having escaped deportation at the hands of the Thermidorians by going into hiding, took advantage of the amnesty in 1799, and was at this time employed by Napoleon to report on the state of public opinion in Paris.]

## 79

## ÉMIGRÉS AND NUNS

### TO M. FOUCHÉ

TRÈVES, *OCTOBER* 7, 1804.

. . .The circular letter to the Prefects of Departments about amnestied persons and *émigrés* would be excellent, only that a certain number of Prefects disregard it. It would have been better to ask the Prefects for the names of those amnestied persons who, as members of Councils or departmental Colleges, have the right to be present at the Coronation; and notes should be added giving information about them: then we can decide what to do. I think there is still time to take this step. Government must be logical. Once a person is admitted to membership of the state, he must be given all the rights of citizenship. I am anxious that the Prefects should send you the lists of amnestied persons and *émigrés* belonging to the Colleges, so that you may submit reports to me, one for each department, and so that those who are recognised as being sensible, harmless, and well-disposed, may receive permits from me, exempting them from supervision, and restoring their civil rights. The art of government consists not only in punishing the wicked, but also in rewarding the good. A great many of these *émigrés*, as you know, returned quite openly; consequently it was impossible to prevent their enjoying their political rights, seeing that there are amnestied persons and *émigrés* in the Senate, the State Council, and other public positions. The general principle is to keep the whole class under supervision, whilst making exceptions in favour of the best behaved; and it is natural to include among the latter those who hold official positions.

I have read carefully the report of the Prefect of Police on the working of the decree of 3 messidor, Year XII, about religious corporations. My chief object was to prevent the Jesuits establishing themselves in France. They assume all sorts of disguises. I want no 'Hearts of Jesus,' or 'Confraternities of the Holy Sacrament,' or anything at all resembling a monastic militia. Under no pretext will I go a step further or admit any ecclesiastics, except the secular clergy. I am equally determined to exclude convents of nuns; but I see no objection, under this head, to the old nuns ending their days in the common life, and wearing what habits they like indoors; but they must not admit novices, or wear their habits out of doors. I except the Sisters of Charity: I am even prepared to let them recruit their Order by establishing novitiates. Two precautions must therefore be taken in the case of nuns. First, we must know who they are, and keep a careful watch on them, to be sure that they are not directed by priests out of communion with their bishop. Any society that breaks these rules deserves punishment without pity. It is on the criminal high road, it is at the mercy of scoundrels; and there is nothing too bad to expect from ill-behaved spinsters. Secondly, we must see to it that they admit no novices. This is not so easy. I see, for instance, that the Sisters of Mercy at No. 529 rue de la Chaise take pupils. How is one to distinguish a pupil from a novice? I must have a guarantee (1) that these pupils do not wear religious habits, but ordinary clothes, (2) that they are not kept there after the age of 18. All those over the age of 18 ought to be sent away from these houses. They must be warned to leave within 6 months: otherwise they will see the house closed and the inmates dispersed. But it would be best to secure some devout and sensible ecclesiastics, approved by the Archbishop, to visit and inspect these establishments; or M. Portalis can commission some members of the monastic underworld to perform this function.

Report to me on the nuns of the congregation of the rue

Saint-Étienne, who are said in the report to be taking in boarders and novices, and who have made a special practice of devotions to the Sacred Heart. Find out whether they are recognised by the Archbishop, and what novices they admit. Make these inquiries through a Grand Vicar, or in some other simple way, without alarming them. You can talk to M. Portalis about them if you like. The report of the Prefect of Police is clear and precise: all the Prefects should furnish similar reports; then you can easily draw up orders, in accordance with the principles that I have just laid down.

[CORRESP., x, 8099. The *émigrés* were those still subject to the various penal laws passed against Frenchmen who had fled from the country during the Revolution.]


## 80

# WEST INDIAN EXPEDITION

## TO GENERAL LAURISTON

PARIS, *DECEMBER* 12, 1804.

The Ministers of War and of Marine have sent you your instructions. You will see that I have strengthened your expedition by the addition of General Reille. I need the frigate 'La Muiron' for another service. It is already rather late in the season. Start at once; justify my confidence in you; and hoist my flag on this fine continent. If, when you have established a footing there, you are attacked by the English, and experience vicissitudes of fortune, never forget three things – to keep your forces together, to be up and doing, and to be firmly resolved to die a soldier's death. These three great principles of the art of war have brought fortune to my side in all my operations. Death is nothing: but to live defeated and inglorious is to die daily. Have no fears for your family: devote all your energies to that part of my family to whose conquest you are bound.

[CORRESP., x, 8209. Lauriston in command of 3,500 men sailed from Toulon with Villeneuve for the West Indies on January 17, 1805.]

## 81

# 'L'EMPIRE, C'EST LA PAIX'

## TO THE KING OF ENGLAND

PARIS, *JANUARY* 2, 1805.

Monsieur my Brother; called to the throne of France by Providence, and by the votes of the Senate, the people, and the army, my first impulse is to pray for peace. France and England are using up their resources. They might indeed go on struggling for centuries. But are not their governments failing in the most sacred of all their duties? And will not their own consciences reproach them with so much useless and aimless bloodshed? I think it no dishonour to make the first advances. I have shown the world enough evidence, I fancy, that I shrink from nothing that war may bring – I see no prospect there for alarm. Peace is the wish of my heart, but war has never been alien to my idea of glory. I beg Your Majesty not to reject the honour of being the world's peace-maker. Do not leave this pleasant task to your children! For in fact there was never a finer occasion or a more favourable moment to silence every passion, and to close the ears to every voice but that of humanity and common-sense. This opportunity once missed, what bounds could one hope to set to a war which all my efforts have failed to end? During the last ten years Your Majesty has gained in territory and in riches more than the whole area of Europe. Your nation is at the zenith of its prosperity. What can it hope to do by war? To form a coalition of some of the continental powers? But the continent will not move, and a coalition would only emphasise the preponderance of France on the continent. To revive our internal disorders? But the times are not what they were. To ruin us financially? But a financial system based on good agriculture is indestructible. To deprive France of her colonies? Colonies are, for France, a matter of secondary importance; and does not Your Majesty already possess more than you can defend? If Your Majesty really thinks about it, you will see that the war has no aim, and offers no results upon which you can count. Why! what a sad prospect it is, to make men fight merely that they may go on fighting! The world is big enough for both our nations to live in, and common-sense is strong enough to find a means of settling all our differences, if both of us have a will to it. In any case, I have fulfilled what my

heart counts a sacred and treasured duty. I beg Your
Majesty to believe in the sincerity of the feelings which
I have expressed, and in my desire to give Your Majesty
proof of it.

[CORRESP., x, 8252. Napoleon had been declared Emperor by
Senatorial decree of May 18, 1804, confirmed by plebiscite of
November 27, and crowned in Nôtre Dame on December 2.]

## 82
## IMPERIAL PICTURES
### TO M. ESTÈVE, KEEPER OF THE PRIVY PURSE

PARIS, *JANUARY* 9, 1805.

You are to make the following payments, on the
Emperor's account:

*(Salon of Year XIII – Napoléon Museum)*

| | *francs* |
|---|---:|
| To M. Gros, for the picture 'The Plague at Jaffa,' commissioned by H.M. the Empress without fixing the price (which ought never to have been done), the sum of 16,000 francs; this will not satisfy the feelings of the artist, in view of the fantastic price paid for Guérin's 'Phèdre'. . . . | 16,000 |
| To M. Rigo, for the picture of the angel El-Mahdi  To | 4,000 |
| M. Serangeli, as a bonus granted him over and above the purchase of his diploma picture. . . | 3,000 |

*(Pictures purchased at the Salon by order of H.M. the
Empress)*

| | |
|---|---:|
| To M. Demarne, for a sea-port and a village cheap-jack. . . . | 2,000 |
| To M. Le Comte, for a landscape representing some knights journeying to the Holy Land. | 1,800 |
| To M. Laurens, for a picture of a young girl at a window, holding a lute | 1,000 |
| To M. Roelm, for a village fair | 1,000 |
| To M. Duperreux, for a view of Eaux-Bonnes | 700 |
| To M. Gérard, for a sketch of the signing of the Concordat, priced at | 1,200 |
| Total | 30,700 |

M. Estève will pay the above sum of 30,700 francs.

[CORRESP., x, 8266.]

# 83

# TURKEY AND RUSSIA

## TO THE EMPEROR OF TURKEY

PARIS, *JANUARY* 30, 1805.

Most Exalted, most Excellent, most Powerful, most Magnanimous and Invincible Prince, Great Emperor of the Moslems, Sultan Selim, in whom abound all honour and virtue, our very dear and perfect friend; may God grant increase of your Greatness and Altitude, and a blessed end.

Have you, a descendant of the great Ottomans, Emperor of one of the greatest empires in the world, ceased to reign? How is it that you allow the Russians to dictate to you? You refuse to render me service for service: are you blind to your own interests in this matter? If Russia has 15,000 men at Corfu, do you suppose that they are aimed at me? Her armed ships have a way of appearing off Constantinople: are you too blind to see that one day, either under pretext of fetching back the Russian troops at Corfu, or of reinforcing them, a Russian fleet and army, with the Greeks on their side, will invade the capital, and your empire will have perished with you? Your dynasty will descend into the night of oblivion. The Reis-effendi is betraying you. Half the Divan is in Russian pay. The death of the Captain-pasha has deprived you of your best friend. I have warned you twice before: this is the third time. Dismiss your Divan, punish the Reis-effendi, and rule in Constantinople: otherwise it is all up with you. For myself, I have tried to be your friend. But if you persistently refuse me the preference which France has always had at Constantinople, and if you would rather remain in slavish submission to your enemies, then I too shall set myself against you; and I have never been a feeble foe. Your Divan is taking no steps to restore order in Egypt and Syria: it allows Mecca and Medina to be lost: it is for ever insulting your friends, and salaaming to your enemies. Persia is at war. She is threatened by Russia. Yet, instead of helping her, the feeble Divan, or rather the traitors who direct it, do nothing even to intervene on her behalf: it is only against me that they show a spark of courage. That is why I am writing to you. You are the only friend France still has in the Seraglio, always provided that my letter is allowed to reach you by men who have occupied all the avenues of the throne. Rouse yourself, Selim. Make ministers of your supporters; dismiss the traitors; trust yourself to your true friends, France and Prussia; otherwise you will destroy your country, your family, and your religion. The Russians are your real enemies, because they want to control the Black Sea, and cannot do it unless they have Constantinople; and because they are of the Greek religion, which is that of half your subjects. I await your answer, to know what I must think and do. If you rule no longer, if the enemies of France have you entirely in their power, I shall lament the blindness and the misguided policy of France's most ancient ally, but I shall understand that the same Destiny which made you so great wills to destroy the empire of such as Soliman, Mustapha, and Selim. For upon earth everything changes and passes away: God alone will never fail. Wherefore I pray God that he may prolong Your Highness's days, and fill them with all prosperity, and give you a blessed end.

Your very dear and perfect friend,

NAPOLEON.

Given at my Imperial Palace of the Tuileries, 10 pluviôse, Year XIII.

[CORRESP., x, 8298. In 1804 Napoleon offered to guarantee the integrity of Turkey against Russia: when the Tsar crossed the Pruth in 1805 he proposed an alliance with Prussia to prevent a Russian conquest of the Balkans.]

# 84

## A TEACHING ORDER
### *Note*

PARIS, *FEBRUARY* 16, 1805.

. . . Perhaps the time will soon arrive for considering the question whether we ought not to form a corporation of teachers. If so should this corporation or order be a religious association, whose members take a vow of chastity, renounce the world, and so on? There does not seem to be any connexion between the two ideas.

As things are, the educational personnel consists of Provisors, Censors, and Professors. A teaching corporation could be formed if all the Provisors, Censors, and Professors in the Empire were under one or more chiefs, like the Generals, Provincials, etc., of the Jesuits; and if it were the rule that no

one could become a Provisor or Censor without first being a
Professor, and no one a Professor in the higher classes who had
not been so in the lower  −  if, in fact, there were regular stages
of promotion in a teacher's career, such as to encourage rivalry,
and to provide, at every time of life, not only enough to live on,
but also something to look forward to. A man who has devoted
himself to teaching ought not to marry until he has passed several stages in his career: marriage ought to be, for him as for
other men, a distant goal that he cannot attain till he has secured
an adequate position and income, by holding a post whose
stipend enables him to support a family without abandoning his
profession. If this were so, the conditions of the teaching profession would be the same as those of other civil careers.

There would be *esprit de corps* among teachers. The most
distinguished members of the corporation could be taken under
the Emperor's protection, and his patronage would raise them
even higher in public esteem than the priests were, at a time
when priesthood passed for a rank of nobility. Everyone knew
how important the Jesuits were. It would not be long before the
same prestige attached to the corporation of teachers, if people
saw a man, whose education had begun in the *lycée*, picked out
for his talents to be himself a teacher, promoted from stage to
stage, and finding himself, before the end of his career, in the
front ranks of state officials.

Of all political questions this is perhaps the most important. There will be no stability in the state until there is a body
of teachers with fixed principles. Till children are taught
whether they ought to be Republicans or Monarchists,
Catholics or Unbelievers, and so on, there may indeed be a
state, but it cannot become a nation. It will rest on vague uncer-
tain foundations. It will be constantly exposed to changes and
disorders.

[CORRESP., x, 8328. The idea here outlined finally took form in the
Imperial University set up in May, 1806, and organised by the decree of
March, 1808. The *Proviseurs* and *Censeurs* were on the administrative staff
of the *lycées*: the *Professeurs* were the teachers.]

85

# AGRICULTURE
*Note*

PARIS, *MARCH* 1, 1805.

His Majesty has abolished the Imperial School of Agriculture, which could only have occasioned idle talk, and useless expenditure. He would like to give some real encouragement to agriculture. In order to do so, one must know the state of agriculture in the different Departments.

It is prosperous in the Upper and Lower Rhine Department, in the North, Belgium, Pas-de-Calais, Somme, Aisne, Oise, Seine and Marne, Seine and Oise, and in most of Eure and Loire, in Lower Seine, Calvados, the Channel, and the Departments that were once Languedoc, in Lot, Vaucluse, the Rhône estuary, Saône and Loire, Upper Saône, part of Côte d'Or, and the six Departments of Piedmont. It will be prosperous, too, in the four new Departments of the Rhine, as soon as the sale of national property puts the land under the control of those who really cultivate it.

It is to the other Departments, then, that we must convey our encouragements. In most of these Departments cultivation is in the hands of labourers or *métayers*, who care for nothing beyond making their living, and who never improve their holdings. These are not the people to be encouraged. It is the rich land-owners, who do something to increase the value of their property, and who are the only class to think about their interests, and to be concerned for the future of themselves and of their children.

People of this kind are not encouraged by grants or money, but by medals, and decorations, and eulogies addressed to them by or on behalf of the sovereign. Every Prefect must therefore get to know which land-owners and agriculturalists in his Department distinguish themselves either by the extent and skill of their farming, or by their superior breeding and rearing of live-stock. Every year the Minister for Home Affairs will distribute, to those who deserve them, either a medal, or the badge of the Legion of Honour (as the case may be), or a letter of congratulation and encouragement from the Emperor.

A certain number of foreign rams, and of specially fine bulls, will be distributed, as has been done already. In the Departments suitable for horse-breeding, prizes will be given to encourage the owners of good stallions. Agriculture, like every other art, owes its improvement to comparison, and to good models.

In those Departments which are still isolated from educational centres, good landlords should be encouraged to send their sons to study the methods in use in Departments where agriculture is flourishing; and they should be stimulated by eulogies and marks of distinction.

Money is no use in a matter of this kind. The greedy class will be coming to apply for grants, and will plead their useless journeys as a ground for fresh subsidies.

[CORRESP., x, 8374. Métayer: a farmer paying rent in kind.]

# 86

## SENATORS ON CIRCUIT
### NOTE FOR THE SECRETARY OF STATE

SAINT-CLOUD, *MARCH* 28, 1805.

M. Maret is to have as many copies made of the enclosed Instructions as there are *sénatoreries*. As I shall sign them personally, 'We' must be put in place of 'His Majesty.' M. Maret will submit them to me for signature.

*Instruction for Senators.*

Monsieur,

His Majesty desires you to go to your *sénatorerie* before the 1st prairial, to reside there continuously for 3 months, and to travel round all the Departments forming its *arrondissement.* The ostensible object both of your journey and of your residence will be to get to know the situation, character, condition, and value of the property from which the income of your *sénatorerie* is derived. Actually your most important duty will be to supply Us with trustworthy and positive information on any point which may interest the Government; and to this end, you will send Us a direct report, once a week, from the capital town of your Department.

You will realise that complete secrecy must be observed as to this confidential mission. If it got about, all enlightened people would avoid you, honest men would refuse to have any communication with you, and you would have nothing to report but treacherous and malicious denunciations. At the same time, the public officials, most of whom deserve Our confidence, would be discredited and discouraged, and these special missions, which are meant to enlighten the Government, would be no better than an odious inquisition, tending to disorganise the public service.

(1) You are to discover what is the character, conduct, and capacity of the public officials, both in the administrative and the judicial departments;

(2) What principles the clergy hold, and how much influence they have;

(3) Who the outstanding men are in each part of your *arrondissement*, in virtue of their character, wealth, opinions, and popular influence; and to what class of society they belong. You will draw up detailed returns of all information about persons, basing your judgments upon genuine and established facts, and send in these returns to Us.

(4) You will investigate, in the different classes and cantons, the state of public opinion on (i) the government; (ii) religion; (iii) conscription; (iv) the road tax; (v) the incidence of indirect taxation.

(5) You will notice whether there are any persons in hiding from conscription; if so, how many; and whether a rising of any kind is to be feared from this cause;

How the Gendarmerie does its work; and what individual members of it are noticeable either for their zeal, or for their neglect of duty;

The number and kinds of criminal offences, and whether they are isolated acts, or the result of public gatherings;

What is generally thought about the institution of the jury, and what its effect is upon criminal trials.

(6) You will look into the state of public education, both in the primary and secondary schools, and in the *lycées*; and inquire why some of these establishments are successful, and some slack. You will draw up one list of teachers of marked ability, and another of those who have done nothing to deserve public confidence.

(7) You will study the state of agriculture, commerce, and manufacture; and find out what individuals are distinguished by intelligence or success in these different spheres.

(8) The state of the food supply, and what is expected of this year's harvest.

(9) You will observe the conditions of the roads, and find out for what general or special reasons they deteriorate.

(10) What the situation is as regards the rearing of horses, wool-bearing animals, and live stock of all kinds; and what encouragements or measures are needed to extend this business, and to make it more prosperous.

You will send Us separate memoirs based on definite knowledge on all these subjects in succession.

[CORRESP., x, 8493. The Senate of 1799 was a body of 60 – 80 members with important constitutional functions. Nearly doubled in size under the Constitution of 1802, its *senatus-consultes* became Napoleon's normal method of legislation. In 1807 it was again reduced in numbers, and lost all constitutional importance.]

# 87

# PERSIA

## TO THE KING OF PERSIA

PARIS, *MARCH* 30, 1805.

BONAPARTE, Emperor of the French, to Feth Ali, Shah of the Persians, Greeting!

I have reason to believe that the Jinn who preside over the destinies of States wish me to support the efforts you are making to uphold the strength of your empire; for the same thought struck both our minds simultaneously. The agents who carried our letters met at Constantinople; and whilst your Governor of Tauris was getting into touch with my commissioner from Aleppo, the latter received orders from me to establish communications with your viziers on the frontiers of Turkey.

It is right to have recourse to the inspirations of Heaven; for Heaven has set up princes to make the peoples happy: and when, from age to age, it produces a few great men, it lays upon them an obligation to co-operate, so that the harmony of their designs may give more brilliance to their glory, and more power to their benevolent intentions.

How else could we view the situation? Persia is the noblest country in Asia: France is the premier empire of the West. To rule over peoples and lands spontaneously beautified by Nature, to enrich them with plentiful produce, to have control over their industrious, witty, and brave inhabitants – is not this the fairest of all fortunes?

But there also exist upon the earth empires in which an ungracious and barren Nature grudgingly produces only what is necessary for the survival of their peoples. In these countries men are by birth restless, greedy, and envious; and woe to the countries favoured by Heaven, if, whilst loading them with benefits, it gives them not also brave and watchful princes, to guard them against the enterprises of ambitious, greedy, and miserable men!

Tired of their deserts, the Russians trespass upon the fairest parts of the Ottoman Empire. The English, thrust away into an island which is not worth the smallest province of your empire, and excited by a thirst for riches, are establishing in India a power which grows more redoubtable every day. Those are the states to watch and fear; not because they are yet powerful, but because they have the need, and an intense passion, to become so. I know the Persians: I believe that they will easily and willingly embrace a policy that ministers both to their safety and to their prestige. At this very moment a foreign army of 25,000 men might be plundering or perhaps subduing their country. But once your citizens learn to manufacture munitions of war, and your soldiers to master the rapid and disciplined movement of military formation, and to support their vigorous attacks with salvoes of light artillery; once your frontiers are defended by a series of fortresses, and the Caspian Sea bears on its billows the flags of a Persian fleet: – then your subjects will be invincible, and your empire beyond fear of attack. . . .

Written in My palace of the Tuileries, this 9th day of Germinal, in the year XIII, being the first of My reign.

NAPOLÉON.

[CORRESP., x, 8502. cf. No. 83. Persia played a similar part to Turkey in Napoleon's anti-Russian and anti-English policy. A Franco-Persian alliance was signed on May 4, 1807, but did not outlast the Treaty of Tilsit the same year.]

# 88

## COURT MOURNING

### TO M. CAMBACÉRÈS

TROYES, *April* 4, 1805.

The King of Prussia has just notified me of the death of the Queen-dowager. The Court must therefore go into mourning. At Berlin they do it for 3 weeks. I don't know what was done under similar circumstances at the Court of Versailles, but I want to follow that usage. M. Ségur, who has written a book on the subject, is not here. But the point must be settled quickly, so that the mourning may be fixed up before my arrival at Milan. Consult the Arch-treasurer, and submit proposals to me as to how I ought to go into mourning, and how it ought to be done by the high officials, the Empress, the ladies of the court, etc. Look into the question whether it ought to include Generals and Prefects; whether liveried servants ought to go into mourning, and, if so, how. I don't think it need take you long to formulate a plan, since what I want to do was done 15 years ago. Draft it in the form of an Instruction that I can print in the *Moniteur*. As I always wear uniform, I don't suppose I shall have to change my dress. When you have settled what mourning the Empress ought to wear, tell Mme Lavalette about it; then she can have the necessary clothes and alterations put in hand at once, so that they can be delivered within 24 hours.

[CORRESP., x, 8522.]

# 89

## MÉSALLIANCE

### TO MADAME MÈRE

CHÂTEAU DE STUPINIGI, *April* 22, 1805.

M. Jérôme Bonaparte has arrived at Lisbon with the woman he is living with. I have ordered the prodigal son to travel by Perpignan, Toulouse, Grenoble, and Turin, and to report himself at Milan. I have told him that if he varies this route he will be arrested. Miss Paterson, who is living with him, has taken the precaution of bringing a brother with her. I have given orders that she is to be sent back to America. If she attempts to evade these orders, and appears either at Bordeaux or in Paris, she will be escorted to Amsterdam, and put on board the first ship for America. As for the young man himself, I shall only give him one interview. If he shows himself unworthy of the name he bears, and seems inclined to persist in his *liaison*, I shall show him no mercy. If he shows no disposition to wipe out the dishonour with which he has stained my name by deserting the colours for a wretched woman, I shall utterly disown him, and perhaps make an example of him, to teach young officers the sanctity of military service, and the enormity of the crime they commit, if they prefer a female to the flag. Assuming that he comes to Milan, I want you to write to him. Tell him that I have been like a father to him. Tell him that it is his sacred duty to obey me, and that his only hope is to do as I command. Get his sisters to write too: for, once I have pronounced his sentence, I shall be inflexible, and his whole career will be ruined.

[LECESTRE, i, 73. Madame Mère is Letizia Bonaparte, Napoleon's mother. Jérôme's naval career (*v*. No. 62) had ended in America, and in marriage (at 19) with a Miss Paterson of Baltimore. Napoleon made him give her up, and marry Catherine of Württemberg, as a qualification for the kingship of Westphalia. cf. No. 153.]

# 90

# CORONATION

## TO M. CAMBACÉRÈS

MILAN, *MAY* 27, 1805.

The Coronation was carried out yesterday in full state. The church looked very fine. The ceremony went off as well as it did in Paris, with the difference that the weather was magnificent. When I took the iron crown, and put it on my head, I added these words: 'God gives it me: woe to him who touches it.' I hope the prophecy will come true.

[CORRESP., x, 8796. On December 4, 1804, Napoleon was crowned Emperor in Paris: at Milan on May 26, 1805, he was crowned King of Italy.]

# 91

# PRESS AND STAGE

## TO M. FOUCHÉ

MILAN, *JUNE* 1, 1805.

. . . The attention of the papers ought to be directed towards attacking England – English fashions, English customs, English literature, the English constitution. This is Geoffroi's only recommendation. Voltaire did us great harm by his constant essays in Anglomania.

It seems to me that the success of the tragedy *The Templars* is turning attention to that incident in French history. That is as it should be. But I don't think we ought to allow plays on subjects of too recent a date. I see in one of the papers that there is talk of putting on a tragedy about Henri IV. That period is not distant enough to rouse no passions. The stage needs a touch of antiquity; and I think that, without interfering with the theatre too much, you ought to veto this particular play; but don't make your intervention public. You might speak to M. Raynouard about it – he seems to be a clever man. Couldn't you commission him to write a tragedy on the transition from the Valois to the Bourbons? Only, instead of being a tyrant, the successor would be the saviour of the nation. That is the kind of play in which the stage can show its new spirit: it would never have been allowed under the old regime. You have the same idea in the oratorio *Saul* – a great man succeeding a degenerate King. . . .

[CORRESP., x, 8821 J. L. Geoffroy, of the *Journal des Débats* (1800 – 14) was the best known critic of the day. Raynouard's tragedy *Les Templiers* was first produced this year.

# 92

# HINTS FOR A VICEROY

## TO PRINCE EUGÈNE, VICEROY OF ITALY

MILAN, *JUNE* 5, 1805.

By entrusting you with the government of Our Kingdom of Italy, We have given you proof of the respect your conduct has inspired in Us. But you are still at an age when one does not realise the perversity of men's hearts; I cannot therefore too strongly recommend to you prudence and circumspection. Our Italian subjects are more deceitful by nature than the citizens of France. The only way in which you can keep their respect, and serve their happiness, is by letting no one have your complete confidence, and by never telling anyone what you really think of the ministers and high officials of your court. Dissimulation, which comes naturally at a maturer age, has to be emphasised and inculcated at yours. If you ever find yourself speaking unnecessarily, and from the heart, say to yourself, 'I have made a mistake,' and don't do it again. Show respect for the nation you govern, and show it all the more as you discover less grounds for it. You will come to see in time that there is little difference between one nation and another. The aim of your administration is the happiness of my Italian peoples; and the first sacrifice you will have to make will be to fall in with certain of their customs which you detest. In any position but that of Viceroy of Italy you may boast of being a Frenchman: but here you must forget it, and count yourself a failure unless the Italians believe that you love them. They know there is no love without respect. Learn their language; frequent their society; single them out for special attention at public functions; like what they like, and approve what they approve.

The less you talk, the better: you aren't well enough educated, and you haven't enough knowledge, to take part in informal debates. Learn to listen, and remember that silence is often as effective as a display of knowledge. Don't be ashamed to ask questions. Though a Viceroy, you are only 23; and however much people flatter you, in reality they all know your limitations, and honour you less for what they believe you to be than for what they hope that you will become.

Don't imitate me in every respect; you need more reserve. Don't preside often over the State Council; you have too little experience to do so successfully – though I see no objection to your attending it, whilst an Assessor acts as president, from his ordinary seat. Your ignorance of Italian, and of legislation too, for that matter, is an excellent excuse for staying away. Anyhow, never make a speech there: they would listen to you, and would not answer you back; but they would see at once that you aren't competent to discuss business. So long as a prince holds his tongue, his power is incalculable; he should never talk, unless he knows he is the ablest man in the room.

Don't trust spies. They are more trouble than they are worth. There is never enough unrest at Milan to bother about, and I expect it is the same elsewhere. Your military police make sure of the army, and that is all you want.

The army is the one thing you can deal with personally, and from your own knowledge.

Work with your ministers twice a week – once with each of them separately, and once with them all together in Council. Half the battle will be won when your ministers and councillors realise that your only object in consulting them is to listen to reason, and to prevent yourself being taken by surprise.

At public functions, and at fêtes, whenever you have Frenchmen and foreigners together, arrange beforehand where they are to be, and what you are to do. It is better never to form a following; and you must take the greatest care not to expose yourself to any sort of affront. If anything of the kind occurs, don't stand it. Prince, ambassador, minister, general – whoever it may be, even if it is the Austrian or Russian ambassador, have him arrested on the spot. On the other hand, such incidents are always a nuisance; and what matters little in my case might have troublesome results in yours.

Nothing is so advisable as to treat the Italians well, and to get to know all their names and families. Don't show too much attention to foreigners: there is nothing to gain by it. An ambassador will never speak well of you, because it is his business to speak ill. Ministers of foreign countries are, in plain words, accredited spies. It is as well to keep them at arm's length. They always think better of those they seldom see than of their professed friends and benefactors.

There is only one man here at Milan who really matters – the Minister of Finance: he is a hard worker, and knows his job well.

Although they know I am behind you, I have no doubt they are trying to gauge your character. See that your orders are carried out, particularly in the army: never allow them to be disobeyed.

The public decree that I have signed defines the powers I am delegating to you. I am reserving for myself the most important of all – the power of directing your operations. Send me an account of your doings every day. It is only by degrees that you will come to understand how I look at everything.

Don't show my letters to a single soul, under any pretext whatsoever. It ought not be to known what I write to you, or even that I write at all. Keep one room to which no one is admitted – not even your private secretaries.

You will find M. Méjan useful, if he doesn't try to make money; and he won't do that if he knows that you are watching him, and that a single act of this kind will ruin him in my eyes as well as yours. He ought to be well paid, and to have good prospects of promotion. But in that case he must be available at all hours: he will be useless to you if he gets into the way of working only at certain hours, and amusing himself the rest of the day. And you will have to rebuke him for a tendency he shares with all Frenchmen to depreciate this country – all the more so as it is accompanied by melancholia. Frenchmen are never happy out of France.

Keep my household and stables in order, and make up all my accounts at least once a week; this is all the more necessary as they have no idea how to manage things here.

Hold a review at Milan every month.

Cultivate the young Italians, rather than the old; the latter are good for nothing. . . .

You have an important position, and will find it pretty hard work. Try to get to know the history of all the towns in my kingdom of Italy; visit the fortresses, and all the famous battlefields. It is likely enough that you will see fighting before you are thirty, and it is a tremendous asset to know the lie of the land.

One last word. Punish dishonesty ruthlessly. The exposure of a dishonest accountant is a victory for the government. And don't allow any smuggling in the French army.

[CORRESP., x, 8852. Eugène Beauharnais was appointed Viceroy of Italy on June 7.]

# 93

# LÈSE-MAJESTÉ

## TO M. FOUCHÉ

FONTAINEBLEAU, *July* 12, 1805.

The baker's apprentice who insulted a sentinel at the gate of the Tuileries deserves severe punishment. Drunkenness is no

excuse. He must be brought to trial. His outrageous act is the
greatest crime a civilian can commit. . . .

[CORRESP., xi, 8975.]

## 94

## GENOESE SAILORS

### TO M. LEBRUN

BOULOGNE CAMP, *AUGUST* 11, 1805.

I was sorry to see your decree forbidding the recruitment of
sailors at Genoa. No doubt it is a way of making yourself very
popular; but it is also a serious blow to the efficiency of the
navy. I mobilised the fleet at Genoa just in order to get sailors,
and yet the only 3 frigates I have in the harbour are not manned.
Why do you suppose I annexed Genoa and admitted her to the
many great advantages she gains by membership of my
Empire? It was not for the money I can get out of her, nor for
the reinforcements she provides for my armies on land: my only
object was to have 15,000 more sailors. It is therefore contra-
vening the whole spirit of the annexation to pass a decree dis-
avowing naval recruitment. I cannot imagine anything more
impolitic. If we had acted so in Piedmont we should not have
got a single conscript. Genoa will never be French until it has
6,000 men serving in my fleets. I want you, then, to set yourself
seriously to procure sailors. Make it understood, by means of a
circular, that this is the only way in which the Genoese can help
me. In fact, this subject ought to be your constant preoccupa-
tion. I repeat it: these people will never be really Gallicized
until I have their sailors on board my ships. What do you imagine I can do with 225 lads from 12 to 20? There are plenty such
in France; it is old sailors I need. I can't agree with you that pro-
fessional sailors are no use – that they are only good for coastal
trade, and are terrified of going to sea in a ship of war. If so, we
must find some way of terrifying them still more. I'm afraid
you have been influenced, in your management of this business,
by the fear of offending the Genoese. Never mind about that.
Whether they wish it or not, I must have them on my vessels;
or else I shall be forced to extreme measures, such as putting an
embargo on their coastal trade, until I have as many sailors as I
want. You are ill informed; and you must think me extremely
ignorant of the Genoese if I suppose that they will be of no use
to me. Nations cannot be governed by weakness; it only does

them harm. I am afraid you have been displaying more of it than is warranted by your character. Did you really expect to manage people without making yourself unpopular? What would you do in France, if you had to organise conscription in such Departments as Calvados, or Deux-Sèvres? You must realise that in matters of government justice demands valour as well as virtue. As for those who say that this measure will make the Genoese troublesome and discontented – I am not the sort of man for such talk. I know well enough what the Genoese are capable of. Do people think I am already so decrepit that they can frighten me with the Genoese? There is only one answer to this despatch – sailors, and again sailors. You know how promptly I make up my mind, and you will understand that this business is not going to make any difference in my friendship and respect for you. But let sailors be the one object of your day's work. Dream of nothing but sailors. Say anything you like on my behalf, but say that I must have sailors.

[CORRESP., xi, 9064. On June 4, 1805, the Ligurian Republic was annexed to France. Napoleon left Lebrun in charge.]

# 95
# PLOMBIÈRES WATER
## TO THE EMPRESS JOSÉPHINE

BOULOGNE CAMP, *AUGUST* 13, 1805

. . .I hardly ever hear of you. It's a pity you forget your friends: I didn't know before that Plombières water has the same properties as the river of Lethe.

I can fancy you drinking this Plombières water, and saying, 'Ah, Bonaparte, if I die, who will be left to love you?' But that's a long way off, isn't it? Everything has its end – beauty, wit, feeling, the sun itself: but what will never end is the happiness that I desire, the good fortune that – who is it? – enjoys, and the kindness of my Joséphine. If you laugh at me, I shall never make love to you again.

Good-bye, darling. I made an attack on the English cruiser yesterday. All went well.

[BROTONNE, ii, 316. Plombières, a health resort in the Vosges made famous by the meeting of Napoleon III and Cavour there in 1858.]

# 96

# VILLENEUVE

(1)

## TO VICE-ADMIRAL DECRÈS

BOULOGNE CAMP, *AUGUST* 22, 1805.

. . . I don't believe Villeneuve has enough character to command a frigate. The man has no energy, no moral courage. A couple of Spanish ships are in collision: a few of his men fall sick: or he has two days' head winds, is sighted by one of the enemy's ships, and hears a rumour that Nelson has joined Calder – and at once all his plans are changed, though there is nothing in any of these things, taken separately. To add insult to injury, he gives no details about the composition of his fleet, and doesn't say a word as to what he is going to do or not to do. He is quite unused to war, and doesn't know how to conduct it. If Nelson had joined Calder, and thought himself sufficiently strong, he would have appeared before Ferrol: that is as obvious as ABC. The English papers, as you know, say that Nelson has been at the Canaries. Under the circumstances a special messenger should be sent to Brest with instructions to Admiral Ganteaume, ordering him, if Villeneuve appears in the roads off Brest, not to let him enter the harbour, but to take over the command of the troops on board, and to fit out for a voyage to Boulogne. If Villeneuve has been at Cadiz, my intention is that, after adding to his fleet the 6 ships there, and taking on board 2 months' provisions, he should sail into the Channel. If it is possible to reinforce himself with the Cartagena squadron, he should do so. I am just going to write my despatch to Ganteaume, and to draft my decree: you shall have them both in a quarter of an hour. I shall postpone my Cadiz despatch until the arrival of tomorrow's messenger. As for the cruisers, I never heard of such lunacy as sending them off with less than 6 months' provisions.

[CORRESP., xi, 9112. On March 30, 1805, Villeneuve with the French fleet at Toulon eluded Nelson's blockade, and reached Cadiz. Thence he crossed the Atlantic, and arrived at Martinique on May 13. Pursued by Nelson, he sailed east again, fought a small action with Calder off Cape Finisterre on July 22, and put into Corunna and Ferrol early in August. When he sailed again, it was not (as Napoleon hoped) north to Brest, but south to Cadiz, which he only left to be defeated at Trafalgar on October 21.]

## (2)
### TO VICE-ADMIRAL VILLENEUVE

BOULOGNE CAMP, *AUGUST* 22, 1805.

I hope you have arrived at Brest. Start, without losing a moment, and sail up the Channel with all the ships you have. England is ours. We are all ready: every man is on board. Appear for 24 hours, and the thing is done.

[CORRESP., xi, 9115.]

## 97

# ENGLAND OR AUSTRIA?

### TO M. TALLEYRAND

BOULOGNE CAMP, *AUGUST* 23, 1805.

The more I reflect on the European situation, the more I see the urgency of taking decisive action. The fact is, I have nothing to hope for from the Austrian explanations. Austria will reply with fine phrases, in order to gain time, and to prevent my doing anything this winter. This winter, under the title of an armed neutrality, she will sign her subsidy treaty, and her act of coalition; and in April I shall find 100,000 Russians in Poland, paid for – horses, guns, and all – by England, besides 15 to 20,000 English at Malta, and 15,000 Russians at Corfu. Then things will be in a pretty pass. So I have made up my mind.

My fleet left Ferrol on the 26th thermidor with 34 sail; there was no enemy in sight. If it obeys orders, joins the Brest fleet, and sails up the Channel, there is still time; England is mine. If on the other hand, my admirals hesitate, manœuvre badly, and fail in their task, I have no alternative but to wait for the winter to get my flotilla across. It is a risky operation; and it would be still more so if pressure of time, and the political situation, obliged me to leave here in April. Things being so, I am off at full speed. I am striking camp, and replacing my fighting battalions with reserves, which in any case give me a formidable enough army at Boulogne; and there I am, on the 1st of vendémiaire, in the middle of Germany, with 200,000 men, and another 25,000 in the Kingdom of Naples. I march on Vienna, and refuse to lay down arms till I have got Naples and Venice, and

have so augmented the Elector of Bavaria's territory that I have
nothing more to fear from Austria. That ought to keep Austria
quiet for the winter. I don't return to Paris till I have reached my
goal.

I thought I had better let you know my intentions, so that
you can draw up a manifesto for me, comprising the official
documents on the Austrian movements: they will show how
absolutely necessary it is for me to act, unless I am to be guilty
of the most heinous of military mistakes. I want you to reiterate
this view in all your conversations with the ambassadors, and to
draft a circular letter in the same sense for my various ministers,
blaming Austria for the beginning of hostilities. Take as your
text the embarkation of my infantry and cavalry: say that Austria chose that moment for ordering armies into Italy and the
Tyrol.

I am acquainting you with my plans so that you may orien-
tate your department accordingly. You are not to say that I am
replying to war by war; but that, fighting having actually begun,
a settlement must be arrived at, and that, unless Austria answers
me, not by words, but by recalling her troops to their Hungari-
an and Bohemian barracks, there is no choice left me but to
repel force by force. All the same, as I want to gain a fortnight,
take M. Otto into your confidence, and warn him that in a few
days' time I am going to send one of my aides-de-camp to Pas-
sau with a letter for the Elector of Bavaria, in which I shall say
that, unless Austria evacuates the Tyrol, I am resolved to put
myself at the head of my army, and that Germany will see more
soldiers than it has ever seen before: but the Elector need not
disturb himself.

[CORRESP., xi, 9,117. Napoleon had just heard (August 22) that Austria
was still arming, and that a new coalition was forming against him.]

## 98

## CARD CATALOGUE

### TO MARSHAL BERTHIER

BOULOGNE CAMP, *AUGUST* 28, 1805.

I want you to have two portable boxes made, and divided
into compartments – one for me, and the other for yourself.
They are to be so arranged that one can find out at a glance, with

the help of cards, the movements of all the Austrian troops, regiment by regiment, and battalion by battalion, even including detached bodies of any considerable size. Divide them up into as many armies as the Austrians possess, and keep compartments for any troops the Emperor may have in Hungary, or Bohemia, or the interior of his states. Once a fortnight you are to send me a list of the changes that have taken place during the previous two weeks, using all the available sources – not only the German and Italian gazettes, but also the various pieces of information that reach you, as well as the Minister for Foreign Affairs; for I want you to co-operate with him for this purpose. The arrangement of the cards in the box, and the fortnightly account of the state of the Austrian army, must be done by the same person.

P.S. – This work ought to be assigned to someone who gives up his whole time to it, who knows German well, who gets all the German gazettes, and makes all the changes accordingly.

[CORRESP., xi, 9148.]


## 99

## PULPIT CENSORSHIP

### TO M. PORTALIS

SAINT-CLOUD, SEPTEMBER 19, 1805.
Inform M. Robert, a priest at Bourges, of my displeasure at the extremely bad sermon he preached on August 15.

[CORRESP., xi, 9243.]


## 100

## ULM

### TO THE EMPRESS JOSÉPHINE

ELCHINGEN ABBEY, OCTOBER 19, 1805.
I am more tired, my dear Joséphine, than I ought to have been. After being wet through every day for a week, and my feet frozen with cold, I'm not feeling particularly well: but I

have stayed indoors all today, and it has given me a rest.

I have carried out my design – destroyed the Austrian army by mere marching, and captured 60,000 prisoners, 120 guns, over 90 flags, and more than 30 generals.

I am going to advance on the Russians. It's all up with them. I am pleased with my army. I have only lost 1,500 men, of whom two thirds are slightly wounded.

Goodbye, my Joséphine. Ever so many compliments. Prince Charles is coming to defend Vienna.

Masséna ought to be just reaching Vicenza. The very moment I am happy about Italy, I will give Eugène some fighting to do. My dearest love to Hortense.

[CORRESP., xi, 9393. Mack capitulated at Ulm on October 17 with 23 – 24,000 men, and his troops laid down their arms on the 20th. Another 15,000 men had been captured in earlier engagements.]

# 101

# THREE EMPERORS

## TO THE EMPEROR OF AUSTRIA

LINZ, *NOVEMBER* 8, 1805.

Lieutenant-General Count Gyulai has handed me the letter from Your Imperial Majesty. Permit me to thank Your Majesty for the kind expressions it conveys on my account. I make bold to say to Your Majesty that the enemies of our two nations could never have rekindled the torch of war unless they had misrepresented my intentions. It was the only course left to England in order to secure for another term her absolute control over the seas and commerce of the world. It is not for me to decide what Your Majesty ought to do in your present situation; but I see with some regret that you agree with the Emperor of Russia; for he has not the same interest in our quarrels as we have, nor do the safety and welfare of his subjects depend upon what is happening at the moment. For Russia this war is mere make-believe; for Your Majesty and myself it is one that absorbs all our means, all our faculties, and all our feelings. I can only repeat to Your Majesty what I said in great detail to Count Gyulai: I desire peace, and I shall think it a happy moment when Your Majesty attends only to the interests of your crown and the good of your peoples, and not to the wishes of a power so differently situated. I do not intend any reflexion on the personal character of the Emperor Alexander. I know too well the extent of the toils into which he has fallen during the last three years to be surprised if his most benevolent intentions produce effects of an exactly opposite kind. He wanted to be the peace-maker and benefactor of Europe: his agents have made him the author and origin of dissension on the continent. I have often been brought into personal contact with the Emperor, and retain affectionate memories of his kindness and good qualities. He is still young; he will gather experience, and achieve all the good he desires for Europe and for the human race. I hope that he will then do more justice to my sentiments, and to the honest friendliness I have shown him in all our intercourse. However, to confine myself to the immediate issue; are the French and German peoples really to be committed to all the anxieties and anguish of war? Count Gyulai did not consider himself empowered to treat for an armistice. He will tell Your Majesty both how willing I am to conclude one immediately, and also how much I fear those delays and intrigues whose full bitterness I have experienced in the past. Our ministers are so well aware of all possible points of difference between us that they could settle them in five minutes. But whatever turn may be given to these preliminaries by the present complex and difficult circumstances, I beg Your Majesty never to doubt that I am always pleased to meet your wishes, and that it is a matter of genuine preference as well as of deliberate purpose on my part to contribute to the happiness of your subjects and of yourself, so long as this is consistent with my duty towards the welfare of my own peoples.

[CORRESP., xi, 9464. Gyulai again represented Austria in negotiating the Treaty of Pressburg, a month later.]


# 102
# AUSTERLITZ

### TO JOSEPH

AUSTERLITZ, *DECEMBER* 3, 1805.

. . . Yesterday, after several days' manœuvring I fought a decisive battle. I routed the allied army under the personal com-

mand of the Emperors of Russia and Germany. The strength of
their army was 80,000 Russians and 30,000 Austrians. I took
nearly 40,000 of them prisoner, including 20 or so Russian generals, 40 flags, 100 guns, and all the standards of Russian Imperial Guard. The whole army covered itself with glory.

The enemy have left at least 12 or 15,000 men on the field
of battle. I don't know my losses yet, but estimate them at 8 or
900 men killed, and twice as many wounded. A whole column
threw itself into a lake, where most of them were drowned: one
can still hear the cries of some of these unhappy men, whom it
was impossible to save. The two Emperors are in a pretty bad
position. You can have a summary of this news printed; but
don't give it as an extract from my letter – that would be incor-
rect. You will get the *Bulletin* tomorrow. Although I have slept
out all this last week, my health is good. I have a bed to sleep
on tonight, in M. de Kaunitz's handsome chateau at Austerlitz,
and it is the first time for a week that I have put on a clean shirt.
My guard and the Russian Emperor's charged one another; the
Emperor's was overwhelmed. Prince Repnin, its commanding
officer, was captured, with part of his regiment, and the standards and guns of the Russian Guard.

This morning the Emperor of Germany sent the Prince of
Liechtenstein to ask me for an interview. Peace may follow
quite quickly. I had fewer troops on the battlefield than the
enemy, but I caught him in the middle of a movement unawares.

[CORRESP., xi, 9538. Kircheisen (*Napoleon*, 336) regards the story of the
lake (which reappears in Army Bulletin No. 30) as a legend. An examination
of the lake a few days later revealed the bodies of 3 men and 138 horses.]

# 103
# PEACE DEMONSTRATIONS
## TO JOSEPH

SCHÖNBRUNN, *DECEMBER* 13, 1805.

It was worse than useless to call so much attention to the
news that the enemy had made overtures for peace, or to fire a
salute. That is just the way to send public opinion to sleep, and
to give foreigners a false idea of the situation in our country.
Peace can't be secured by shouting for it. I didn't even mention
the word in any of my bulletins: there are still better reasons

for not proclaiming it in the theatres. The word 'peace' means nothing. It is a particular kind of peace that we want – peace with glory. I can't imagine anything, therefore, more unwise or more unreal than this performance at Paris.

[JOSEPH, i, 341.]

# 104

# BRIDE FOR EUGÈNE

## TO PRINCE EUGÈNE

MUNICH, DECEMBER 31, 1805.

Here I am at Munich. I have arranged your marriage with Princess Augusta, and it has been announced in the papers. The princess came to see me this morning, and I had a long talk with her. She is very pretty. I am enclosing a portrait of her on a cup; but it doesn't do her justice. . . .

[CORRESP., xi, 9636. Eugène was in Italy, and had not been consulted. He married Princess Augusta Amelia of Bavaria on January 13, 1806. For the sequel, v. Nos. 106, 113.]

# 105

# EMPEROR AND POPE

## (1) *Direct*
## TO HIS HOLINESS THE POPE

MUNICH, JANUARY 7, 1806.

Most Holy Father; I am in receipt of a letter from Your Holiness under date November 13. 1 cannot but be keenly affected by the fact that, when all the powers in English pay banded together to wage an unjust war against me, Your Holiness should lend your ear to ill advice, and write to me in such immoderate terms. Your Holiness is perfectly free either to keep my minister at Rome, or to dismiss him. The occupation of Ancona is an immediate and necessary consequence of the military incompetence of the Holy See. It was better for Your Holiness to see that fortress in my hands than in those of the Turks or English. Your Holiness complains that since your return from

Paris, you have had nothing but disappointments. The reason is that all those who used to call themselves my friends, only because they feared my power, have since then taken heart from the strength of the coalition, and changed their tune: thus, since Your Holiness returned to Rome, I have met with nothing but refusal on your part, whatever the occasion; and this even in matters of the first importance for religion, as, for instance the question of preventing a revival of Protestantism in France. I have always considered myself the protector of the Holy See; and it was in this capacity that I occupied Ancona. I have always considered myself like my Valois and Bourbon predecessors, as the eldest son of the Church and as the sole bearer of the sword with which to protect it, and to put it beyond danger of defilement by Greeks and Moslems. I shall continue to protect it, whatever the mistakes, ingratitude, and ill-will of the men whom these last three months have unmasked. They thought I was done for; but by the success with which he favoured my arms, God has signally demonstrated his protection of my cause. So long as Your Holiness consults the true friends of religion, and your own heart, I shall be your friend. I repeat; if Your Holiness wishes to dismiss my minister you are free to do so; and free to summon, if you prefer them, the English, and the Caliph of Constantinople. Only, as I do not wish to expose Cardinal Fesch to such affronts, I shall send a layman in his place. Besides, Cardinal Consalvi shows him so much dislike, that he has never met with anything but rebuffs, whilst every favour has gone to my enemies. Yet, God knows, I have done more for religion than any other prince alive.

Hereby I pray God, Most Holy Father, to preserve you for many years in the rule and government of our Holy Mother Church.

Your devoted son, Emperor of the French and King of Italy.

[CORRESP., xi, 9655. Ancona was occupied by French troops before the Austrian campaign of 1805. The Pope's protest reached Napoleon just before Austerlitz. This is his answer. Cardinal Consalvi was the Papal Secretary of State.]

## (2) *Indirect*

### TO CARDINAL FESCH

MUNICH, JANUARY 7, 1806.

The Pope has written to me, under date November 13th, a quite ridiculous and lunatic letter: these people thought I was dead. I occupied Ancona because, in spite of your representations, nothing had been done to defend it; besides, things are so badly organised that, whatever had been done, it could never have been held against anyone. Make it clearly understood that I won't stand any more of this nonsense, and that I won't tolerate the presence of a Russian or Sardinian minister at Rome. It is my intention to recall you, and to replace you by a layman. As these imbeciles see no harm in a Protestant occupying the French throne, I shall send them a Protestant ambassador. Tell Consalvi that, if he has any care for his country, he must either do what I required of him, or resign his post. Tell him that I'm religious, but that I'm no bigot. Remind him that Constantine distinguished the civilian sphere from the military, and that I too can nominate a senator to command in my name in Rome. It is a nice idea, all this talk of religion, by those who have admitted the Russians, and rejected Malta, and are now trying to get rid of my minister! These are the people who prostitute religion. Is there any such thing as an apostolic nuncio in Russia? Tell Consalvi, tell the Pope himself if you like, that he may want to turn my minister out of Rome, but that I can equally well come and put him back there. Can nothing be done with these fellows except by force? They are letting religion go to ruin in Germany by refusing to finish the business of the Concordat: it is the same in Bavaria, the same in Italy. They are becoming the laughing-stock of courts and peoples. I have given them good advice, but they would never listen to it. I suppose they thought that the Russians and English and Neapolitans would have respected the Pope's neutrality! For the Pope's purposes, I am Charlemagne. Like Charlemagne, I join the crown of France with the crown of the Lombards. My empire, like Charlemagne's, marches with the East. I therefore expect the Pope to accommodate his conduct to my requirements. If he behaves well, I shall make no outward changes: if not, I shall reduce him to the status of bishop of Rome. They complain of my arranging Italian affairs without consulting them. Do they want things to be as they are in Germany, where there are no services left, no sacraments, and no religion? Tell them that, unless they make an end of their present behaviour, I shall hold them up to all Europe as mere egoists, and shall settle the affairs of the church in Germany with the Arch-chancellor, and without them. Really, there is nothing in the world so utterly unreasonable as the Court of Rome.

[CORRESP., xi, 9656. To this the Pope replied, on March 21, that Napoleon was 'Emperor of the French, and not of Rome. There is no Emperor of Rome.']

# 106

# PATERNAL

## TO PRINCESS AUGUSTA

STUTTGART, *JANUARY* 19, 1806.

My daughter; your letter is as nice as yourself. My feelings of devotion to you will only grow greater every day. I am sure of this, because it is such a pleasure to remember all your good qualities, and because I am always wanting to hear you tell me that you like us all, and that you are happy about your husband. However busy I am, there will never be anything I care about more than the means of making my children happy. I assure you, Augusta, I love you like a father, and I count on your loving me like a daughter. Take care of yourself on your journey, and in the new climate you are going to; get as much repose as you can. You have been rushing about all this last month: I don't want to have you falling ill. I end, my daughter, by giving you a father's blessing.

[CORRESP., xi, 9683. *v.* No. 104 above.]

# 107

# CHURCH PAPERS

## TO M. FOUCHÉ

PARIS, *FEBRUARY* 7, 1806.

M. Portalis has informed me that there are a number of Church papers, and has pointed out the awkwardness that might result from their editorial temper, and above all, from their differences of opinion about religion. It is therefore my intention that the Church papers shall cease separate publication, and be combined into a single paper, which will be sent to all their subscribers. As the special object of this paper is to be the education of the clergy, it will be called the *Journal des curés*. Its editors will be appointed by the cardinal-archbishop of Paris.

[CORRESP., xii, 9769.]

## 108

# LITURGIOLOGY

### NOTE FOR THE MINISTER OF PUBLIC WORSHIP

PARIS, *FEBRUARY* 12, 1806.

Considering how necessary it is to give a religious sanction to solemn occasions, whilst at the same time diminishing the number of festivals which distract people from their work, two feasts may be suggested: –

(1) On August 15th, the Feast of St. Napoléon, which would celebrate at the same time the Emperor's birthday, and the ratification of the Concordat; with this festival could be associated acts of thanksgiving for the prosperity of the Empire; and one could try to give the procession, which would still take place on this day, a character tending to efface its old associations.

(2) On the first Sunday following the day corresponding to the 11th frimaire one could commemorate both the success of the Grand Army and the occasion of the Coronation; and one of the clergy could preach a sermon making special mention of local citizens who fell in the battle of Austerlitz.

[CORRESP., xii, 9803.]

## 109

## 'BUY FRENCH'

### TO PRINCESS ÉLISA

PARIS, *FEBRUARY* 22, 1806.

My Sister, I should like you to insist that no dresses are worn at your Court except those made of silk or batiste, and to prohibit cotton and muslin, so that a preference may be given to the products of French industry, and they may become fashionable.

[CORRESP., xii, 9870. Marie-Anne (Elise) Bonaparte, Napoleon's sister, married Felice Baciocchi in 1797: in 1805 he was made Prince of Lucca and Piombino.]

## 110

## BERTHIER

### TO MARSHAL BERTHIER

LA MALMAISON, *APRIL* 1, 1806.

I am sending you the *Moniteur*: you will see there what I have done for you. I only attach one condition to it, namely, that you get married; and that is also a condition of my continued friendship. Your love affair has lasted too long, and has become absurd. I have a right to expect that a man whom I have called my companion in arms, and whom posterity will always picture at my side, shall no longer abandon himself to an unprecedented weakness. I want you to get married, then; if you don't, I will never see you again. You are fifty, I know; but you come of a race that lives till eighty; and those thirty years are just the time when you most need the amenities of married life.

When circumstances allow, you must go to Strasbourg, and thence to your principality, to see about everything there. It yielded 50,000 crowns to Prussia, it ought to yield you twice as much. You know that no one is fonder of you than I am: but you are also aware that no one can have my affection who has not first my respect. You have well deserved it hitherto: continue to be worthy of it by falling in with my plans, and becoming the root of a fine big family tree. . . .

[CORRESP., xii, 10046. After the victories of 1805 Napoleon rewarded

Berthier, his Chief of Staff, with the Principality of Neuchâtel, ceded by Prussia. Berthier's mistress was Mme. de Visconti.]

# 111

# DISCIPLINE

## TO MARSHAL BERTHIER

LA MALMAISON, *APRIL* 10, 1806.

I am annoyed at your sending your brother to Paris. I didn't want to see him, and I won't receive him. Write and tell him to clear out at once. The fact that he has made two millions in Hanover is no reason why he should give himself such airs. If, now that he is a rich man, he thinks he can play fast and loose with his duties; he will soon find he is mistaken. I call it dishonourable for a general to leave his troops. As for his wife's *accouchement*, I can't go into details like that. My wife might have died at Munich or Strasbourg: it wouldn't have made one quarter of an hour's difference to my plans, or to my opinions. Don't you suppose that every military man in Germany – and not least yourself – would be only too glad to get back, and that there are plenty of reasons, quite apart from the needs of the service, why I should like to have you in Paris? But the army is becoming effeminate, and I refuse to make concessions. If General Berthier had come without your leave, he would have been arrested on the spot. . . .

[CORRESP., xii, 10074.]

# 112

# ITALIAN BUDGET

## TO PRINCE EUGÈNE

SAINT-CLOUD, *APRIL* 14, 1806.

I have received your letter of April 7th. It is natural enough that the decree of annexation should have been unpopular at Milan. They are always wanting impossibilities in that country: they would like to pay no taxes, have no troops, and be the greatest nation in the world – all pure fantasy; and sensible people are bound to agree with me. My policy fits the circumstances, and the needs of the country, because I have higher aims. The only reward that the army has won from unparalleled successes, or France from unremitting efforts, is the district of Venice. Everything that consolidates my system in France consolidates it also in Italy, and everything that France does to keep Venice is in the interests of my Italian crown.

As for the taxes, the answer is quite simple. Are they paying more there than here? It is obvious that my French subjects pay much heavier taxes than my subjects in Italy: that being so, the latter have nothing to grumble about. I have just started levying duties on salt, and have further increased French taxation. My budget is before the Legislative Body: you will get it tomorrow in the *Moniteur*. You had better have it put into the papers. Then they will see how much the French pay.

I am sending you the balance-sheet from the Minister of Finance. The $2\frac{1}{2}$ million francs a month to be paid me by my Kingdom of Italy fall far short, I can assure you, of meeting the expenses of my army: were Italy to be taxed to the extent of a third of its resources, it would certainly not be too much for the defence of the country. The defence of France absorbs half its revenues. Besides, one must look further ahead. Europe will change: the present hatreds will die down: the new countries will in time become established and consolidated. Then I shall reduce my army by 50 per cent; I shall withdraw my troops from Italy; and my Italian subjects will only pay a million a month to my French treasury, or perhaps nothing at all. You know well enough that $2\frac{1}{2}$ millions a month won't pay for my army, and that I shall be obliged to send money from France – a costly affair, and one that will drain my resources: for it is only fair to say that what the French nation has done to set up and embellish the throne of Italy involves the duty of maintaining a much stronger military establishment in that country.

As regards the succession, it is not my custom to look to other people's advice for my political opinions; and my Italian subjects know me too well to forget that there is more in my little finger than in all their heads put together. In Paris, where people are more enlightened than in Italy, they hold their tongues, and bow to the judgment of a man who has proved that he saw further and more clearly than they did. I am surprised that in Italy they are less obliging.

[CORRESP., xii, 10097. The Italian legislature was suppressed for criticising this first budget.]

## 113
# EUGÈNE MARRIED
### TO PRINCE EUGÈNE

SAINT-CLOUD, *APRIL* 14, 1806.

My Son, you are working too hard; your life is too monot-onous. It is all right for yourself, because you ought to regard work as a form of recreation. But you have a young wife, and she is expecting a baby. I think you ought to manage to spend the evening with her, and to ask a few people in. Why don't you use the royal box at the theatre once a week? I think you should also keep a small stable and go hunting at least once a week. I will gladly ear-mark a sum in the budget for this purpose. There ought to be more gaiety in your home: it is needed for your wife's happiness, and for your own health. One can get through a lot of business in a short time. I live much as you do; but then I have an old wife, who doesn't need me to amuse her; and I have more work to do. Yet I'm sure I find time for more amuse-ment and dissipation than you do. A young wife needs to be amused, especially when situated as yours is. You were fond enough of enjoying yourself in the old days; you must cultivate those tastes again. You might not do this for yourself, but you really ought to do it for the Princess. I have just settled in at Saint-Cloud. Stéphanie and the Prince of Baden are quite fond of one another. I spent the last two days with Marshal Bessières, and we disported ourselves like children of fifteen. You used to be in the habit of getting up early: you ought to take to it again. That would not inconvenience the Princess, provided you went to bed with her at 11; even if you finished your work at 6 in the evening, you could still secure a 10 hours' working day by get-ting up at 6 or 7. The Cattaro affair is postponing the May fêtes, but I think only for a month. I hope you and the Princess will come to Paris then. I have had the Pavillon de Flore made ready for you: you will be on the first floor, the Prince of Baden on the second. Tell the Princess how pleased people will be to see her in Paris. By that time her pregnancy will have taken a more settled form, and won't prevent her travelling by short stages. Provided the weather is fine, it can do her nothing but good.

[CORRESP., xii, 10099. Soon after Eugène's marriage Napoleon had arranged a match between Stephanie Beauharnais, Josephine's niece, and Charles Louis Frederick, Crown Prince of Baden. The Pavillion de Flore was a wing of the Tuileries, occupied in 1794 by the Committee of Public Safety. Napoleon was 37 at this time, Bessières 38. The 'Cattaro affair' arose out of the failure of Austria to hand over Cattaro, though included in the cession of Dalmatia by the treaty of Pressburg.]

# 114

# FORCED LABOUR

## TO DEJEAN

SAINT-CLOUD, APRIL 25, 1806.

A thousand Neapolitan convicts will remain at Alexandria to work on the fortifications there; 300 are to be sent to Mantua, and 300 to Legnano, for the same purpose; and 600 to Genoa, where they will embark for Corsica, to be employed, among other things, on repairing the roads and draining the marshes. The remaining 1,200 will be sent to Rochefort, and put at the disposition of the Bridges and Forests department, to work on the draining of the Rochefort marsh-lands. Of the 4,000 Neapolitan prisoners, 2,000 are to remain at Alexandria, to be employed on the work there, and the other 2,000 will be sent to Languedoc, to do any work needed by the Minister for Home Affairs.

[CHUQUET, i, 672. This is the sequel to Joseph's entry into Naples in February.]

# 115

# HISTORY

## TO M. FOUCHÉ

SAINT-CLOUD, MAY 7, 1806.

Millot has just published a fourth volume, containing all kinds of ridiculous nonsense, and depreciating our victories. It is the height of indecency that such an ignoramus should write in the grand manner about contemporary events. Have the book suppressed. . . .

[CORRESP., xii, 10209. Millot's *Élements de l'histoire de France* first came out in 1767.]

# 116

# ARC DE TRIOMPHE

*Note*

SAINT-CLOUD, *MAY* 14, 1806.

The triumphal arches would be a futile and pointless piece of work, and I should never have had them put up, unless I had thought of them as a means of encouraging architecture. My idea is to use them to subsidise architecture in France for 10 years, to the tune of 200,000 francs. M. Denon is to present me with a plan. The Minister of the Interior is having another triumphal arch built in the Place de l'Étoile. It is essential that all the designs should conform to the same general description. One of the first two must be a Marengo arch, and the other an arch of Austerlitz. I shall have another erected somewhere in Paris, to be the arch of Peace, and a fourth to be the arch of Religion. With these four arches I am confident that I can finance French sculpture for 20 years. But it is as well that M. Daru should know of the existence of all four arches, so that he may not put work into one that is only suitable for another.

Will M. Daru please let me know on which of the arches the statue of Charlemagne has been placed? Will he also come to an agreement with M. Cretet on the subject of the two fountains which are to be erected, one in the Place de la Révolution, and the other on the site of the Bastille? They are of a monumental character, and ought to have statues and bas-reliefs: the subjects for these can be taken in the first instance from the Emperor's life, and afterwards from the history of the Revolution, and of France. Generally speaking, no opportunity should be missed to humiliate the Russians and the English. William the Conqueror and Duguesclin may be given places of honour on these monuments.

[CORRESP., xii, 10235. The Arc de Triomphe in the Place de l'Étoile is that through which German troops marched in 1871, and French in 1919, and under which is the Tomb of an Unknown Warrior.]

# 117

## ORDERS

### TO JOSEPH

SAINT-CLOUD, *MAY* 21, 1806.

I have received your letters of May 10 and 11. I had
thought, like you, of an Order of St. Januarius. Send me a note
on its constitution and duties. But it seems to me a bit too religious; and at first sight I don't like the idea of an Order attached
to the Bourbons as its founders. Institutions of this kind ought
to be newly created, and to correspond from the start, so far as
possible, to the needs of the age. The mere name of St. Januarius raises a smile all over Europe. We ought to find something
that inspires respect, and gives rise to imitation. The English
themselves are just trying to start something over there on the
lines of the Legion of Honour. . . .

[JOSEPH, ii, 245. The miraculous liquefaction of the blood of St. Januarius was the chief event in the ecclesiastical year at Naples.]

# 118

## BODY-GUARD

### TO JOSEPH

SAINT-CLOUD, *MAY* 31, 1806.

Don't allow any one to be in sole command of your Guard.
Nothing could be more dangerous. Sooner or later you will
have to revise the arrangement, and it is better not to start off on
the wrong lines. I have told you before and I tell you again, that
you trust the Neapolitans too much. I am thinking particularly
of your kitchen arrangements, and of your body-guard, where
you are running the risk of poisoning or assassination. It is my
deliberate desire that you should keep your French cooks, that
you should have your own waiters, and that your domestic
arrangements should provide for your being always under
French protection. You haven't seen enough of my private life
to know how, even in France, I am constantly under the eye of
my oldest and most trusted soldiers. Of all the people you mention there isn't one I know, unless it's the Duke of San
Théodoro, whose letters to the Queen I saw, when he was at

Madrid. Whatever he may be like, I don't object to your nomi-
nating him Grand Master of the Ceremonies. But do make sure
that your valets, your cooks, and the sentries who sleep in your
apartments, or who call you during the night to give you
despatches, are Frenchmen. It should be impossible for anyone
to enter your room at night, except your aide-de-camp; and he
ought to sleep in the room opening into your bedroom. Your
door should be locked on the inside; you ought not to open it
even to your aide-de-camp, unless you are sure you recognise
his voice; and he ought not to knock at your door until he has
been careful to close that of his own room, to make sure that he
is alone, and that no one can follow him.

  These precautions are important: they give no trouble; and
they inspire confidence; besides, they may really save your life.
It is an arrangement which you ought to start at once, and
always keep up: you don't want to be forced to adopt it by particular circumstances; that is embarrassing both to your self-
respect, and to your suite. Don't rely too much upon your own
experience. The Neapolitan reputation has been the same
always and everywhere; and you have to reckon with a woman
who is the personification of crime. . . .

[JOSEPH, ii, 260. In 1801, Naples had been forced into a treaty with
France. When war broke out in 1803 it was occupied by French troops. The
landing of an Anglo-Russian expeditionary force there in 1805 gave Napoleon
an excuse to depose Queen Maria Carolina, the effective ruler, since Ferdinand IV was an imbecile. On February 15, 1806, Joseph entered Naples at the
head of a French army, as its new king. The reference in the last sentence is
to the Queen.]


# 119

# NEW NOBILITY

## TO JOSEPH

SAINT-CLOUD, *JUNE* 5, 1806, 11 *A.M.*
  The behaviour of the Roman Curia bears every mark of
insanity. I wanted to show them at the start what they had to fear
from me. Besides, I thought that under any circumstances the
Benevento and Ponte-Corvo *enclaves* could only be a source of
trouble to your Kingdom, so I turned them into two Duchies
that of Benevento for Talleyrand, and that of Ponte-Corvo for

Bernadotte. I know that they are poor districts: but I will give grants in aid – or rather, I will do so in Bernadotte's case: Talleyrand is rich enough to do without. Occupy these districts, then, and do so with troops in the first instance. You will realise that, if I have given Bernadotte the titles of Duke and Prince, it is on your wife's account. There are other generals in my army who have served me more faithfully, and on whose attachment I can better rely: but I thought it proper that the brother-in-law of the Queen of Naples should rank high at your court. As for the other six Duchies, I shall soon be in a position to appoint to them. Masséna and Jourdan would both be suitable men. Imperfections disappear in time, but titles that recall such victories as Fleurus or Zürich are immutable, and will be the first thought of those who see their children. When you are master of Sicily, found three more fiefs, one of them for Reynier – especially as I think you are putting him in command of the expedition; and this will be no small encouragement to him, if he has any doubts about my friendly feelings towards him.

Tell me what titles you would like attached to the Duchies in your Kingdom. They are titles, and no more: the essential thing is the money that goes with them: 200,000 livres a year will have to be set aside for this purpose. I have made it a further condition that each holder of a title shall keep up a house at Paris; for that is the centre of the whole system, and I want to have there 100 fortunes, which have all been built up alongside the throne, and which are the only estates of any size remaining in the country: for they are gifts by trust, whereas all others, under the working of the Civil Code, gradually disappear.

Introduce the Civil Code at Naples, and at the end of a few years all the fortunes not attached to you will be destroyed, and any that you wish to preserve will be consolidated. That is the great advantage of the Civil Code. If you don't like the idea of divorce at Naples, I see no objection to your deleting that article. I think it's useful, all the same. Why should the Pope denounce the granting of divorce on account of impotence, or some other compelling cause, which has no ecclesiastical bearing? However, if you think necessary, change it. And you can leave the registration of civil acts to the clergy. With these modifications you had better introduce the Civil Code. It consolidates your power, for by its means all wealth not in the form of gifts by trust disappears, and no great families remain except those you transform into fiefs. That is why I recommend a Civil Code, and why I established it. . . .

[JOSEPH, ii, 274. For Bernadotte v. No. 9.]

## 120

# TURKISH EMBASSY

## TO M. DE TALLEYRAND

SAINT-CLOUD, *JUNE* 9, 1806.

General Sebastiani's instructions fall under two heads. One consists of information on the geographical and political situation of the Ottoman Empire, extracted from the minister's letters; this you need not submit to me. The other must be his instructions proper, of which the following are the outlines.

(1) My ambassador at Constantinople must endeavour at all times and by every available means to produce in the Porte a feeling of confidence and security; and to make them realise that I do not want any part of the empire of Constantinople, but that my wish is to do all I can to pacify, reorganise, and re-establish the whole of this formidable empire, which, even in its weakest moments, impinges upon Russia, and holds her in check.

(2) The object of my policy all through is to make a triple alliance of myself, the Porte, and Persia, aimed indirectly or by implication against Russia.

(3) I want to be treated as the most favoured power. But I should like the influence I have lost to be regained by tact, subtlety, and trust, not by arrogance, force, or threats. I want my ambassador to be liked and trusted. I shall know that he has inspired confidence, and carried out his instructions, every time the Porte informs him of the demands of Russia or England.

(4) I shall not support any rebel against the Porte, nor any of my old friends in Egypt or Syria, nor any Greek. My policy is perfectly simple – whole-hearted alliance with the Porte.

(5) I want to stand well with the Porte by the creation of confidence, and the expression of friendly feelings; but that is not enough. I want this relationship to be known in Russia, in England, and all over Europe; every element of friendship in it advertised, every scrap of coolness and discontent concealed.

(6) My ambassador must always be on the look-out for

opportunities to put Russia out of favour. He must depreciate the strength of her army, and the courage of her troops, whenever and in whatever way he can. He must adopt a distant attitude towards the Russian legation – show it little attention, and treat it with disdain rather than condescension. Whatever the relations of Russia and France elsewhere, the French legation at Constantinople must be on cool terms with the Russian. On the other hand, once peace is made, it can be friendly with Austria, Prussia, and England.

(7) All our negotiations ought to aim at these points:(1) closing the Bosphorus against the Russians, and prohibiting the passage of their vessels from the Mediterranean to the Black Sea, whether they are armed or unarmed (for it is an utter fraud to close the ports of a warship and call it a troopship); (2) forbidding any Greek to sail under the Russian flag; (3) fortifying or arming every position against the Russians; (4) subduing the Georgians, and re-establishing the absolute rule of the Porte over Moldavia and Wallachia.

(8) I don't want to partition the empire of Constantinople: even if I were offered a three-quarters share, I should refuse to do so. I want to strengthen and consolidate this great empire, and to use it, as it is, against Russia.

[CORRESP., xii, 10339. Sebastiani (*v.* No. 64) is being sent as French ambassador to Constantinople in order to form a Franco-Perso-Turkish alliance against Russia. In August Selim deposed the Russophil Hospodars of Moldavia and Wallachia, and in October a Russian army marched on the Danube.]

# 121
# MOUNTED SCOUTS
## *Note*

SAINT-CLOUD, *JULY* 9, 1806.

Submit a scheme for organising 4 regiments of Scouts, each composed of 4 squadrons 200 strong.

The Scouts will be not more than 5 ft. tall, and they will use horses standing from 4 ft. to 4 ft. 3½ ins. at most.

The horses will have only their fore feet shod.

The bridles will be as simple as possible.

They will have cushions in place of saddles; but, of course, the stirrups and other indispensable accessories will be adapted to the cushions.

The scouts will wear uniforms – a tunic, with breeches or trousers, as well as a stable jacket. They will also have a cloak which will serve them in place of an overcoat. The knapsack will be as small as possible, and the weight of its contents will have to be cut down to 4 lbs.

The boots will be something like those of the hussars, but without any ornamentation.

The Emperor's object in forming this new regiment, is to utilise small horses, and to diminish the wastage of the larger kinds.

These corps will be able to do the scouting work that has hitherto been done by the hussars and chasseurs. It will be possible to increase their number very easily in any district, because at any time, and almost everywhere, there will be opportunities for procuring horses of this size, and in the field these corps can be remounted on horses of any sort.

Once these regiments are set on foot, men below the height of 5 ft., who are too small to serve in the dragoons, will be utilisable in the cavalry, as they are already in the infantry, owing to the formation of companies of *voltigeurs*; at the same time these Scouts will be comparatively cheap. . . .

It is the Emperor's intention that the Scouts' horses should be kept out in all weathers, and should graze on open ground, and be given no oats. It is an experiment worth trying, and one that offers no difficulties in France during 8 or 9 months of the year; but for 3 or 4 months it will have to be modified in most parts of France, owing to the hard frosts, and snow-fall: and it will be indispensable, in my opinion, to have, on the pastures, sheds closed on 2 or 3 sides, and to keep the horses there on dry fodder whilst the hard frost or snow lasts.

The only place I know in France which is an exception to this is the Ile de la Camargue: there the sheep and horses pass the whole winter in the open without shelter.

The Emperor's plan would be to have a fixed depot for each of these corps, where, in course of time, enough land could be bought to provide grazing.

The Ile de la Camargue would be one of these 4 depots.

Every 6 or 8 years the corps would exchange depots.

Whilst *en route*, the horses would be put in stables or barns.

His Imperial Majesty has been led to make these proposals

by the considerations stated above, and also by what he saw in the armies of Italy and Egypt. The 22nd regiment of *chasseurs* joined the Italian army with 200 horses from la Camargue, purchased for 150 francs each; they only stood 4 ft. 2 ins., and they were shod only on their fore feet. Owing to their training they came through all the hardships of the mountain campaign in Italy. They have since been tried in Egypt, and have shown more powers of resistance than other horses.

[CORRESP., xii, 10473. The Ile de la Camargue is part of the delta of the Rhone.]

# 122

# ENEMY BOOKSELLERS

## TO MARSHAL BERTHIER

SAINT-CLOUD, *AUGUST* 5, 1806.

I imagine that you have arrested the Augsburg and Nuremberg booksellers. My intention is to bring them before a court-martial, and to have them shot within 24 hours. It is no ordinary crime to spread defamatory writings in places occupied by the French armies, and to incite the inhabitants against them. It is high treason. The sentence must declare that, since, wherever an army may be, it is the duty of its commander to see to its safety, such and such individuals, having been found guilty of trying to rouse the inhabitants of Swabia against the French army, are condemned to death.

You will parade the guilty men in the centre of a division, and appoint seven colonels to be their judges. In the sentence, you must mention that the defamatory writings originally came from the booksellers Kupfer of Vienna and Enrich of Linz, and that they are condemned to death in their absence; the sentence to be carried out, if they are captured, wherever the French troops may happen to be. You are to have the sentence published all over Germany.

[CORRESP., xiii, 10597. Palm, Schöderer, and Meikle were condemned to death by a French military court at Braunau on August 25, for publishing and disseminating a pamphlet deploring the French occupation of Germany; and Palm was shot.]

## 123

# MUSTER-ROLLS

## TO THE KING OF NAPLES

RAMBOUILLET, *AUGUST* 20, 1806.

. . . I advise you to take a pleasure in reading your muster-rolls. The splendid state of my armies is due to the fact that I spend an hour or two every day doing this; and when they send me the monthly return of my troops and fleets, which take up about 20 big files, I give up every other occupation to study them in detail, and to see what difference there is between one month and another. I get more enjoyment out of reading these returns than a young girl does out of reading a novel. . . .

[CORRESP., xiii, I0672.]

## 124

# THE JEWS

## TO M. DE CHAMPAGNY

RAMBOUILLET, *AUGUST* 23, 1806.

I send you some notes which will show you what direction I want to give to the Jewish Congress, and what the government representatives attached to the Congress have to do at the present juncture.

### *Notes*

It is the first time, since Titus' capture of Jerusalem, that so many enlightened men belonging to the religion of Moses have been able to foregather. Hitherto the Jews, persecuted and dispersed, have been expected to do nothing but receive punishment, abjure their faith, or make contacts or concessions equally unfavourable to their interests and to their beliefs. The present situation is unlike any of the epochs which have preceded it. The Jews are neither being asked to abandon their religion, nor to accept any modifications contrary to the letter or spirit of Judaism.

When they were being persecuted, or were in hiding to escape persecution, different kinds of doctrine and custom crept in. The Rabbis, indeed, claimed the right to expound the principles of the faith, whenever explanation was required. But the right of legislation, in matters of religion, cannot belong to any individual; it can only be exercised by a General Assembly of Jews, legally and freely brought together, including in its body Spanish, Portuguese, Italian, German, and French Jews, and thus representing the Jewries of more than three-quarters of Europe.

It seems to me, therefore, that the first thing to do is to constitute the Congress at present assembled in Paris into a Great Sanhedrin, whose decisions will rank alongside the Talmud as articles of faith and principles of religious legislation.

This first point thus settled, all Jews, of whatever nationality, will be invited to send deputies to Paris, and to contribute their ideas to the work of the Great Sanhedrin. A notification, in the form of a sort of proclamation, will therefore be issued to every synagogue in Europe – officially, in the case of French synagogues. Certain questions will then be proposed to this gathering, and the answers given will be made into theological rulings or instructions, so that they may have the force of ecclesiastical and religious law, and form a second Jewish dispensation, preserving the essential character of that of Moses, but adapting itself to the present condition of the Jews, and to the customs and usages of the day.

The following questions have been propounded: –

*1st Question.* Is it lawful for Jews to marry more than one wife? – The answer must be a plain negative, and the present Congress or Great Sanhedrin must prohibit polygamy in Europe.

*2nd Question.* Is divorce permitted by the Jewish religion? And is divorce invalid unless it has been pronounced by courts, or in virtue of laws, which take a radically different view from that of the French people? – The Congress constituted as the Great Sanhedrin must prohibit divorce, except in the cases provided by the Code Napoléon, and it cannot take place unless it has been previously granted by the civil authority.

*3rd Question.* Can a Jewess marry a Christian, or a Christian woman a Jew? Or does the law only allow Jews to marry among themselves? The Great Sanhedrin must declare that a religious marriage has to be preceded by a civil marriage, and that Jews and Jewesses can marry Frenchmen or Frenchwomen. The Great Sanhedrin must go further, and recommend such unions as a means of protection for Jews, and as a proper thing for them to do.

*4th Question.* Do Jews regard Frenchmen as brethren, or as strangers? – The Sanhedrin, after recognising, as the Assembly has done, that Frenchmen and Jews are brothers, will lay down this principle: that the Jews recognise as brethren the inhabitants of all countries which grant them not merely toleration, but also protection, and in which they are admitted to the enjoyment of all the privileges attached to political and civil status. It will recognise, in this connection, the difference which exists between French and Italian law and that of other countries.

*5th Question.* In any case, what duties does their law prescribe to Jews towards Frenchmen who are not of the Jewish religion? – The answer to this question follows from what was said above.

*6th Question.* Do Jews who were born in France, and who have the legal status of French citizens, regard France as their fatherland? Is it their duty to defend it, to obey its laws, and to accommodate themselves to all the provisions of the Civil Code? – The Sanhedrin must declare that it is the duty of Jews to defend France as they would defend Jerusalem, since they are treated in France as they would be treated in the Holy City; that substitution can only be allowed for half the number of conscripts each year, and that the rest must serve in person.

*7th Question.* Who nominates the Rabbis? – The Sanhedrin must decide by whom the Rabbis are to be nominated, and how they are to be organised and paid; and it must establish in Paris a Council of Rabbis, whose members will be regarded as the Superiors and Supervisors of the Jews. This committee will reside in Paris, and will be called the Rabbis' Committee, or something of that kind.

*8th Question.* What police jurisdiction do the Rabbis exercise over the Jews? What kind of police magistracy do they recognise among themselves?

*9th Question.* Are the forms of election and jurisdiction of the police magistrates laid down by Jewish law, or merely consecrated by custom? – The Sanhedrin must draw up the regulations required to determine the method of election, the functions, the jurisdiction, etc., of the Rabbis.

*10th Question.* Are there any professions prohibited by Jewish law?

*11th Question.* Does the law forbid Jews to practise usury

in dealing with their brethren?

*12th Question*. Does it forbid or does it allow them to practise usury in dealing with strangers? – The Sanhedrin must prohibit usury in dealing with Frenchmen, or with the inhabitants of any countries where Jews are allowed to enjoy civil rights. It will expound the Mosaic Law on these lines, laying it down that Jews ought to behave, in all places where they are citizens, as though they were in Jerusalem itself; that they are strangers only where they are persecuted or ill-treated by the law of the land; and that it is only in such places that illicit gain can be tolerated by religious legislation. When this point has been regulated by the Sanhedrin on these lines, we must look further into the matter for some means of limiting and repressing this habit of speculation, which is nothing but a system of fraud and usury.

All this is meant simply to serve as instructions for the Commissioners. They will realise what is wanted, and will begin by looking for means to secure it, by having private talks with the most influential members of the Assembly. When they are clear in their own minds, they will go to the Assembly; they will say that I am pleased with the zeal that animates its proceedings; they will emphasise the uniqueness of the occasion, and explain that I am anxious to do all I can to prevent the rights restored to the Jewish people proving illusory – in a word, that I want them to find in France a New Jerusalem. They are then to ask for the formation of a committee of nine members chosen from amongst the most enlightened members of the Assembly, with whom they can co-operate, with the hope of reaching important results. This Committee will report to the Assembly. It will begin by suggesting the formation of the Great Sanhedrin.

[CORRESP., xiii, 10686. The National Assembly of 1789 had given the Jews civic rights, but had not dealt with the consequential problems. The Great Sanhedrin met on February 9, 1807, but two months later Napoleon dissolved it, and settled the whole question by an Imperial edict of March 17, 1808.]

## 125

# PRUSSIA – PEACE OR WAR?

TO M. DE TALLEYRAND, PRINCE OF BENEVENTO
MINISTER FOR FOREIGN AFFAIRS

*Note on the present situation*

SAINT-CLOUD, *SEPTEMBER* 12, 1806.

It is not in my interest to trouble the peace of the continent.
Austria is not in a position to attempt anything. Russia and
Prussia are kept apart by every kind of rivalry and dislike. Austria's wounds are still unhealed. It may be assumed that no considerable force of Russians can appear in Europe just yet. They
might go to some lengths to attack the Porte: they might keep
reserves in Poland: but 1 don't think they will again run the risk
of sending 100,000 men into Germany.

The idea that Prussia could take me on single-handed is too
absurd to merit discussion. It is impossible for me to have a
genuine alliance with any of the great European powers: Prussia is only my ally through fear. Her cabinet is so contemptible,
her king so weak, and her court so dominated by young officers
in search of adventure, that no one can depend upon her. She
will go on acting as she has acted – arming today, disarming
tomorrow; standing by, sword in hand, while the battle is
fought, and then making terms with the conqueror.

The fact that Prussia should be arming at this moment
astonishes all Europe: yet the motive is the same as it has been
at any time during the last twelve years. That being so, we must
give her plenty of time to regain confidence, and to disarm
again peacefully. All the same, it might so happen that, after
arming from the fear of me, and regaining confidence through
my kindness, Prussia might become alarmed on her own
account, and make alliances with the other European powers –
flimsy alliances, no doubt, but I shall have to keep my eyes
open.

Two courses are open – first, to reassure Prussia, and to
look for the easiest means to restore her previous peacefulness;
or secondly, to do everything I can to reinforce my German
armies with men and arms. But these two courses are incompatible. If Prussia is already afraid of my army, she will be still
more so when it is reinforced. She must therefore disarm in a
mood of reassurance, but of reassurance touched with fear. That

is the language she understands. That is the only form of appeal that really moves her.

M. de Lucchesini's arrival at Berlin will be an important move in the game. M. de Talleyrand must call his attention to my review of the Guard yesterday, and at Meudon (whence the cavalry has already marched) the day before. He must if possible give such a turn to the conversation as to induce M. de Lucchesini to ask for a letter giving positive assurance of the pacific intentions of the French government; and he must promise to hold back the Guard's marching orders until Lucchesini's arrival at Berlin – I could not in any case give such orders without informing the Senate and the general public. If M. de Talleyrand prefers, the letter might be written, for the new minister, before M. de Lucchesini starts, and it might promise that the Emperor will take no extraordinary steps until the return of the messenger with the reply to Sunday's interview.

My object, in this *démarche*, is to change my tone. Instead of saying 'Disarm or fight,' which Prussia might still find rather alarming, I shall say 'Disarm, if you don't want me to reinforce.' This way of putting it is a little more reassuring:there is even a touch of friendliness in it. It suggests no hostile intention against Prussia. It makes the French moves dependent on the Prussian. This procedure is half encouragement and half threat. The first part puts fear to sleep: the second wakes it up ever so little. Such half-and-half measures are just the medicine Prussia needs.

[LECESTRE, i, 124. Influenced by the Queen and the war party, by the diplomatic humiliations of 1805-6, and by the rumour that Napoleon was contemplating a separate peace with England, Frederick William of Prussia mobilised his troops on August 9, 1806. Napoleon expressed his pacific intentions to the King (as well as to Talleyrand), on September 12; but on the 18th he determined to fight, and on October 14 he defeated the Prussians at Jena and Auerstadt. Jerome, Marquis de Lucchesini, was the Prussian ambassador.]

# 126

# AUSTRIAN ALLIANCE

TO M. DE LA ROCHEFOUCAULD, AMBASSADOR AT THE
COURT OF H.M. THE EMPEROR OF AUSTRIA

WÜRZBURG, OCTOBER 3, 1806.

I have been at Würzburg since yesterday, and have had an opportunity for a long talk with His Royal Highness. I have informed him of my firm resolve, whatever the outcome of the present situation, to break off all ties of alliance that bind me to Prussia. The latest news from Berlin is that there may be no war after all; but I am resolved not to be the ally of such a change-able and despicable power. Doubtless I shall remain at peace with her, because I have no right to shed my subjects' blood for reasons of no importance. But this is the point. I must have an ally on the continent, so as to be able to concentrate attention on my fleet. Circumstances had made me the ally of Prussia: but that power is just the same today as it was in 1740, and has always been – without any consistency or sense of honour. The Emperor of Austria has commanded my respect, even in the midst of his reverses, and of the events that came between us: I believe he is a man who knows his mind and keeps his word. You should express yourself, but without misplaced emphasis, in those terms. I am too strong and too well situated to be afraid of anyone: all the same, the enormous efforts I have made are a burden upon my subjects. I must have one of the three powers – Russia, Prussia or Austria – for an ally. Prussia, in any case, cannot be trusted: there remain Russia and Austria. France had a fine fleet once, owing to the advantages of an Austrian alliance. Austria, too, needs rest – a feeling which I share whole-heartedly.

The kind of alliance I should like would be one founded upon the independence of the Ottoman Empire, a guarantee to respect the integrity of our states, and understandings which would give me a chance to concentrate on my fleet. The House of Austria has often hinted at such an alliance. Now is the ideal moment, if she knows how to take advantage of it. I need add no more: I have expressed myself in greater detail to the Prince of Benevento, who will not fail to give you instructions. All I will say is that your mission will be accomplished when you have conveyed, as delicately as possible, the idea that I am not averse to a *rapprochement* with Austria.

Don't fail to keep an eye on Moldavia and Wallachia, so that you can warn me of any Russian movements against the Ottoman Empire.

[CORRESP., xiii, 10932. The references to the fleet show that Napoleon has not given up his idea of an invasion of England. For the position in Turkey, *v.* No. 120.]

## 127

# EVE OF JENA

### TO THE EMPRESS

GÉRA, *OCTOBER* 13, 1806, 2 A.M.

I am at Géra today, darling. Things are going well, and everything is as I could wish it. I fancy that in a few days, God helping me, the poor King of Prussia will be in a terrible situation. I am sorry for him personally: he is a good fellow. The Queen is at Erfurt with him. If she wants a battle, that cruel pleasure will not be denied her.

I am wonderfully well. I am already fatter than when I started, in spite of travelling 20 or 25 leagues every day, on horseback, in my carriage – in all kinds of ways. I go to bed at 8, and am up again at midnight: sometimes I remember that you are not in bed yet.

All my love.

[CERF, 80.]

## 128

# WOMEN

### TO THE EMPRESS

BERLIN, *NOVEMBER* 6, 1806, 9 P.M.

Thank you for your letter. You seem to be upset by the unkind things I say about women. It is true, there is nothing I dislike so much as a meddlesome woman. I am used to good-natured, gentle, and agreeable women, and I like them so. If they have ever spoilt me, it is your fault, not mine. Besides, I will give you an instance to show how nice I can be to a woman who behaves in a really dutiful and sympathetic way. Take Mme de Hatzfeld. When I showed her her husband's letter, she said to me, with the simplicity of deep feeling, and in a voice broken with tears, 'Yes, it is indeed his writing.' The tones in which she read it touched my heart. She made me feel so unhappy that I said, 'Madam, you can throw that letter into the fire: I shall never be strong enough to punish your husband.' She burnt the letter, and I think she was happy. From that moment her husband was a free man. Two hours' delay, and it would have been all up with him. That shows you that I like women who are sweet, simple, and dutiful. It is because they resemble you. Goodbye, my dear. I am quite well.

[CORRESP., xiii, 11191. The 'meddlesome woman' is the Queen of Prussia, with whom Napoleon was the more angry since the discovery of compromising papers at Charlottenburg. Prince Hatzfeld, the Governor of Berlin, was brought before a military court on account of a letter he had written to an officer staying with the Queen.]

# 129

## POETRY TO ORDER

### TO M. CAMBACÉRÈS

BERLIN, *November* 21, 1806.

. . . Whilst the army does all it can for the glory of the nation, it must be admitted that our writers are doing their best to dishonour it. I was reading yesterday some shocking bad verses sung at the opera. Really, it's a perfect farce. How do you come to allow these extemporised songs at the opera? They're too bad for anything but vaudeville. Express my displeasure to M. de Luçay. He and the Minister for Home Affairs might very well set about getting some decent stuff written; but in that case they mustn't expect it to be ready for production less than three months after it has been commissioned. People complain that we have no literature: it is the fault of the Home Minister. It's ridiculous to order an eclogue from a poet as one orders a muslin frock from the dressmaker's. . . .

[CORRESP., xiii, 11287.]

# 130

# POLAND

## TO M. CAMBACÉRÈS

POSEN, *DECEMBER* 1, 1806.

I have received your letter of the 21st. You will see, from today's bulletin, that my troops have entered Warsaw. All Poland is up in arms. It is difficult to convey a proper idea of the national movement in this country. The Poles are raising regiments as fast as they can. The richest are the keenest. Priests, nobles, peasants – they are all of one mind. Poland will soon have 60,000 men under arms. The great nobles of the country are all men with incomes of 100 – 500,000 francs, and it is they who are meeting the cost of their army. Amidst all the marching and moving of this great host, and the excesses which accompany it, we are having a regular round of balls. I am going to one tomorrow given in my honour by the local gentry. I have held a court for the women: they have all come in from their country estates, and it is the first time they have appeared here since the partition of Poland. Everyone at all well off speaks French, and the peasantry love France.

[CORRESP., xiv, 11333. Napoleon refused to proclaim the independence of Poland unless they put 30,000 men in the field. By 1808 there were about 5,000 serving in Germany and 8,000 in Spain.]

# 131

# 'ONLY ONE WOMAN'

## TO THE EMPRESS

POSEN, *DECEMBER* 2, 1806.

Today is the anniversary of Austerlitz. I have been to a town ball. It is raining. I am quite well. I love you and want you. My troops are at Warsaw. There has been no cold weather yet. All the Polish women here are quite French. There is only one woman in the world for me. Did you ever know her? I could describe her for you to the life: but unless I flattered her you would not recognise yourself. And yet, to speak the truth, I could find nothing for you in my heart but pretty speeches.

How long the nights are here, all alone!

All my love.

[CORRESP., xiv, 11365. A month later he met Marie Walewska; *v.* No. 134.]

# 132

# PROPAGANDA

## TO M. CAMBACÉRÈS

POSEN, *DECEMBER* 11, 1806.

. . . Have all the bulletins of the Grand Army during this campaign and the last translated into Turkish and Arabic, and send large quantities of them to Constantinople. Get 6,000 copies printed. Have a short 10 – page pamphlet produced, in good style; revise it yourself, and call it 'An old Ottoman to his brethren.' It is to be a manifesto against the Russians, depicting their policy and their aims. Have 10,000 copies of this printed in the same languages. It must be ready within a week. Send 1,000 copies to the Viceroy, who will distribute them in Dalmatia; 1,000 to Marseille, to be given to ships sailing for the Levant; 1,000 to my minister at Constantinople; 1,000 to my minister at Vienna; and send another 1,000 to me. When the work is written, see that the Turkish ambassador gets a view of it, indirectly, so as to know what he says of it, and whether it is well written.

[CORRESP., xiv, 11434.]

# 133

# JOSÉPHINE

## TO THE EMPRESS

WARSAW, *JANUARY* 23, 1807.

I have received your letter of January 15. 1 can't possibly allow a woman to undertake the journey here. The roads are too bad – unsafe, and deep in mud. Go back to Paris; be happy and cheerful; and perhaps I will come soon. Your remark, that you married a husband in order to live with him, makes me smile. I thought, in my ignorance, that the wife was made for the husband,

and the husband for the country, the family, and glory. Forgive my ignorance. There is always something one can learn from the fine ladies of today.

Good-bye, my dear. Remember how much it costs me not to let you come. Say to yourself, it shows how much he cares for me.

[CERF, 99. His real reason for not wanting her at Warsaw is seen in the next group of letters.]

## 134

# MARIE

### TO MADAME WALEWSKA

WARSAW, *JANUARY*, 1807.

I saw no one but you, I admired no one but you, I want no one but you. Answer me at once, and assuage the impatient passion of

N.

### II

Didn't you like me, Madame? I had reason to hope you might. . . . Or perhaps I was wrong. Whilst my ardour is increasing, yours is slackening its pace. You are ruining my repose! Ah! grant a few moments' pleasure and happiness to a poor heart that is only waiting to adore you. Is it so difficult to let me have an answer? You owe me two.

N.

### III

There are times – I am passing through one now – when hope is as heavy as despair. What can satisfy the needs of a smitten heart, which longs to throw itself at your feet, but is held back by the weight of serious considerations, paralysing its keenest desires? Oh, if only you would! . . . No one but you can remove the obstacles that keep us apart. My friend Duroc will make it quite easy for you.

Ah! come! come! You shall have all you ask. Your country will be dearer to me, once you have had pity on my poor heart.

N.

### IV

Marie, my sweet Marie, my first thought is of you, my first

desire is to see you again. You will come again, won't you? You promised you would. If you don't, the eagle will fly to you! I shall see you at dinner – our friend tells me so. I want you to accept this bouquet: I want it to be a secret link, setting up a private understanding between us in the midst of the surrounding crowd. We shall be able to share our thoughts, though all the world is looking on. When my hand presses my heart, you will know that I am thinking of no one but you; and when you press your bouquet, I shall have your answer back! Love me, my pretty one, and hold your bouquet tight!

N.

[MASSON, 'Napoleon et les femmes,' 199. Marie Walewska was the young wife of an old Polish noble, whom Napoleon met at a ball at Warsaw, and who soon became his mistress. She was with him again at Finkenstein the same year, at Paris in 1808 and 1810, at Vienna in 1809: and she visited him at Elba. Their son, Count Florian Walewski, was born on May 11, 1810. Of these notes, 1 – 3 were written after the ball, and 4 after their first time together.]

# 135

# CONTINENTAL SUNDAY

## TO M. PORTALIS

OSTERODE, *March* 5, 1807.

It is contrary to divine law to prevent men, who have Sunday needs as well as week-day needs, working on Sundays to earn their daily bread. The government could not enforce any such law, unless it gave free meals to those who would otherwise go without. Besides, the besetting sin of the French people is not overwork. There is nothing for the police or the government to do in the matter. The Holy Fathers themselves only prescribe Sunday rest to people in easy circumstances, or to those who can arrange their work during the week so that they need do none on Sunday. The proof of this is that it used to be understood in all Christian countries that one could work on Sunday with the leave of the bishop and the parson. Would it be the right of the bishop, or of the magistrates, to give this permission nowadays? In our own days we have seen troops employed going about the towns and countryside to make people keep the Tenth Day, and work on Sunday. If we aren't careful we shall find ourselves driven, one of these days, to using the gendarmes

to stop a man working on Sunday, when he must either work or
starve. Both are examples of superstition on the part of the
authorities – the one political, the other religious. God has made
it men's duty to work, because he does not allow them any of
the fruits of the ground unless they work for them. He intends
them to work every day, because he has given them needs
which revive daily. One must distinguish, in what the priests
prescribe, between real laws of religion and duties which have
only been invented in order to extend the authority of the clergy.

It is a law of religion that Catholics should go to mass every
Sunday: but the clergy, to extend their authority, ruled that no
Christian may work on Sundays without their leave. This leave
they granted or withheld at will, to prove their power; and one
knows that in many parts it could be obtained by paying for it.
Once more, such practices were superstitious, and more calculated to injure religion than to serve its true interests.

Wasn't it Bossuet who said, 'Eat beef, and be a Christian?'
The observance of the Friday fast and the Sunday rest is a rule
of secondary and insignificant importance. The essential laws
of the Church are, 'Thou shalt not hurt Society,' 'Thou shalt do
no ill to thy neighbour,' and 'Thou shalt not misuse thy liberty.'
It is no good arguing with priests who insist on such rules: one
can only laugh at them. I am not going to compel them, against
their will, to grant absolution: but neither am I going to let them
force me to imprison a peasant who works for his own living,
and his family's, whatever day of the week it may be.

They appeal to authority: it must then be competent to settle the question. I am authority; and I give my people permission, once and for all, not to interrupt their work. The more they
work, the less vicious they will be. The more fully they provide
for their necessities, the better they will satisfy their bodily
needs, and the demands of nature. If I *were* to meddle in these
matters, I should be more inclined to order that after church-
time on Sundays the shops should be open, and the workmen
should return to their jobs. When one looks at the various classes
that make up society, one sees to what an extent the Sunday rest
does more harm than good. One sees in how many arts and professions this interruption of work has disturbing effects. Society
is not an Order of Contemplatives. Certain legislators have tried
to turn us all into monks, and to put us under rules fit only for
the cloister. People must eat every day. They should be allowed
to work every day.

M. Portalis must not forget that, once this concession is granted, others will be asked for. Once the government has been induced to intervene in matters which are out of its sphere, they will try to get us back to the disastrous era of the 'confession cards,' and to those wretched times when the *curé* thought he had the right to abuse every citizen who didn't go to mass.

The power of the clergy lies in preaching and confession. People should never be forced to church by imprisonment and the police.

[CORRESP., xiv, 11936. It is printed in parallel columns with Portalis's letter, and headed *Décision*. Under the Revolutionary Calendar of 1793 the 'Tenth Day' (*décadi*) took the place of Sunday. 'Confession cards' were the certificates of orthodoxy issued to Catholics by the *Archbishop* of Paris during the Jansenist controversies of 1747 – 57.]

# 136

# PLAIN WORDS TO LOUIS

## TO LOUIS NAPOLÉON, KING OF HOLLAND

OSTERODE, *March* 30, 1807.

The news I hear is so extraordinary that I cannot believe it is true. They tell me that you have restored to the nobles in your states their titles and privileges. Is it possible that you are so short-sighted as not to see how fatal such a step would be to you, to your people, to France, and to myself? How could you, a French prince, have violated your simplest vow – to maintain equality among your subjects? [I refuse to believe it can be true.]

You are as good as renouncing the French throne: for a man who has broken his oath, a man who has robbed a nation of the fruit of fifteen years' fighting, toil, and endeavour, would be unworthy of such a position. I have, too, my own just grounds of complaint. For a long time past you have consistently acted against my advice. This cannot go on. My ambassador has instructions to inform you in so many words that, unless you revoke this measure, he is under orders to leave Holland, and I have done with you. You are an ungrateful brother, and the advisers under whose influence you have fallen are a pack of criminals. Further, I tell you this plainly, since you care nothing for good advice, that I will not have Frenchmen wearing your

Order: so you can save yourself the trouble of conferring it on anyone. I have asked my ambassador for a copy of the act re-establishing nobility: if this measure is not rescinded, I shall look upon you as an inveterate foe. But perhaps I am making mountains out of mole-hills. The simple truth is, you have lost your head. Unless you retract this measure, look out for the consequences. You shall no longer be a French citizen, nor a prince of my blood. Haven't you sense enough to see that if your claim to the Dutch throne were to rest on noble birth, you would be at the bottom of the list? Is this all I am to expect of you? At the present rate, the next claim to a title will be to have fought against France, and to have sold ships to the English. Every local grandee will take up old claims to a title. Could nobody make you realise that you were alienating the people of Amsterdam – indeed, every Dutchman? An order of nobility is bearable in a military country: in a commercial one it is intolerable. I think better of the humblest shop-keeper in Amsterdam than of the highest noble in Holland.

[LECESTRE, i, 144. In revising the letter Napoleon inserted the sentence in square brackets, and struck out all that follows.]

# 137

# THE PAPERS AGAIN

## TO M. FOUCHÉ

FINKENSTEIN, APRIL 4, 1807.

Most of the papers are badly conducted. It may be difficult to remedy this. All the same, I should like you to see that they never talk about the interests of the new dynasty, which they treat rather as though they were a party affair. That dingy publication, the *French Courrier*, can insult the *Empire Journal* as much as it likes; but they mustn't bring *me* into the business. Both these papers follow the same plan. The *Journal* blames philosophy for all the evils of the Revolution, as though there hadn't been civil war, oppression, and persecution in every age. All this is silly enough; but it is quite as absurd for the *Courrier* to pose as my champion, and the defender of my cause, in the interests of Champfort, Diderot, and the Encyclopaedists. Is it too much to ask that, if they are allowed to attack each other with as many bad arguments as they like, they should at least keep off current questions? Everybody reads the *Journal*, and if it does do the government harm, we don't need the *Courrier* to tell us all about it beforehand. I have no wish to start the charge of *lèse-majesté* again: I attach no importance to these gutter-press debates. But I won't let any paper speak of the Bourbons, or of the present dynasty, as the *Courrier* does. Can't it defend its case without bringing in the government? A man can be as atheistical as Lalande, as religious as Portalis, or as famous a philosopher as Regnaud, without being any less a supporter of the government, and a good Frenchman. Then why in the world should we allow the papers to go and tell these men that they are bad citizens? That is the kind of thing that *Brothers and Friends* does; indeed, if it said what it really thinks, you would find its own little set proclaimed as my only friends. The clergy, I suppose, and the 20 million devout Catholics, all belong to the *ancien régime*!

The first time this paper mentions the Bourbons, or my interests, suppress it. As for the *Journal des Débats*, there can be no doubt that it pushes partisanship to the verge of persecution. The time will come when I shall take steps to put this paper, which is the only one that people read in France, into more reasonable and less impulsive hands. Party spirit is dead, and I can only regard it as a calamity that less than a dozen scoundrels, without an ounce of talent or genius among them, should be constantly raking up accusations against the most respectable men in the country. But my interest in the matter is purely literary. Keep the papers within limits: forbid them to mention either the Bourbons or the Napoleons.

[CORRESP., xv, 12285.]

# 138

# LOUIS AGAIN

## TO THE KING OF HOLLAND

FINKENSTEIN, *April* 4, 1807.

I have received your letter of March 24. You say that you have 20,000 men with the Grand Army. You don't really believe it? Why, there are not 10,000 of them; and what men! It is soldiers you must produce, not counts, marshals, and knights. If you go on like this, the Dutch will laugh at me.

Your government is more like that of a monk than of a king. Royal benevolence should be redolent of the palace, not of the cloister. Nothing could be worse than all these journeys to the Hague, unless it is this Inquiry you are having made all over your kingdom. A king gives orders, he does not ask anyone to do anything. He is supposed to be the fountain of power, and to have such resources that he need never draw on another's purse. But all these fine distinctions are beyond your comprehension.

I recall certain ideas about the re-establishment of the nobility, as to which I am still not at all clear. Am I to suppose that you have lost your head over this point, and forgotten your obligations to me? Your letters are always talking of obedience and of respect; but it is deeds I want, not words. Respect and obedience consist in not going so fast in such important matters without my advice: for European opinion cannot imagine you so undutiful as to take action without first asking what I advise. I shall be obliged to disown you. I asked for the document about the re-establishment of the nobility. You must expect some public expression of my serious displeasure.

Don't make any naval expedition: it is too late in the year. Recruit National Guards to defend your country. Pay off my troops. Levy plenty of national conscripts. A prince who gets a reputation for good nature in the first year of his reign, is laughed at in the second. The love that kings inspire should be virile – partly an apprehensive respect, and partly a thirst for reputation. When a king is said to be a good fellow, his reign is a failure. How can a good fellow – or a good father, if you prefer it so – bear the burdens of royalty, keep malcontents in order, and either silence political passions, or enlist them under his own banner? The first thing you ought to have done – and I advised you to do it – was to introduce conscription. What can you possibly do without an army – for you can't give that name to a mob of deserters? How could you ever fail to see that, in the present state of your army, the creation of marshals was as unsuitable as it was absurd? The king of Naples hasn't got any. Do you suppose, to take an analogous case, that if 40 French vessels were added to 5 or 6 Dutch barques, Admiral Ver Huell, in his capacity as marshal, could take command of them? None of the smaller powers, such as Sweden or Bavaria, have marshals. It is much too important a title to give to men who never deserved it.

You are going too fast, and refusing to take advice. I have offered you mine: you reply with fine compliments, and go on making a fool of yourself.

Your quarrels with the Queen are becoming public property. If only you would keep for family life the fatherly and effeminate disposition you exhibit in the sphere of government, and apply to public affairs the severity that you display at home! You drill your young wife like a regiment of soldiers. Distrust your suite: they are all nobles, and the views of that class are always the exact opposite of public opinion. Be careful: you are already losing your popularity at Rotterdam and Amsterdam. The Catholics are beginning to fight shy of you. Why don't you give some of them employment? Isn't it your duty to protect your religion? All this shows a lack of character and determination. You show too much favour to one part of the nation, and cold-shoulder the rest. What have your 'knights' done to deserve their decorations? Where are the wounds they received in the country's service, or the talents that marked them out for distinction – I don't say all of them, but even three out of four? Many of them deserve well only of the English party, and are the cause of their country's misfortunes. I don't say you should penalise them; you want to be friends with everybody. There are *émigrés* at my court too: but I don't let them be cock of the walk. They may think they are going to score a point, but they are even further from doing so than when they were in exile; for I govern by system, and not by concessions.

You have the best and worthiest wife in the world, and yet you are making her unhappy. Let her dance as much as she likes: she is just the age for it. I have a wife in her forties, and I write to her from the battlefield, telling her to go to balls. Do you expect a wife of twenty, who sees her life slipping away, and dreams of all she is missing, to live in a nunnery or in a nursery, with nothing to do but bath her baby? You spend too much time at home, and too little in your office. I wouldn't say all this, only I am concerned about you. Make Hortense happy – she is the mother of your children. The only way is to treat her with all possible trust and respect. It's a pity she is so virtuous: if you were married to a flirt, she would lead you by the nose. But she is proud to be your wife, and is pained and repelled by the mere idea that you may be thinking poorly of her. You ought to have had a wife like one I know in Paris. She would have brought you to heel, and tied you to her apron-strings. I've done my best. I have often talked to your wife about it.

Very well, then; you can play the fool in your own kingdom – that's as may be: but I can't have you doing it in mine. You are offering your decorations to Tom, Dick, and Harry: yet I hear from numbers of people who haven't a title between them. I am sorry that you should not realise what disrespect this shows for my interests. I am determined not to wear these decorations myself, and I won't allow them to be worn at my court. If you ask me why, I answer that you have never done anything to justify people wearing your portrait. Again, you introduced the Order without my permission, and you are bestowing it too freely. Besides, what have they done – those people round you, to whom you are giving it? What have they *done?*

[CORRESP., xv, I2294. Louis Bonaparte had married Hortense Beauharnais, Josephine's daughter, in 1802. Their eldest son, Napoleon-Charles, died in 1807. Their youngest became Napoleon III.]

# 139

# DISSOLUTION OF MONASTERIES

## TO JOSEPH

FINKENSTEIN, *APRIL* 14, 1807.

. . .As you wish me to speak of what has been done at Naples, I must say that I was not particularly pleased with the preamble to the suppression of the monasteries. Documents dealing with religious matters should be expressed in language of a religious and not of a philosophical tone. There lies the art of statesmanship, and it is one that an author or a man of letters doesn't possess. Why speak of the services that the monks have rendered to science, or to art? It was not that which made them deserving, but the way they administered the consolations of religion. The whole preamble is philosophic, and I don't think that is the issue. It is adding insult to the injury of expulsion. This preamble would have been all right, if it had only been written from a monastic point of view. It is easier to put up with unpleasantness from a man of one's own way of thinking than from one who takes an entirely different point of view. What should have been said was that the great numbers of the monks made it difficult for them to subsist; that, for the credit of the state, they must have enough to live on, and hence the need of reform; that some of them must be kept for the necessary work of administring the sacraments, and some of them be reformed, etc. I recommend this to you as a matter of general principle. I think poorly of a government whose edicts are always literary compositions. The thing is to give each edict the style and character of the special subject to which it applies. An educated monk who believed in the suppression of monasteries would not express himself as you have done. Men put up with injury if it is not accompanied by insult, and when the blow does not appear to have come from the enemies of their profession. Now it is precisely the philosophers and men of letters who are the enemies of the monastic life. Not that I am any fonder of them myself – as you know, I have destroyed them everywhere. . . .

[Joseph, iii, 335.]

# 140

# HIGHER EDUCATION
## REMARKS ON A SCHEME FOR ESTABLISHING A FACULTY OF LITERATURE AND HISTORY AT THE COLLÈGE DE FRANCE

FINKENSTEIN, *April* 19, 1807.

. . .Education in the true sense of the word has a number of objects. One must learn to speak and write correctly – what is generally called grammar and *belles-lettres*. This need is met in every *lycée*, and every educated man has been through a course in rhetoric.

After the need of correct speech and writing comes that of counting and measuring; and this the *lycées* have met by their mathematical classes, covering the various branches of arithmetic and mechanics. There follow the outlines of several other studies, such as chronology and geography; and some ideas of history are also included in the curriculum of the *lycées*.

Thus the institution of three stages of education enables every well-to-do citizen to have been through his courses of rhetoric and mathematics, and to have acquired some ideas about history, geography, and chronology. A youth who leaves his *lycée* at 16 knows not only the rules of French, the classical writers, the construction of a speech, the forms of rhetoric, the methods of calming and exciting the feelings of an audience, and in fact all that is taught in a course of *belles-lettres;* he knows also the chief eras of history, and the geographical divisions of the world; he can measure and calculate; and he has a general idea of the most striking phenomena of nature, and of the principles of balance and movement in solid and fluid bodies.

If he wishes to go to the Bar, to enter the Army or the Church, or to take up literature; if he intends to join one of the expert departments, and become a geographer, an engineer, or a surveyor – in all these events he has had the general education necessary as a ground-work for the advanced study that his profession requires; and it is at the moment of choosing a profession that an opportunity is given for specialization.

Does he want to devote himself to the art of war, engineering, or artillery? If so, he enters the specialised school of mathematics, i.e., the Polytechnic. What he learns there is the corollary of what he learnt in his elementary studies of mathematics; but the knowledge so acquired has to be developed and applied, and he proceeds to the various branches of Higher Mathematics. It is no longer merely a matter of general education, as in the *lycées*, but of a science to be mastered. The Observatory is another specialised school of mathematics.

The Natural History Museum, up to a certain point, may be counted in the same class, for there is a real analogy between the way in which different branches of knowledge are acquired and compared in botany and the other natural sciences, and it is in virtue of this that they have been classed among the exact and positive sciences. If it were possible to teach a smattering of botany, natural history, chemistry, and astronomy in the *lycées*, it could only be on the educational (as distinct from the scientific) level; for such elementary ideas would never make anyone a botanist, an astronomer, or a chemist.

Are there enough specialised schools for the exact sciences nowadays? Has this department been treated on a broad scale, like the rest of the educational programme? These are questions that the Home Secretary should be investigating, if it has not been done already.

After the specialised schools of mathematics come those of law and medicine. These have been organised with special care, and need no extension. Law and medicine cannot avoid specialisation; for they are studied only by those who are going to practise the professions for which they are indispensable.

Generally speaking it is not the business of the specialised schools to give the preliminary instruction, which, to be adequate, must include the elements of most branches of knowledge, and which, as given in the *lycées,* fits young people, when they reach the age of discretion, to adopt one or other of the professions. On the contrary, it is their special business to teach some particular branch of knowledge from A to Z, so as to make a well-educated young man useful to society in some particular profession.

It follows that a school for advanced study is not an educational establishment, in the ordinary sense, but an establishment devoted to the instruction of men destined for some particular science or learned profession.

Mathematics, physics, natural history, medicine, and jurisprudence are all sciences, because they involve facts, observation, and comparison; because the discoveries which they make one by one accumulate, and form a series, linking age with age, and extending every day the scientific domain; and because the facts and their relationship, the art of classifying them, and the method of observing and comparing them, can be taught and understood.

The Minister wishes to have schools for the advanced study of literature: yet if the above considerations are sound, it is difficult to attach any meaning to the term. It is intended to teach eloquence, to teach poetry. But what remains to be taught in these subjects, beyond what every young man has learnt in his rhetoric class at school? It only takes a month or two to understand the structure of poetry, or to learn how to analyse a speech. To write well in verse and prose constitutes eloquence; but there is nothing in this art which can be taught in a more advanced way than in the *lycées.* There one is taught to write correctly, and to know and appreciate the best models; one is introduced to the canonical literature of good taste, and set to study the rules of composition, whether for tragedies or comedies, songs or epics: but one is never taught actually to compose any of these things. The creative talent in literature, as in music and painting, is an individual gift: it belongs to those personal faculties whose development is perhaps fostered by special circumstances, or by the customs of a particular age. In these creations of mind and genius, the mind or genius arrives at its finest achievements suddenly, and by means known only to

itself. In tragedy, comedy, and epic poetry we have never sur-
passed the Greeks; they are still our models: whereas in the
exact sciences, which rest upon the observation and comparison
of facts, every enlightened age has made fresh advances. All
this is so well understood, that a teacher of eloquence will not
waste his time explaining the principles of the various *genres* of
intellectual expression: he might just as well teach grammar
and rhetoric, a knowledge of which has already been acquired
at the *lycées*. Instead, he lectures, comments, quotes examples,
and criticises model compositions; and whether it be done in an
Athenaeum, a club, or a drawing-room, the result is no more
than glorified table-talk. Is that a time for criticising the clas-
sics? What can be said that hasn't been said before? For criticising modern books, then? – the last thing anyone would do.
There is therefore no meaning to be attached to a 'school for the
advanced study of literature,' as there is to a club, a *salon*, or
even an academy for teaching or lecturing. The whole business
belongs, not to education in the proper sense, or to any specialised profession, but to the social amenities. What is needed,
then, to prevent literary talent and genius being arrested in its
development? Good class-teaching, especially in rhetoric; and
this is already provided for in the *lycées*. Compare a teacher of
literature with a teacher of mathematics. The latter will teach
the rules of astronomy, optics, and mechanics; he will demon-
strate stone-cutting, and in fact, all those things that are not
taught at lycées, because the pupils are too young, and because
they need greater maturity for the instruction appropriate to the
profession which they may choose, but have not yet chosen.
The teacher of literature amuses his audience, if he is witty, and
interests it, if he is clever; but he doesn't bring out a single new
principle, or new idea; he lays down no positive rules; he tells
you nothing you didn't learn at school; and if he went on teaching for forty years, he would be no wiser himself at the end than
he was at the beginning. He will know his authors better, and
criticise them more acutely; but this is no more than his individual opinion; it is no sign or promise of progress in the literary art.

   Grammar would seem to be more suitable for advanced
study than literature; for it is based upon wider observation and
comparison, and it deals with the origin of sensations – the
kinds of speech corresponding to the kinds of feeling. But the
science of speech is still confused with that of ideas, and is so
little understood that it has been usefully applied only to the

treatment of mutes: the real school for the advanced study of grammar is the Home for the Deaf and Dumb.

Thus eloquence and poetry are not appropriate material for advanced study, because there is nothing really positive about them, and because, in point of education, Corneille and Racine knew no more about such subjects than any promising boy in a rhetoric class: taste and genius cannot be taught.

The specialised schools for Oriental languages, whether ancient or modern, are simply a special kind of *lycées* for the study of foreign languages, and are thought necessary in order to link our age to past ages, and our land to foreign lands. They are private institutions, proportionate to the small number of men likely to need the instruction that they offer. But there are other branches of literature which do give occasion, up to a certain point, for the establishment of schools for advanced study – namely geography and history. Geography, whether physical or political, has many of the characteristics of an exact science – abundance of facts, plenty of debatable issues, and frequent changes; its field expands with each advance of the human mind; it is enriched by discovery, and subject to modification by political as well as physical revolutions. The elements of the subject, learnt at school, are as nothing compared to the science as a whole. If at some central point, such as Paris, there existed a number of teachers of geography who could collect, compare, and sift out the scattered information on this subject, and if one could safely consult them for fuller information on geographical points, it would be well worth while to have such an institution.

Instead, therefore, of any further institutions specially devoted to literature, one would prefer to establish 4 chairs in Geography – one for each quarter of the world. In these information bureaux (as it were) for Europe, Asia, Africa and America, one could lay one's hand on the most accurate facts, the most definite ideas as to new discoveries and recent changes. Each of these professors would be a kind of guide-book, and their lectures would be full of usefulness and interest to everyone desiring or needing instruction.

History, for similar reasons, can be classed with the sciences which would benefit by a school of advanced study. The reading of history is a science in itself. Everything has been said over and over again. There is such a glut of apocryphal histories, and so much difference exists between one book written at

an earlier date, and another written at a later date, and making
use of the labours and the ideas of previous historians, that a
man who wants to look up the best account of some event, and
plunges into a big historical library, loses himself in a regular
maze. To know what remains of the ancient historians, and what
has been lost, and to distinguish original authorities from the
additions made to them by good or bad commentators – this
alone, if not a science, is at least an important subject of study.
Thus the knowledge and selection of good historians, good
memoirs, and genuine chronicles, is a real and useful acquisition. If, in a great capital like Paris, there were a school of
advanced study in history, and if its first course were one in bibliography, a young man need no longer waste months in the
misleading study of inadequate or untrustworthy authorities; he
would be directed to the best books, and would, with less time
and trouble, acquire a better knowledge of the subject.

There is, besides, a part of history, namely the most recent
periods, which cannot be learnt from books. No historian comes
down to our own day. For every man of 25 there is a period of
50 years before his birth of which no history has been written.
This gap presents many difficulties. It needs hard work – work
that is always imperfect, and often unremunerative – to link up
past events with the present day. To do so would be an important duty of the professors at the advanced school. They ought
to know not only what has happened from the beginnings of
national life up to the point at which historians stop writing, but
also up to the time at which they are teaching.

There should be a number of such professors – in Roman
history, Greek history, the history of the Empire, Church history,
American history, and several more for the history of France,
England, Germany, Italy, and Spain.

History would also be divided into the various branches
suitable for teaching. First would come the history of legislation. The professor of this subject would have to go back to the
Romans, and follow on from that period, dealing with the
reigns of the French kings in chronological order, down to the
Consulate. Then would come the history of the art of war in
France. The professor would expound the different plans of
campaign adopted at various periods of our history, whether for
invading other countries or for defending our own; the causes
of victory and of defeat; with the authors and memoirs in which
his facts can be found, and his conclusions verified. This branch

of history, which interests everyone, and is essential for soldiers, would also be extremely useful to statesmen. The art of
attacking and defending fortified positions can be explained at
the specialised School of Engineering: the art of war as a whole
can't be expounded, because it has never yet been put on paper
– if, indeed, it ever will be. But a chair of history devoted to
explaining how the great commanders defended our frontiers in
various wars could not fail to be of the greatest benefit.

One might, then, consider the organisation of a sort of Literary University, including in this term not merely *belles-lettres*, but also history and geography – for one cannot think of
the former without the later. This University could be found in
the existing *Collège de France;* but it would have to consist of
some 30 chairs, so well correlated that they formed a kind of
personal office for instruction and advice, at which anyone who
wanted to know all about a particular century could ask what
books he ought to read and to avoid, and what memoirs or
chronicles he ought to consult; and at which anyone who
wished to travel in a particular country could obtain definite
information either as to the routes he ought to follow, or as to
the government in control of any district in which he might
wish to pursue his researches.

Something is surely lacking in a great state, if a young student cannot get competent advice on the subject he wishes to
study, and is obliged to grope his way, wasting months or years
in fruitless reading, whilst he searches for the information he
really needs.

Something is surely lacking in a great state, if, in order to
get definite information about the situation, government, and
present condition of any part of the globe, one has to go either
to the Foreign Office, which (whatever treasures may be buried
there) only knows part of the facts, or to the Admiralty, which
very often can't answer all one's questions.

I want this University: it has been in my mind a long time,
because I have done so much work myself, and have felt the
need of it. I have read a lot of history, and I have often wasted
a deal of time in useless reading, just for lack of direction. And
I have paid enough attention to geography to know that there is
no single man in Paris who is perfectly up to date in the discoveries which are made every day, and in the ceaseless
changes of that subject. I am certain that the proposed institution would be a great help to education in general, even for the

best educated people; whereas courses in literature would have none of these advantages – my experience being that they teach nothing more than one knows at the age of 14. . . .

The reasons given in this Note for a Literary University, primarily for the teaching of history and geography, are not the only motives that influence me. It will be easily guessed that my private idea is to gather together, not historians of philosophy or of religion, but men who will write the history of events, and carry it on up to the present day. Our young people have more facilities for getting to know the Punic Wars than the American War of 1783. They can more easily find out about the events of past ages than about things which have happened during their own lifetime.

One objection is constantly raised in this connexion: it is said that contemporaries are bad historians. I don't agree. I should, if what is meant is a satirical treatment of current events: I should, if it were the history of a living man, or of one whom the historian had known personally; for history must not be turned into panegyric. But it is as easy one year as it is a hundred years after the event to say when or under what circumstances a state was forced to take up arms; at what moment it compelled the enemy to make peace; or in what month such and such a fleet sailed on such and such an expedition, and what engagements it lost or won. It makes little difference whether the historian is near the facts, or far away from them. If he is really close to the facts he is likely to be all the more truthful, because he knows that his readers can judge of what happened in their own life-time. There is no inconvenience in this, whilst there is a real advantage, especially for young people, who can find nobody to instruct them in the events of 20 or 30 years ago. For instance, without this type of teaching, soldiers will have to wait a long time before they can learn to profit by the faults which have led to defeat, or to appreciate the dispositions which would have prevented it. The whole Revolutionary war should be full of lessons: yet one often devotes long hours to persistent research and fails to gather them. The reason is, not that there is no detailed description of the facts – for they have been described in all kinds of ways and in all kinds of places, but that it is nobody's business to make research easy, and to give the guidance which is needed if it is to be done intelligently.

To sum up: it would be feasible to set up at the *Collège de France* a big institution or school of higher study for subjects other than the mathematical sciences, jurisprudence, medicine, etc. But, if one is to make it a specialised school of literature, with courses of history and geography in all their branches, such an institution will need at least 20 or 30 professors.

[CORRESP., xv, 12416. This belongs to the period between the inauguration and the organisation of Napoleon's Imperial University.]

# 141

# HISTORY AND CRITICISM

REMARKS ON THE HOME SECRETARY'S REPORTS ABOUT
THE ENCOURAGEMENT OF LITERATURE

FINKENSTEIN, *April* 19, 1807.

The Emperor has received three Reports dealing with the encouragement of literature. The first report includes a draft decree under six heads. The first of these heads deals with the establishment of two or more Official Historians.

France has had official historians: but the truth is, they did nothing either for France or for history. Racine was official historian under Louis XIV, but none of his work has lived. We haven't many good historians, and they don't include the present holders of the title which it is proposed to re-establish. Such an institution might, indeed, be of some use; but it would not produce historians. Above all, we must avoid the phrase 'official historians.' If it be agreed that a historian is a judge, and one who expresses the verdict of posterity, then he must possess so many qualities, and so many perfections, that it is difficult to believe that good history can ever be produced to order. What *can* be expected of sensible men, with some degree of talent, is historical memoirs based on scholarly research, and containing original material, with critical remarks designed to throw light upon the events of history. If these researches, documents, and materials are embodied in a good narrative, the work will have many points of likeness to history; yet its author will not be a historian in our sense of the word.

The second head of the draft decree has the effect of instituting Poets Laureate or Poets Caesarian. The object of this is clear enough – it is to create posts for our poets. But the institution ought to harmonise better with our habits; in particular it must give no occasion for ridicule, such as Frenchmen seize so maliciously. It is really easier to imagine the creation of official historians; because in appointing historians, though one leaves them free either to praise or to blame, one does at least impose upon them the necessity of speaking the truth. But will official poets be allowed to write satires on the court to which they are attached? Or will it be their duty to eulogise it? In either case it is not obvious what is the use of employing them. Poetry is the child of society. It is only as society remodels itself on lines of public peace and private happiness that it can teach its poets that good taste, and that grace and perfection of style, which are the ornament of literature and art. Besides, poetic production carries so many rewards with it that there is no need for the state to intervene. Whether a poet writes a tragedy or a comedy, an opera or a farce, an elegy or a romance, he is rewarded by the praises of his admirers, and the support of the public whom he interests or entertains. The Institute too provides a means of rivalry; the poet who gains a place in it becomes a public character. Did Corneille ever receive any particular marks of court favour? Did those that Racine received inspire his masterpieces? Was the flight of his genius restricted by his failure to receive others? Generally speaking, no form of creation which is merely a matter of taste, and which all the world can attempt, needs official encouragement.

However, if there were any way of paying a distinguished compliment to some contemporary poet, whilst being careful not to make him ridiculous, I should raise no objection. For instance, why not attach certain poets to the Théâtre Français, and give them honorary titles, carrying stipends, and the right to be consulted about the plays produced? There would be little to object to in such an arrangement. They have it at the Opera. But in this case it would need to be instituted in a specially flattering and solemn manner. This would give us a means of awarding distinctions to certain authors. But it would be a mistake to think that this is the way to produce poets. What does the art of government consist in, whether for sovereigns or ministers? It consists in advertising anything well done. Decrees are not enough: one must take some definite action about it. For instance, several good odes have been published. Why not call public attention to their authors? Why not give them that confidence in themselves which would encourage them, stimulate their efforts, and lead to their producing still better work? If

Italy has had so many good poets, it is because she possessed such a number of petty courts, so many idle and rival societies. Besides, in this range of ideas it often happens that one man who becomes famous enables another to become famous after him. Perhaps Racine and Boileau would not be held in such esteem if the fame of Corneille had not preceded them. Perhaps Laharpe, Marmontel, and other highly commendable authors owed their enterprise, if not their talents, to the successful example of Voltaire. Cardinal de Richelieu's criticism of *Le Cid* was undoubtedly beneficial: it still wins approval. His action in the matter has, indeed, been attributed to motives of the lowest kind – perhaps rightly, but very possibly not; for might one not suppose that the minister intended public discussion to stimulate a movement for the purification of French taste and the French tongue?

Our journalistic critics might contribute to the same end, if they were not inspired, sometimes by hatred, more often by a satirical turn of mind, and always by a desire to entertain idle readers, rather than to edify the serious public. Is it desirable that Frenchmen should learn to speak their language elegantly, and to acquire a liking for discussions about the improvement of taste and style? If so, let the Minister get the Second Class of the Institute to criticise one of the best books issued in the last 20 years. The public will become interested in this work, and perhaps even take sides for and against the criticism – never mind which: its attention will be directed to these interesting debates; it will talk about grammar and poetry; literary taste will be educated and perfected; and the original purpose will be achieved. If it be well understood beforehand that the choice of a particular book for enlightened and kindly criticism is a proof that it deserves the approval of men of taste; if it is by the Emperor's own request that the Institute criticises (let us say) the Abbé Delille's *Georgics* (not as a translation from the Latin, but as a masterpiece of French language, poetry, and taste), or the finest canto of Esménard's *Navigation*, or Lebrun's best odes, or even (to show how impartial it is) the most beautiful piece of verse from the pen of Fontanes, it may be that the author who is criticised will be a little hurt at first, but he will soon see that the choice of his work is a form of commendation; whilst the general public, the spectators of this useful contest, will be interested, edified, and formed into a school of taste. This is one of the most important duties the Institute can undertake. Such a system of criticism, once begun in the formal way I have described, will soon be desiderated by the authors who find themselves honoured by it. A new tragedy is produced, and is a success on the stage; it will lack only one ingredient of fame – that the Minister should ask the Institute, on the Emperor's behalf, to report on it by the rules of dramatic art, taste, and style. Such is the only real criticism – an honourable criticism, quite different from that exercised by our mountebank magazines, in which contemporary authors are treated, not with serious criticism but with sarcasms which are intentionally dishonest or malicious, and which have no bearing either on art or taste. The only reason for putting up with a form of criticism which does more harm than good, and for doing nothing to remedy such an abuse, is the fear that government intervention may produce even worse results, or that excesses of criticism which hurt an author's self-esteem may be better for literature than uncritical admiration. But, once a system of intelligent criticism has been set up, it will be possible to prohibit the present method, or at least to correct its abuses. The Institute is a splendid weapon for the Minister: if he uses it properly, it will do all that the Government requires. . . .

The Minister's second Report deals with the establishment of a literary paper. It seems useless to do this, for there are too many papers already, people only read them for amusement, and the more sarcastic a literary criticism is, the more amusing they find it. In a state like France there must of course be *one* paper, such as the *Moniteur*, and this must be made to pay. There is no reason why its back page should not be given up to articles or literary criticism, written by men selected by the Minister. The *Moniteur* is expensive but plenty of people read it without subscribing to it, or combine to take it in; it is copied by the provincial papers, it is translated into the foreign press. The part of the *Moniteur* set aside for literature ought to be quite distinct from the rest, in view of the serious subjects of which the latter is full. Both ideas – the Emperor's and the Minister's – would thus be combined in the one paper; for it would include critical articles such as might appear in a specialised literary review, as well as more serious and detailed criticisms asked for by the Minister from the Institute at the Emperor's request.

One cannot ignore the further advantages of this second idea. There are at the moment great differences of opinion about literature. In order to escape from this anarchy we must purify tradition and good taste, and give them back their rights. There could be no better means of doing this than the serious criticism of good books by a body containing all the distinguished talents still available, and bound to obey a superior authority, whose choice would in itself be proof that the book was popular, and evidence that it was approved. This criticism need not be applied to more than 4 or 5 publications a year: it would then have immense, and indeed decisive effects. There is no better way of learning to speak our language than to read the criticism on *Le Cid*, or Voltaire's comments on *Corneille*. There is therefore nothing new in the idea underlying the present proposals; but we have wandered so far from the right path, that an institution designed to bring us back to it would have the attraction of novelty, as well as the interest attaching to a good debate, and the advantage of raising high-class work out of the common rut.

The Institute will raise no objection to our demands. It is obliged by its constitution to do anything the Home Minister asks of it; and the Minister, writing to it in the Emperor's name, and in accordance with the present Remarks, will simply inform it that, such and such a work having deservedly won public attention, it is worth while to enquire what faults the author may have committed against the canons of art and the genius of the French tongue, and to prevent the corruption of taste and language by vices of thought and expression which may have crept in under cover of an elegant style. . . .

[CORRESP., xv, 12415. Delille (1738 – 1813) was a poet of Nature; Lebrun (*Odes républicaines*, 1795) and Fontanes (1757 – 1821), members of a literary circle influencing Châteaubriand. Cardinal de Richelieu took part in the controversy aroused by Corneille's *Le Cid*, and compelled the Academy to publish a criticism of it (1638). J. E. Esménard's *Navigation*, a poem in 8 cantos, came out in 1805.]

# 142

# PRESS CAMPAIGN

## TO M. FOUCHÉ, MINISTER OF POLICE

FINKENSTEIN, *April* 21, 1807.

I want you to get up a great agitation, especially in the provincial press of Brittany, Vendée, Piedmont, and Belgium,

against the persecutions which the Irish Catholics are suffering
at the hands of the Anglican church. For this purpose you must
collect all the features that represent the persecution in its
strongest colours. I will get M. Portalis to make private arrangements with some of the bishops, so that, when these newspaper
articles have had time to produce their effect, intercessions may
be offered for the stoppage of the persecutions. But the whole
affair must be managed very tactfully, from the government
side. You must make use of the papers without their suspecting
the end we have in view. The editors of the *Journal de l'Empire*
are the very people for the job. You must make people realise
the cruelties and indignities committed by England against the
Irish Catholics, whom they have been massacring in St.
Bartholomew's Eve fashion for the last hundred years. Don't
talk of 'Protestants'; say 'the Anglican Church': for there are
Protestants in France, but there are no Anglicans.

[LECESTRE, i, 150. Daniel O'Connell's agitation for Catholic rights in
Ireland began in 1805.]


# 143

## JEALOUSY

### TO THE EMPRESS

FINKENSTEIN (?), *MAY* 10, 1807.

I have received your letter. I don't understand what you say
about my lady correspondents. There is only one person I love,
and that's my little Joséphine. She's kind, she's capricious, she
easily takes offence. Her quarrels are as graceful as everything
she does; for she is always adorable, except when she is jealous,
and then she becomes a regular little devil. But to return to
these ladies of yours. If I were to waste my time on any of them,
you can be sure they would have to be as pretty as rose-buds.
Does that fit the ladies you mean?

I want you never to dine with people who have not dined
with me. Keep to the same list for your private parties. Never
invite ambassadors or foreigners to Malmaison: I should be
angry with you, if you did. And don't let yourself be imposed
upon by people whom I don't know, and who wouldn't come to
see you if I were there.

Good-bye, my dear. All my love.

[CERF, 118. Mme Walewska was at Finkenstein.]

## 144

# A GIRLS' SCHOOL
*Note*

FINKENSTEIN, *MAY* 15, 1807.

The buildings at Écouen ought to be as handsome, and the curriculum as simple as possible. Beware of following the example of the institution at Saint-Cyr, where vast sums were spent, and the girls abominably educated.

The first problem that needs your attention is the employment and distribution of time. What are the girls brought up at Écouen going to be taught? You must begin with religion in all its strictness. Don't allow any compromise on this point. Religion is an all-important matter in a public school for girls. Whatever people may say, it is the mother's surest safeguard, and the husband's. What we ask of education is not that girls should think, but that they should believe. The weakness of women's brains, the instability of their ideas, the place they will fill in society, their need for perpetual resignation, and for an easy and generous type of charity – all this can only be met by religion, and by religion of a gentle and charitable kind. I did not lay special stress on religious observances at Fontainebleau: and in the *lycées* I only prescribed the necessary minimum. At Écouen matters must be entirely different. Nearly all the exact knowledge taught there must be that of the Gospel. I want the place to produce, not women of charm, but women of virtue: they must be attractive because they have high principles and warm hearts, not because they are witty or amusing. We must therefore have, as headmaster at Écouen, a man of ability, good character, and a sufficient age; and every day the pupils must have regular prayers, hear mass, and learn the catechism. This is the part of their education with which most care must be taken.

In addition the girls must be taught writing, arithmetic, and elementary French, so that they may know how to spell; and they ought to learn a little history and geography: but care must be taken not to let them see any Latin, or other foreign languages. The elder girls can be taught a little botany, and be taken through an easy course of physics or natural history. But that too has certain embarrassments. The teaching of physics must be limited to what is necessary to prevent gross ignorance and silly superstition, and must confine itself to the facts, and not indulge in reasoning which directly or indirectly touches on first causes.

You must go into the question whether all girls who have reached a certain class should be given a dress allowance. They could then practise economy, calculate prices, and keep their own accounts.

But the main thing is to keep them all occupied, for three-quarters of the year, working with their hands. They must learn to make stockings, shirts, and embroidery, and to do all kinds of women's work. These young girls should be regarded as belonging to provincial families with incomes of 15 – 18,000 livres, and as unable to bring their husbands a dowry of more than 12 – 15,000 francs; and they should be treated according-ly. That is why one realises that manual labour in the home can-not be ignored.

I don't know whether it is possible to give them some idea of medicine and pharmacology, at any rate that kind of medical knowledge commonly required for nursing invalids. It would be a good thing, too, if they knew something about the work done in the Housekeeper's room. I should like every girl who leaves Écouen, and finds herself at the head of a small house-hold, to know how to make her own frocks, mend her husband's things, make clothes for her babies, provide her little family with such occasional delicacies as can be afforded by a provin-cial housekeeper, nurse her husband and children when they are ill, and know in these matters, because she has been taught it beforehand, what invalids have learnt by experience. All this is so simple and obvious that it does not require much considera-tion.

The girls ought to wear uniform. Choose quite common material, but a good pattern of frock. In that respect I don't think the present fashions can be improved upon. But of course they must have long sleeves, and such other modifications as health and modesty require.

As for their food, it can't be too simple: some soup, some boiled beef, and a small *entrée* – that's plenty.

I wouldn't dare insist on the pupils cooking their own

meals, as I did at Fontainebleau: there would be too much opposition to it. But they might be made to dish up their own dessert,
and any special food given them for a treat, or on holidays. And
if I let them off cooking, I insist on their doing the baking. The
advantage of all this is that they are given practice in everything
they are likely to be called on to do, and that their time is normally filled up with sensible and useful occupations.

The girls ought to furnish their own rooms, make their own
chemises, stockings, and frocks, and do their own hair. I attach
a great importance to all this. I want to make these young persons into useful women, and I am sure that in that way I shall
make them attractive wives. I don't want to *aim* at making them
attractive: the only result would be to turn them into leaders of
fashion. Making your own clothes teaches you how to hold
yourself: afterwards it becomes a habit to do it gracefully.

Dancing is necessary for the health of the pupils; but it
must be a cheerful sort of dancing, not the kind they indulge in
at the opera. They may have music too, but only vocal music.

You can take as your model, up to a point, the school at
Compiègne. At Écouen, as at Compiègne, you must have mis-
tresses to teach sewing, cutting out, embroidery, etc., as well as
the parts of pharmacology and household management I mentioned above.

If I am told that this institution will not be particularly popular, I reply that I don't want it to be: for in my opinion the best
education of all is that which a mother gives her daughters; and
my principal object is to do something for those girls who have
lost their mothers, and whose people are too poor to bring them
up properly. In fact, if wealthy members of the Legion of Honour are too snobbish to let their daughters go to Écouen, whilst
poor parents are glad to send them there, and if these young persons return to their country homes with the reputation of making good wives, I shall have done absolutely all I want: I shall
be confident that the institution has every chance of winning a
high and solid reputation.

This is a matter in which we must risk a little ridicule. I am
not bringing up shop assistants, or chambermaids, or house-
keepers, but wives – wives suitable for poor and humble homes.
Among the poor it is the mother who looks after the whole
house.

With the single exception of the Headmaster, all men must
be excluded from the school. No man must ever enter within its

walls, under any pretext whatsoever. Even the gardening must be done by women. My intention is that in this respect, the establishment should be as strictly ruled as a convent. The Headmistress herself must not be allowed to receive men, except in the parlour; and if it is impossible to exclude the girl's relations in cases of serious illness, at least they must only be admitted by special permission of the Grand Chancellor of the Legion of Honour.

I have no time to write more about this establishment. It is more original than Compiègne, as I view it; and Compiègne is unlike anything of its kind before.

I need hardly say that the only women employed in the school must be elderly spinsters, or widows without children; that they must be entirely under the control of the Head-mistress; and that they must never receive men, or go outside the walls of the school.

It would, no doubt, be equally superfluous to remark that nothing is worse, or more open to censure, than the idea of let-ting young girls appear on the stage, or stimulating rivalry among them by allowing them to take places in form. It is good for men, who may have to make speeches, and who, having to master so many subjects, need the support and stimulus of com-petition. But in the case of young girls, competition should be banned: we don't want to rouse their passions, or to give play to the vanity which is one of the liveliest instincts of their sex. Light punishments, and a word of praise from the Headmistress to those who do well, seem to me all that is needed. I can't think it has a good effect to distinguish the girls by different coloured ribbons, unless the object is merely to classify them by age; oth-erwise it might establish a kind of precedence among them.

[CORRESP., xv, 1258.]

# 145

## POST-HASTE

### TO THE EMPRESS

DRESDEN, *JULY* 18, 1807, MIDDAY.

My dear; I got to Dresden yesterday at 5 p.m., feeling very well, though I had been 100 hours on the road without leaving my carriage. I am staying here with the King of Saxony, with whom I am well pleased. So you see I am more than halfway back to you. One of these fine nights I may turn up at Saint-Cloud in the rôle of the jealous husband; I give you fair warning. Good-bye, my dear. It will be a great pleasure to see you. All my love.

[CORRESP., xv, 12912. He is on his way back from Tilsit.]

# 146

# TITLES FOR ELECTORS

## TO M. CAMBACÉRÈS

SAINT- CLOUD, *AUGUST* 12, 1807, 2 P.M.

I want you to bring me this evening, at 8 o'clock, the proposed *sénatus-consulte* about the Tribunate, and the draft of the decree on Titles. I also want you to read through the enclosed memorandum, and to bring it back this evening with any remarks you have to make upon it.

### *Memorandum*

Nowadays the Electoral Colleges of the Departments are the connecting links between the government and the people. If a necessity arose for dismissing the Legislative Body, it would be for them to elect the elements of which the new legislature would be composed. True, they carry out this duty in conjunction with the Colleges of the *arrondissements*; but it is none the less certain that, if they chose good men, the Senate could nominate from among their candidates, and it would not matter if the Colleges of the *arrondissements* chose badly.

Thus there exists in the state a large body of persons nominated by the choice of the people, selected from amongst men of property, appointed for life, and having an important influence upon public order; and it would be entirely consistent with our general scheme of government if membership of an Electoral College carried with it the qualification to hold a title. If this were so, all past or present Chairmen of Colleges might be given a title; but it would be a purely personal one, and would become hereditary only when permission was obtained to establish an entailed estate bringing in 10 – 20,000 livres a year.

Members of Colleges who could prove possession of a freehold with a net revenue of not less than 10,000 francs, and who had held their office for more than six years, could petition the Emperor for a hereditary title, with every likelihood of obtaining it.

Amongst other advantages, this institution would attach more prestige to membership of the Electoral Colleges, and would distinguish between fortunes made by legitimate means, and of some standing, from fortunes of recent origin, derived from business or speculation.

Distinctions of this kind, so bestowed, would be very generally coveted, because it is only human nature to want to leave to one's children some memorial of the reputation one has enjoyed, as well as an adequate and honourable fortune.

It won't be so easy to become a member of a College, because there are not more than 300 members to a Department; so that a man might not reach the position till he was already pretty old, and his career might be over before the end of the necessary six years.

To sum up: the sovereign bestows titles, or allows the establishment of entails, in the case of citizens who have distinguished themselves by public spirit and important services. He is the sole judge, and no private considerations can set limits to his freedom of action. As for other citizens, who do not combine these qualifications to such an eminent degree, the sovereign can bestow the same favour on them too, but they must necessarily be marked out by their wealth, since they are among the principal tax-payers; they must have obtained the votes of their fellow-citizens, since the members of the Colleges are nominated by the cantonal assemblies; and they must have occupied for some time a position in the public eye, as one of the conditions is that they shall have held their office for more than six years.

To these general considerations it may be added that this scheme is the only means by which the old nobility can be completely rooted out. The titles of Duke, Marquis, and Baron are reappearing: coats of arms and liveries are coming into use again. It was easy to foresee that, unless one replaced these old customs by new institutions, they would soon begin all over again. In any case, what public inconvenience can be caused by creating a new currency in which to reward services and success, to add prestige to popular election, and to make it understood that military distinctions are not the only kind, and that, if the army is the most brilliant career, it does not make us forget honourable and useful work in other spheres?. . .

[CORRESP., xv, 13020.]

# 147

# COPENHAGEN

## TO THE EMPEROR OF RUSSIA

SAINT-CLOUD, *AUGUST* 28, 1807.

I wrote to Your Majesty a few days ago on the Copenhagen affair. I have at this moment received letters of August 21st from which I learn that the city is formally invested. I am deeply incensed at this horrible crime, and I feel a great desire to make the English Government sorry for it. It seems to me that what we ought to do is first of all to force Sweden to declare war on England, and then to compel Austria to dismiss the English ambassador from Vienna, and to shut the port of Trieste against English commerce. If Your Majesty agrees with these views, it will only be necessary to send instructions to your minister at Vienna: then our two ambassadors will combine to ask for an interview with the Austrian Minister for Foreign Affairs, and will do their utmost to persuade him that it is in the interests of all the powers to break off communications with a people that tramples the most sacred rights of humanity under foot. If, at the end of several talks, the Austrian court still refuses to act, they will declare that they have orders to leave Vienna, unless the English Minister has himself quitted the city before a certain date. I am assuming that Austria will not face a war with both our states at once; if she did, she would soon be sorry for it.

As for Sweden, I cannot conceive how her present sovereign can remain indifferent to what is happening at Copenhagen. The only possible explanation lies in that prince's character. In any case it is difficult for him to remain neutral. If he sides with the English, I fancy Your Majesty has told me that you have treaty obligations to help Denmark. I shall certainly give her all the help I can; and the Danish army in Norway could make a diversion while Your Majesty attacks Sweden.

[CORRESP., xv, 13086. In consequence of information from Tilsit as to Napoleon's designs on the neutrality of Denmark, the British Government proposed a defensive alliance with that country, and the temporary surrender of its fleet. Denmark refusing, English troops landed near Copenhagen, in August, 1807, and on September 2 an English fleet bombarded the city.]

# 148

# LOCAL INDUSTRIES

## NOTE FOR M. CRETET, MINISTER FOR HOME AFFAIRS

SAINT-CLOUD, *SEPTEMBER* 2, 1807.

The Minister is requested to write to the syndics of Lyon, and to inform them that the local factories are not doing their work in such a way as to maintain their reputation. The green hangings edged in rose and gold tissue, which were put up in His Majesty's study at Saint-Cloud not much more than a year ago, have already worn out. The syndics are to visit the manufacturer, find out where the fault lies in the method of manufacture, and make a report to be submitted to His Majesty personally. Foreigners who see quite modern decorations in such a state are bound to form a very bad impression of the Lyon factories.

[CORRESP., xvi, 13100.]

# 149

# INSULT TO THE ARMY

## TO MARSHAL BERTHIER, PRINCE OF NEUCHÂTEL, MAJOR-GENERAL OF THE GRAND ARMY

RAMBOUILLET, *SEPTEMBER* 7, 1807.

You must be sure to inform Marshal Soult, by special messenger, of the incident at Königsberg, where two actors, appearing on the stage as French officers, were hissed by the audience. You will tell Marshal Soult that I have demanded satisfaction from the King of Prussia for this insult, and that I have required that the two chief culprits shall be shot. Marshal Soult is to inform the officer opposite him of the base and despicable character of the outrage of which I have had to complain, and of the explicit terms in which I have demanded satisfaction.

[LECESTRE, i, 172.]

# 150

# CENTENARIES

### TO M. CRETET, MINISTER FOR HOME AFFAIRS

FONTAINEBLEAU, OCTOBER 2, 1807.

Please inform the Prefect of Troyes of my displeasure, because, without your permission, he has authorised a kind of fête that they want to have in honour of Thibaut, Comte de Champagne. It is absurd to go and revive, centuries afterwards, the memory of men who never had any outstanding merits.

Find out from the Prefect of Tours what this monument is that they want to put up to Agnès Sorel. It seems to me most unsuitable. If I remember aright, Agnès Sorel was a king's mistress, and has little title to fame except the poem *La Pucelle*. Write to the Prefect and tell him that I am not going to allow any such monument. . . .

[CORRESP., xvi, 13207. Thibault, Count of Champagne, became King of Navarre in 1234. Agnès Sorel was Charles VII's mistress, and plays a large part in Voltaire's *La Pucelle*.]

# 151

# PORTUGAL

### TO CHARLES IV, KING OF SPAIN

FONTAINEBLEAU, OCTOBER 12, 1807.

At a moment when Holland, the various states of the Confederation of the Rhine, Your Majesty, the Emperor of Russia, and I are united in an attempt to exclude the English from the continent, and to exact all possible vengeance for the crime that they have just committed against Denmark, Portugal offers the spectacle of a power that has been in the English pay for sixteen years. In Lisbon England has possessed an inexhaustible spring of wealth, and a constant resource, both as a port of call, and as a base for naval expeditions. It is time that Porto and Lisbon were closed against her. I calculate that before November 1st the army under General Junot's command will be at Burgos, along with Your Majesty's army, and that we shall be in a position to occupy Lisbon and Portugal in force. I will arrange with Your Majesty to dispose of this country in whatever way is convenient to you: in any case it shall be placed under your suzerainty, as you appear to desire. We cannot secure peace except by isolating England from the continent, and by shutting every European port against her commerce. I count on Your Majesty's energetic co-operation in this particular; for England must be forced to make peace, if tranquillity is to be restored to the world.

[CORRESP., xvi, 13243. For 'the crime committed against Denmark,' v. No. 147. On July 19 (before the Copenhagen affair) Napoleon had demanded the closing of all Portuguese harbours against British ships, the seizure of British subjects and property, and the breaking off of relations with England. The Prince Regent of Portugal – ruling for the Queen, who was insane – refused the second of these demands. On October 12, Napoleon ordered troops at Bayonne under Junot to march into Spain.]


# 152
# OCCUPATION OF LISBON

## TO GENERAL JUNOT, O.C.
## THE ADVANCE GUARD OF THE GIRONDE

FONTAINEBLEAU, *NOVEMBER* 12, 1807.

I have received your letter of November 3. You will have learnt from two despatches I sent you by special messenger what my intentions are as regards your march on Portugal. They fit in well enough with the plans of which you inform me. It is my hope that in any case you will seize the Portuguese fleet. I enclose a list of the naval officers who are under orders to join you.

If (as I expect) the Portuguese do not oppose your entry, this is how you should proceed: occupy the harbour, encamp your troops in good positions, seize the fleet, hoist the French flag, put 200 infantrymen on board every vessel, and distribute among the fleet the naval officers I am sending you. I am giving orders to the Minister of Marine to despatch as quickly as possible a battalion of naval gunners, to man the ships. You must at once arm such vessels as are fit for it, keep the crews on board at full strength, and provision them, so that I may have 7 or 8 battleships ready to sail anywhere.

The moment you have taken possession of the fleet and fortresses, you must proceed to disarm the Portuguese troops.

Inform the Prince Regent that he must go to France; and try to induce him to do so willingly. Assign him officers whose overt instructions are to escort him, but whose real duty will be to keep him prisoner. Tell me when you reach Lisbon, and wait there for my orders. Treat all claimants to the throne in the same way, and send them off, without troublesome restrictions, to Bayonne. If there are any Swiss soldiers, incorporate them in your Swiss regiments, and send the officers to Paris, to be placed in my Swiss regiments, if I have room for them.

Deport some of the most prominent men, and those most likely to give you trouble, under instructions to go to Paris. They ought all to wait at Bayonne for further orders.

You can go so far as to mobilise a body of 5 – 6000 officers and men from the Portuguese army, and to send them off towards France in columns of 1,000 strong, telling them that I am taking them into my service. Make them take the oath; draft a few French officers among them; and give new names to their regiments; and I really will take them into my service. By this means you will get rid of a crowd of undesirables. Be careful to send them off by different routes.

The Portuguese taxes must be collected in my name. M. Herman is to be Administrator-general of finance. I am giving orders to the Minister of the Public Treasury to send you a Collector of Taxes, who will be under his orders.

I need not advise you to give no occasion for complaints: it is for you to set an example of impartiality that everyone can imitate. Above all take care to provide for the payment of the army. The proceeds of prize-money, jewellery, and shops containing English goods will go, half to the Privy Purse, and half to the army; the latter half will enable the generals and chiefs of staff to be content with their pay.

English goods are to be confiscated, individual Englishmen arrested and sent to France, and English property, such as houses, vineyards, estates, etc., sequestrated in my name.

One thing I insist upon; you must be as correct in your conduct as I should be myself, and set an example of absolute incorruptibility. It is better to have a fortune you have won by your merits, and that you can openly avow comes from me, than one made by illegitimate and disgraceful means. Portugal is not a country in which you are likely to win much military renown: so you must acquire the reputation of an honest and blameless administrator. And, to do that, you must set a good example.

Your chief of staff is an unscrupulous man: he took a lot of money at Fulde. Insist upon his observing a strict rule, and make it known that if there is any thieving, I shall punish it.

Hoist the French flag at Lisbon, and hold on there.

Your army must be paid to the last penny. The pay of generals, colonels, and commandants should be on the scale of the Grand Army, but not more.

All objects of value that you capture are to be packed in cases and sent to the bank. Their exact destination will be the one I gave in my letter.

[CORRESP., xvi, 13351. On Junot's approach, the Prince Regent fled with the Portuguese fleet to Brazil. Junot occupied Lisbon, and remained there till defeated at Vimiero in August, 1808. F.A. Herman was a diplomatist trained under Louis XVI.]


# 153

# WESTPHALIA

## TO JÉRÔME NAPOLÉON, KING OF WESTPHALIA

FONTAINEBLEAU, *NOVEMBER* 15, 1807.

I enclose the Constitution for your Kingdom. It embodies the conditions on which I renounce all my rights of conquest, and all the claims 1 have acquired over your state. You must faithfully observe it. I am concerned for the happiness of your subjects, not only as it affects your reputation, and my own, but also for its influence on the whole European situation. Don't listen to those who say that your subjects are so accustomed to slavery that they will feel no gratitude for the benefits you give them. There is more intelligence in the Kingdom of Westphalia than they would have you believe; and your throne will never be firmly established except upon the trust and affection of the common people. What German opinion impatiently demands is that men of no rank, but of marked ability, shall have an equal claim upon your favour and your employment, and that every trace of serfdom, or of a feudal hierarchy between the sovereign and the lowest class of his subjects, shall be done away. The benefits of the Code Napoléon, public trial, and the introduction of juries, will be the leading features of your government. And to tell you the truth, I count more upon their effects, for the extension and consolidation of your rule, than upon the most resounding victories. I want your subjects to enjoy a degree of liberty, equality, and prosperity hitherto unknown to the German people. I want this liberal regime to produce, one way or another, changes which will be of the utmost benefit to the system of the Confederation, and to the strength of your monarchy. Such a method of government will be a stronger barrier between you and Prussia than the Elbe, the fortresses, and the protection of France. What people will want to return under the arbitrary Prussian rule, once it has tasted the benefits of a wise and liberal administration? In Germany, as in France, Italy, and Spain, people long for equality and liberalism. I have been managing the affairs of Europe long enough now to know that the burden of the privileged classes was resented everywhere. Rule constitutionally. Even if reason, and the enlightenment of the age, were not sufficient cause, it would be good policy for one in your position; and you will find that the backing of public opinion gives you a great natural advantage over the absolute Kings who are your neighbours.

[CORRESP., xvi, 13361. Jérôme, at the age of 22, deprived of Miss Paterson (v. No. 89) and betrothed on October 22, 1807, to Princess Catharine of Wurttemberg, arrived at Cassel as King of the newly created state of Westphalia on December 10. For the sequel v. No. 157.]

# 154

# PRUSSIAN MANNERS

## TO MARSHAL VICTOR, GOVERNOR OF BERLIN

VENICE, *DECEMBER* 6, 1807.

I have received your letter informing me that Prince Augustus of Prussia is misbehaving himself at Berlin. I am not surprised to hear it. He is a good-for-nothing. He has been wasting his time at Coppet, making love to Mme de Staël, and can have picked up nothing but bad principles there. We can't let it go on. Tell him that the first time he opens his mouth you will arrest

him, and shut him up in a castle, and send Mme de Staël there
too, to console him! A Prussian prince is the greatest bore in the
world!

[BROTONNE, i, 227.]

# 155

# LUCIEN'S DAUGHTER

## TO JOSEPH

MILAN, *DECEMBER* 17, 1807.

I saw Lucien at Mantua, and had several hours' talk with
him. No doubt he has told you in what state of mind he left me.
His ideas, and his way of expressing them, are so unlike my
own, that I found it difficult to understand what he wanted; but
I think he told me he wished to send his eldest daughter to Paris,
to be with her grandmother. If this is still his inclination, I
should like to be informed of it without delay; and the young
person must reach Paris during January, whether Lucien escorts
her himself, or whether he leaves it to a governess to bring her
to Madame's. Lucien seemed to me to be swayed by contrary
feelings, and to be too weak to make up his mind. I exhausted
all the means I knew – and, after all, he is still quite a young
man – to make him devote his talents once more to myself, and
to the country. If he wants to send me his daughter, she must
start without delay, and, in consideration of my taking her, he
must send me a declaration putting her entirely at my disposal.
For there is not a moment to lose; events hurry on, and my destiny must be fulfilled. If he changes his mind, then, too, I must
be told about it at once; for I shall have to make some other
arrangement.

Tell Lucien that I am touched by his trouble, and by what
he told me of his feelings; but that I am all the more sorry that
he won't be reasonable, or contribute to his own peace of mind
as well as to mine. . . .

[JOSEPH, iv, 80. Lucien, unlike Jerome, refused to give up his second wife,
Alexandrine de Bleschamp (1803) for a throne (that of Portugal), in spite of
pressure from 'Madame' (his mother), and the rest of the family. This interview took place on December 13. By his first marriage with Christine Boyer
('1794) Lucien had two daughters. Charlotte, the elder, was now 12.]

## 156

# SWEDEN AND INDIA

TO ALEXANDER I, EMPEROR OF RUSSIA

PARIS, *FEBRUARY* 2, 1808.

General Savary has just arrived, and I have spent two whole hours with him talking about Your Majesty. Everything he said touched my heart; I cannot lose a moment in thanking you for all the kindness that you have shown him, and that you are extending to my ambassador.

Your Majesty will have seen the latest speeches in the English Parliament, and its decision to carry on the war to the bitter end. This being so, I am writing direct to Caulaincourt. If Your Majesty will condescend to have a talk with him, he will explain my views. Nothing but measures on a really large scale will now enable us to secure peace, and to carry out our common designs. Your Majesty ought to enlarge and strengthen your army. All the help and assistance at my disposal will be freely given you; I have no feeling of jealousy towards Russia; my only desire is for her prosperity, her glory, and the further extension of her frontiers. Will Your Majesty graciously listen to the advice of one who claims to be honestly and affectionately attached to you? Your need is to remove the Swedes further from your capital. Extend your frontiers as far as you like in their direction. I am ready to help you in this with all the means in my power.

A Russo-French army of 50,000 men, including perhaps a few Austrians, marching viâ Constantinople into Asia, would no sooner appear on the Euphrates, than it would put England into a panic, and make her beg for mercy from the Continental powers. I am within striking distance in Dalmatia, Your Majesty on the Danube. Within a month of our plans being made this army could be at the Bosphorus. The blow would be felt in India, and England would collapse. I should refuse no preliminary stipulations that would enable me to achieve so great a result. But the reciprocal interests of our States must be balanced and combined. This can only be done in an interview with Your Majesty, especially if it is preceded by frank discussions between Romanzof and Caulaincourt, and by the despatch to Paris of someone who is really in our confidence. M. de Tolstoi is a fine fellow, but he is full of prejudices and distrust where France is concerned, and he is far from understanding the full significance of what happened at Tilsit, or the new orientation given to the world by the close friendship between Your Majesty and myself. The whole thing could be decided, and the agreement signed, before March 15. By May 1 our army could be in Asia, and Your Majesty's troops at Stockholm. Then the English, threatened in India, and expelled from the Levant, will be crushed under the weight of the events with which the atmosphere would be charged. Your Majesty and I should, no doubt, have preferred the pleasures of peace, and a life spent in the midst of our vast empires, regenerating them and making them happy by the arts and blessings of good government. This the enemies of the world will not allow: they must aggrandise themselves at our expense. Prudence and policy therefore dictate that we should do as destiny demands, and go whither we are led by the irresistible march of events. If we do so, this cloud of pygmy powers, whose only interest is to see whether the events of today can be parallelled in the newspaper accounts of the eighteenth century, will accommodate themselves to the movement imposed by Your Majesty and myself; whilst the Russian people will be grateful for the glory, the wealth, and the fortunes flowing from these great events.

Thus, in a few lines, I tell Your Majesty my inmost thoughts. What was done at Tilsit will rule the destiny of the world. Perhaps a touch of cowardice on Your Majesty's part, as well as on my own, led us to prefer a certain and immediate benefit to a better and more perfect settlement: but, since England will not have it so, let us recognise that the moment has come for great changes and great events.

[CORRESP., xvi, Appendix (i). Hearing at the end of January, 1808, that England is determined to go on fighting, and counting on the Tsar's anger at the bombardment of Copenhagen (*v.* No. 147), Napoleon revives his plan for an attack on India. If the Tsar will co-operate, he may annex Finland ('remove the Swedes further from your capital') and even part of Turkey ('I should refuse no preliminary stipulations'): but 'the reciprocal interests of our States must be balanced,' i.e., Napoleon wants Silesia. General Savary is Napoleon's aide-de-camp, sent to St. Petersburg to negotiate for an alliance; Count Peter Tolstoi is the Tsar's representative at Paris.]

## 157

# JÉRÔME AND HIS MINISTERS

### TO JÉRÔME NAPOLÉON, KING OF WESTPHALIA

PARIS, *MARCH* 6, 1808.

I have read your letter to Beugnot. I fancy I told you that you could keep Beugnot and Siméon as long as you want them: but is it absurd to make them take an oath. No sober-minded Frenchman, who seriously considered the results of such an act, would do so. I pardon their taking the oath only because I cannot believe they did so *ex animo.* If it is an oath of fidelity to your person, that is already contained in the oath of fidelity to mine taken by every Frenchman. If it is an oath taken as a subject of Westphalia, you are asking something that would be refused by the humblest drummer-boy in my army. No such oath has been taken by the Senators or State Councillors employed at Naples. Frenchmen employed in the King's household have sworn fidelity to him as a French prince. And even supposing these reasons were not enough, this is not the moment, when you are surrounded by foes and foreigners, to ask of men who might be useful to you the criminal act of renouncing their fatherland. I have seldom seen anyone with so little sense of proportion as yourself. You know nothing, yet you never take advice. You decide nothing by reason, everything by impulse and passion. I have no wish to correspond with you more than is indispensable for matters involving foreign courts; for there you put yourself forward, and publish your disagreements with me to all Europe: and that I am hardly disposed to allow. As for your financial and home affairs, I repeat, as I said before, that nothing you do squares either with my opinions or with my experience: if you go on as you are doing you will get nowhere. All the same, I should be obliged if you would practise a little less pomp and ostentation in *démarches* whose consequences you fail to appreciate. Nothing could be more absurd than the audience you gave to the Jews. Nothing could be worse than your parody of the French *Moniteur.* I have undertaken to reform the Jews; but I have made no attempt to attract more of them into my states. Far from it. I have been careful to do nothing suggesting a good opinion of the most despicable race in the world.

P.S. – My dear fellow, I'm very fond of you, but you're a

mere babe. Keep Siméon and Beugnot for at least a year longer,
oath or no oath. Then we shall see what we shall see!

[LECESTRE, i, 237. The P.S. was added in Napoleon's own hand. Counts
Beugnot (afterwards Imperial Commissioner in the Duchy of Berg) and
Siméon had introduced the Napoleonic regime into Westphalia.]

## 158

# THE SPANISH THRONE

### TO LOUIS NAPOLÉON, KING OF HOLLAND

SAINT-CLOUD, *MARCH* 27, 1808, 7 P.M.

The King of Spain has abdicated. The Prince of the Peace
has been put in prison. An insurrection has broken out at
Madrid. Whilst all this was happening, my troops were 40
leagues away from the capital; but the Grand Duke of Berg
should have entered it with 40,000 men on the 23rd. The people
have been loud in their appeals to me throughout the crisis. Convinced as I am that I shall never secure lasting peace with England until I set the whole of Europe in motion, I have determined to put a French prince on the throne of Spain. The Dutch
climate doesn't suit you. Holland can never rise again from its
ashes. Whether there is peace or not, it hasn't the means to
defend itself in this whirlwind of a world. Things being so, I am
thinking of you for the throne of Spain. There you will be sovereign of a generous nation of 11 million souls, and of important colonies overseas. Given economy and energy, Spain might
have 60,000 men under arms, and 50 warships in its ports. Tell
me in so many words what you think of this plan. You understand that it is still only in the air, and that, though I have
100,000 men in Spain, the circumstances may be such that I can
go straight ahead, and get it all done in a fortnight, or such that
I may have to proceed slowly, and only reach my hidden objective at the end of several months' operations. Give me a plain
answer. If I appoint you King of Spain, do you accept? Can I
count on you? As your messenger might come too late to find
me in Paris and might then have to follow me across Spain, and
be liable to mischances that cannot be provided against, give
me your answer in one of these two forms: – 'I have received
your letter of Such and such a date: my answer is 'yes''; and
then I shall count upon your doing what I wish: or 'no': which

will mean that you do not accept my proposal. You can follow this up with a letter explaining your views and wishes in detail; and this you had better address under cover to your wife in Paris. If I am there, she will forward it to me; if not, she will send it back to you. Don't take anyone into your confidence, and don't mention the subject of this letter to a single soul. A thing like this must be done, before one admits to having thought of doing it.

[CORRESP., xvi, Appendix (3). Charles IV became King of Spain in 1788. His Queen, Maria Luisa of Parma, took, as one of her lovers, Manuel de Godoy of the Royal Guard, and made him chief minister and generalissimo. He was called 'Prince of the Peace' from the conclusion of the Peace of Basle in 1795. Ferdinand, the heir to the throne, was on bad terms both with his mother and with her lover. On March 19, 1808, as the result of a popular rising at Aranjuez, Godoy was dismissed, and Charles IV abdicated in favour of his son, who became Ferdinand VII. On March 23, Murat (the Grand Duke of Berg), entered Madrid.]


# 159

# OFFICIAL HISTORY

## NOTE FOR M. CRETET, MINISTER FOR HOME AFFAIRS

BORDEAUX, *April* 12, 1808.

His Majesty disapproves of the principles laid down in the Minister's note. They were true 20 years ago; they will be true 60 years hence; but they are not true today. Velly is the only author who has written anything like a detailed history of France. President Hénault's *Chronological Summary* is a good old classic. It would be well worth while to bring them both up to date. Velly ends with Henri IV, and the other historians don't go beyond Louis XIV. Everything depends upon the spirit in which the continuations are written. Young people can hardly avoid accepting whatever version of the facts is presented to them. To fob them off with nothing but memoirs is to provide them with a store of future errors. His Majesty has ordered the Minister of Police to see to the continuation of Millot: he wishes the two Ministers to co-operate in arranging for continuations of Velly and President Hénault. The work must be entrusted not merely to authors of real ability, but also – and this is even more important – to adherents of the Government, who

will present the facts from their right angle, and lay the foundations of healthy education, taking up the old historians at the
point where they stop, and carrying on the history up to the Year
VIII.

His Majesty regards expense as of no consideration. It is
indeed his intention that the Minister should make it known that
no study is more likely to merit the Emperor's protection than
that of history.

Every line of the history must bring out the effects of the
influence of the Court of Rome, of the 'confession cards,' of the
Revocation of the Edict of Nantes, of the absurd marriage of
Louis XIV to Madame de Maintenon, and so on. The weakness
through which the Valois kings fell from their throne ought to
rouse the same feelings as that through which the Bourbons let
the reins of government slip from their hands. Justice should be
done to Henri IV, Louis XIII, Louis XIV, and Louis XV, but
without flattery. The September massacres and the horrors of
the Revolution should be painted with the same brush as the
Inquisition, and the massacres of the Sixteen. In speaking of the
Revolution, care must be taken to avoid reaction of any kind.
Nobody could oppose the Revolution. The blame for it belongs
neither to the victims, nor to the survivors. No single power
could have changed conditions or prevented happenings which
were the natural outcome of circumstances.

Attention should be called to the constant financial disorders, the chaotic state of the provincial assemblies, the preten-
tions of the *parlements*, and the lack of administrative method
and energy, which made the patch-work France of those days,
with its disunity of law and government, more like a congeries
of twenty kingdoms than a single state; and thus, when the reader comes to the epoch that enjoys the benefits of one law, one
land, and one government, he will breathe again. Realising how
weak the government always was under Louis XVI, Louis XV,
and even Louis XIV, he will feel bound to support the work we
have recently accomplished, and the supremacy we have
achieved. So too, the knowledge that we have re-established
Catholic worship and the Catholic altars should inspire appre-
hension lest the peace that France now enjoys be destroyed by
some ambitious Confessor, or some foreign priest.

No work could be more important. Every passion and party
in the country can produce reams of misleading literature: but a
work like Velly, or like Hénault's *Summary*, requires more than

one continuator. Once this book appears, well edited, and written with a right tendency, no one will either want to write or have the patience to write another, especially when its composition, far from being favoured, is discouraged by the police.

If the view expressed in the Minister's note were adopted, it would mean abandoning this important work to private enterprise, and to publishers' speculations – a bad plan, the result of which could only be disastrous.

If any individual historian offers his services, the one question to ask is whether he possesses the necessary talents, and is a man of good sense, and whether we can rely upon his researches and writings being directed by sound opinions.

[CORRESP., xvi, 13735. Hénault's *Abrégé* (1744), Velly's *Histoire de France* (1755), and Millot's *Élements de l'Histoire de France* (1767) were the most popular old-fashioned histories of France in the eighteenth century.]

# 160

# SPANISH COURT

## TO M. TALLEYRAND, PRINCE OF BENEVENTO, VICE-GRAND ELECTOR

BAYONNE, MAY 1, 1808.

I have received your letter of April 27. The Spanish minister has written a quite ridiculous letter to Champagny complaining of the statement in the papers that King Charles was forced to abdicate. Tell him that he ought to have read the *Moniteur*; that I have seen King Charles and the Queen, and that they gave their sons a very bad reception: that for several hours they went in fear of their lives, and that if the King had not signed his abdication they would have been assassinated. Make the same statement to the assembled ambassadors, and add that the King has been much surprised that the foreign ministers at Madrid should have recognised the new king; that the French minister, representing the only power in a position to control his affairs, has not recognised him; that when this minister asked the King whether his abdication had been voluntary, he replied: 'That is a subject which I am keeping for a letter to my brother the Emperor of the French'; that this hint was enough for M. de Beauharnais, who had the good sense not to recognise Ferdinand VII; that the King's life, and the Queen's, were only saved at the price of abdication: and that the following day he made his daughter, the Queen of Etruria, write to the Grand Duke of Berg; hence the document that appeared in the *Moniteur*.

The Prince of the Asturias is a brute, a bad lot, and an enemy of France. You can imagine that, with my experience of managing men, his 24 years quite failed to impress me; indeed my mind is so clear about him that nothing less than a long war would induce me to recognise him as King of Spain. Further than that, I notified him that, as King Charles was on the French frontier, I could not have any more dealings with him. In pursuance of this attitude I arrested his messengers, and found on them letters full of venomous hatred against the French, whom he repeatedly described as 'these damned Frenchmen.'

The Prince of the Peace is here. King Charles is a fine fellow. I don't know whether it is his position or circumstances, but he has the air of an honest and good-natured old man. The story of the Queen's infatuation is written on her face: there is no need to say more. The affair passes imagination. They are both dining with me today. The Prince of the Peace looks rather like a bull: there is something of Daru about him. He is beginning to recover his nerves after the unparalleled barbarity with which he was treated. It is as well that the untrue imputations against him have been withdrawn; but it is inevitable that he should still be treated with veiled contempt.

[CORRESP., xvii, 13777. The Prince of the Asturias is Ferdinand VII, whose accession (*v*. No. 158) Napoleon refused to recognise, since he intended the throne for one of his own family.]

# 161

# ENTERTAINING SPANISH PRINCES

## TO M. DE TALLEYRAND, PRINCE OF BENEVENTO, VICE-GRAND ELECTOR

BAYONNE, *May* 9, 1808.

The Prince of the Asturias, his uncle the Infant Don Antonio, and his brother the Infant Don Carlos leave here on Wednesday, spend Friday and Saturday at Bordeaux, and will be at Valençay on Tuesday. I want you to be there by Monday evening. My chamberlain Tournon is posting there, to get everything ready for their reception. Arrange for the provision of table and bed-linen, and all that is needed for the kitchen. They will have eight or ten persons in attendance on them, and as many, or perhaps twice as many servants. I am ordering the General who is acting as Senior Inspector of the Paris Gendarmerie to go there, and to organise the police service.

I want these princes to be received without public ceremonial, but decently and attentively. You must do all you can to keep them amused. If there is a theatre at Valençay, and you could arrange for some actors to come there, it wouldn't be a bad idea. Then you could get Mme Talleyrand to come, with four or five other women. If the Prince of the Asturias were to form an attachment to some good-looking woman, whom one could depend upon, so much the better: it would give us an additional means of watching him; and I am particularly anxious that he should commit no political indiscretions: that is why I want him to be occupied and amused. If I were vindictive I should shut him up at Bitche, or in a fortress of some kind. But as he has thrown himself on my mercy, and promised to do nothing without my orders, and as everything in Spain is going well, I have decided to send him to this country place, and to surround him with pleasures and spies. The arrangement need only last during May and a part of June: by that time the situation in Spain will have declared itself, and I shall be able to tell what to do. Your own part in the business is honourable enough. To entertain and amuse three illustrious personages is thoroughly in character with your nation and with your rank. Eight or ten days spent in their company will acquaint you with their thoughts, and help me to decide what I ought to do. . . .

[LECESTRE, i, 278.]

# 162

# SHIP-BUILDING

## TO REAR-ADMIRAL DECRÈS, MINISTER OF MARINE

BAYONNE, *MAY* 22, 1808.

I have received your letter of the 18th, referring to the Spanish-American expedition. The Spaniards are despatching

from Cadiz every ship they can. If the French took the trouble
to fit out expeditions in their ports, it would, I suppose, only
result in giving the alarm? Nonsense! Your one business is to
despatch ships from Bordeaux, Bayonne, and every available
port. I can't give orders to a minister as I should to an ordinary
official: when I give a minister an order, I leave it to him to find
means to carry it out. However, you need not send an expedition to America. Nor, by the way, need you compare me with
God. The way you put it is so extraordinary, and shows so little
respect for me, that I can't believe you thought what you were
saying. I am sorry for your judgment. . . . But I will say no more
about it. Send me lists, with plenty of details, showing me how
far the work has gone, to what classes the vessels under construction belong, and what I can get built; for it seems that if I
want a single schooner to sail I shall have to design it myself!
If I had a sensible minister at the head of my navy, there would
have been 40 vessels at sea by this time – brigs, corvettes,
scouts, schooners, two-masted sloops, lateen-rigged ships, and
the rest; and if all 40 had been captured, at any rate the minister would have done his duty. As it is, only 3 vessels have
sailed, and it was I who despatched them. One must be something of a fool, after that, to think there is nothing superior to
one's own ideas but miracles, and the mind of God! . . .

[CORRESP., xvii, 13960. This concerns Napoleon's scheme for a Franco-
Spanish expedition against Egypt, in connexion with the attack on India outlined in No. 156.]

# 163

# SPANISH APOLOGIA

## TO ALEXANDER I, EMPEROR OF RUSSIA

BAYONNE, *JULY* 8, 1808.

I send Your Majesty the Constitution just passed by the
Spanish Junta. Disorder in this country had reached a degree
difficult to imagine. Compelled to intervene in its affairs, I have
been led by the irresistible force of events to a system which
guarantees both the happiness of Spain and the tranquillity of
my own states. In her new situation Spain will really be less
dependent on me than she was before; but I shall derive this
advantage, that, when she finds herself normally situated, and

with nothing to fear on land, she will use all her resources to rebuild her navy. I have reason to be satisfied with all the people of rank, fortune, or education. Only the monks, who occupy half the land, and who foresee that the new regime means the destruction of abuses, as well as the many agents of the Inquisition, who are apprehensive that their occupation will soon be gone, are still agitating the country. I am well aware that my action in Spain will open a vast ground for discussion. People will fail to make allowances for the circumstances, or for the facts of the situation: they will allege that the whole thing was a premeditated plot. But in fact, if I had thought of nothing but the interests of France, it would have been quite simple to extend my southern frontiers at the expense of Spanish territory; for everyone knows that ties of blood go for little in calculations of policy, and are null and void at the end of 20 years. Philip V went to war with his grandfather. The addition to France of such a province as Catalonia or Navarre would have been a greater increase of her power than the change which has just taken place, and which in fact benefits no country but Spain herself. . . .

[CORRESP., xvii, 14170. On June 11 the Spanish authorities at Madrid, under military pressure, recognised Joseph as King of Spain: but the Juntas of Asturias (May 25) and of Seville (June 6) had already declared war on the French: and soon the whole country was in revolt. Philip's 'grandfather' should be his father-in-law, the Duke of Savoy.]

## 164

## JÉRÔMES DEBTS

### TO JÉRÔME NAPOLÉON, KING OF WESTPHALIA

BAYONNE, *JULY* 16, 1808.

You owe the bank two millions. You allow your notes to be repudiated. It is thoroughly dishonest of you. I will not be let down like this. You must sell your diamonds and your plate. There must be an end to the mad extravagance which already makes you the laughing-stock of Europe, and will end by rousing the indignation of your subjects. Sell your furniture, sell your horses, sell your jewellery, and pay your debts. Honour is the best currency. It is bad form to leave your debts unpaid, whilst everyone can see the kind of presents you give. The luxury you indulge in bewilders and shocks your subjects. You are young and light-headed, and care nothing for the value of money – and that at a time when your people are suffering from the after-effects of war.

[LECESTRE, i, 318.]


# 165

## HUNDRED BEST BOOKS

### TO M. BARBIER, THE EMPEROR'S LIBRARIAN

BAYONNE, *JULY* 17, 1808.

The Emperor wishes to provide himself with a portable library of 1,000 volumes, in small 12° size, and good type. His Majesty's intention is to have works specially printed for his own use, and without margins, so as not to waste space. The volumes should contain 5 or 600 pages each, and should be bound with loose backs, so that they open flat, and in the thinnest possible boards. This library would be composed of about 40 volumes on religion, 40 of epics, 40 of plays, 60 of poetry, 100 of novels, and 60 of history. The balance, up to 1,000, would be made up with historical memoirs of all ages.

The religious works would be the *Old* and *New Testaments* in the best translations: a selection of the Epistles and other most important works of the Church Fathers; the *Koran*; some mythology: select treatises on the sects which have had most historical influence, such as the Arians, Calvinists, Reformed bodies, etc.; and a history of the Church, if there is room for it within the thousand volumes.

The Epics should be Homer, Lucan, Tasso, *Télémaque*, the *Henriade*, etc.

The Tragedies: of Corneille, only the plays that have stood the test of time; Racine; but leave out the *Frères ennemis*, *Alexandre*, and the *Plaideurs*; of Crébillon, only *Rhadamiste*, and *Atrée et Thyeste*; and what has survived of Voltaire.

History: put in some good books on chronology, and the chief ancient authorities – sufficient for a detailed history of France. You can include under the head of history Machiavelli's *Discours sur Tite-Live*, the *Esprit des Lois*, the *Grandeur des Romains*, and whatever is worth keeping of Voltaire's historical writings.

Novels: Rousseau's *Confessions*, and *Nouvelle Héloise*. There is no need to mention the masterpieces of Fielding, Richardson, Lesage, etc., which are of course included. The *Contes* of Voltaire.

*Note.* – Don't put in Rousseau's *Émile*, or the whole crowd of letters, memoirs, speeches, and useless treatises that he wrote. The same remark applies to Voltaire.

The Emperor wishes to have a descriptive catalogue of the library, with notes pointing out the best books, together with a memorandum saying what would be the cost of printing and binding these 1,000 volumes, what proportion of an author's works each volume would contain, what each volume would weigh, how many boxes of what size would be needed to hold them all, and how much space they would take up.

The Emperor would also like M. Barbier to collaborate with one of our best geographers in editing memoirs on the campaigns which have been fought on the Euphrates and against the Parthians, from that of Crassus down to the 18th century, including those of Antony, Trajan, Julian, etc.; and in marking, on maps of a convenient size, the route followed by each army, with the names (both ancient and modern) of the districts and principal towns, remarks on the geography of the country, and historical narratives of each expedition drawn from orginal sources.

[CORRESP., xvii, 14207. For second thoughts on this library, cf. No.183.]

# 166

# THE WAR IN SPAIN

## TO JOSEPH NAPOLÉON, KING OF SPAIN

BORDEAUX, *JULY* 31, 1808, 11 P.M.

I have received your letters of the 24th, 25th, and 26th. I don't like the tone of that of the 24th. There is no question of dying, but of fighting and winning. You are fighting: you will win. In Spain I shall find the Pillars of Hercules, but not the limits of my power. In all my military life I have never come across anything so despicable as these Spanish bands and troops. In any case troops and reinforcements of every kind are coming to your aid. You have a third more forces than you need, if only they are managed with proper efficiency. Apart from Moncey, with his disgraceful retreat and his cowardly council of war, I am very pleased with my troops. Savary has a good head and heart: he has made mistakes in strategy, because he is unaccustomed to supreme command: all the same, he is superior to anyone that you have. Caulaincourt has done splendidly at Cuenca. The town has been looted – by right of war, since it defended itself against capture.

Russia has recognised you: the letter was sent to M. Strogonoff. When I reach Paris I shall no doubt hear that Austria has done the same. As a King your position may be painful: as a general it is brilliant. There is only one thing to fear: take care you don't destroy the spirit of the army by refusing to allow retaliation upon the Spaniards. It is impossible to show consideration towards brigands who murder my wounded, and commit every kind of outrage. It is only natural to treat them – I have said so before, and I say it again – as the army does. . . .

[LECESTRE, i, 333. Joseph was 'recognised' as King of Spain. After suppressing the revolt of May 2 at Madrid, Moncey was sent with 7,000 men to capture Valencia. After two attempts, he withdrew, with a loss of 1,000 men. Napoleon had not yet heard of the disaster at Baylen on July 23.]

# 167

# BAYLEN AND SPANDAU

## TO MARSHAL SOULT, SECOND IN COMMAND OF THE GRAND ARMY, AT STETTIN

SAINT-CLOUD, *AUGUST* 23, 1808.

Dupont has utterly disgraced himself and my arms. He conducted his operations at the end of July like a fool and a coward, and completely lost his head. He has upset all my plans in Spain. But the harm done is nothing to the dishonour. The details of the affair, which I prefer to keep to myself, would make your blood boil. One of these days they shall be published, and the honour of our arms shall be avenged.

I believe the agreement for the evacuation of Prussia will be signed tomorrow, or the day after. The evacuation itself will be carried out towards the end of October. I think it would be as well if you were to blow up Spandau; but you must do it secretly, and do it soon, so that there may be no excuse for claiming compensation. You will want some miners; and you must get the whole job done in five days, before Berlin gets wind of it. You can say, if you like, that a magazine blew up, or that the explosion was due to powder stored in the cellars. I am keeping the forts at Glogau, Stettin, and Cüstrin until the indemnities are paid, and the situation clears up.

[LECESTRE, i, 341. The capitulation of General Dupont's army to the Spaniards at Baylen on July 23 – Napoleon heard of it on August 2 – was a serious blow to French prestige. By an agreement signed on September 8 Prussia paid a heavy indemnity, reduced her forces, and promised help against Austria, in return for a partial withdrawal of the French army of occupation.]

# 168

# ERFURT

## TO THE EMPRESS JOSÉPHINE

ERFURT, *October* 9, 1808.

Thank you for your letter, my dear. I am glad to see you are well. I have just been hunting on the battlefield of Jena. We lunched on the spot where I slept out, the night before the battle. I have been to a ball at Weimar. The Emperor Alexander dances, but I don't. Forty *is* forty. My health is really excellent, in spite of a few small ailments. Good-bye, my dear. All my love. Hoping to see you soon.

[CORRESP., xvii, 14366. Napoleon entered Erfurt, for a conference with the Tsar, on September 27. On October 6 he went to Weimar for a *battue* and a ball.]

# TEMPLE OF JANUS

## TO PRINCE CAMBACÉRÉS,
### ARCH-CHANCELLOR OF THE EMPIRE

ARANDA, *NOVEMBER* 26, 1808.

. . . I have put up a monument at the Madeleine in honour of the Grand Army. The Legislature ought to erect on the heights of Montmartre a sort of Temple of Janus, with an inscription to the effect that 'This temple was erected by the Departmental Deputies of the Legislature, and by the members of the Electoral Colleges of the French Empire, etc.' The temple should be used for the first solemn declarations of peace, and for the distribution of decennial prizes. It would be a kind of Temple of Janus. It can hardly cost less than 30 or 40 millions. The Legislature must petition me to ask for a law by which each member of the Electoral Colleges (there are 30 or 40,000 of them) is invited to subscribe 1,000 or 3,000 francs, according to his means, to be paid in 5 annual instalments. By this means 30 or 40 millions will be available in the course of 5 years; the money will be employed to hurry on the work; and we shall make this Temple one of the finest buildings in the whole world. It will not inconvenience the Electors, for they are rich men: and anyhow they can spread their payments over 5 years, and give only 1,000 francs instead of 3,000, if they cannot afford more. I will pass on the petition to the State Council, and they will draft a law. The subscription-list will be opened at once, and work will begin next year.

[CORRESP., xviii, 14510.]

# 170

# STEIN

## TO M. DE CHAMPAGNY, MINISTER FOR FOREIGN AFFAIRS

MADRID, *DECEMBER* 16, 1808.

Forward the annexed order to all my ministers attached to the Princes of the Confederation of the Rhine, and inform them that Stein is still intriguing with the English in his fantastic plots against the Confederation. Request the Prince of Nassau to sequestrate his property. Inform the Prussian Court that my ministers will not visit Berlin unless Stein is banished from that capital, and from Prussia. But that is not enough. You are to write to the Prussian minister, demanding that the fellow be handed over as a traitor, and as an agent employed by the English to embroil the two courts. Speak strongly in this sense to the Prussian minister in Paris. Instruct my consul at Königsberg to speak to the King about it. Give them to understand that, if Stein falls into French hands, he will be shot.

[LECESTRE, i, 385. The news of Baylen (v. No. 167) encouraged the Prussian patriots. A compromising letter by their leader, Stein (August 15) reached Napoleon. Nassau was Stein's native place.]

# 171

# WATER-WORKS

## TO M. CRETET, MINISTER FOR HOME AFFAIRS

MADRID, *December* 21, 1808.

I see from the papers that you have laid the foundation-stone of the fountain on the site of the Bastille. I assume that the elephant will stand in the centre of a huge basin filled with water; that it will be a handsome beast, and big enough for people to be able to get inside the *howdah* on its back. I want to show how the ancients fixed these *howdahs*, and what elephants were used for. Send me the design for this fountain. Have plans drawn for another fountain representing a handsome galley with 3 banks of oars, e.g., that of Demetrius, of the same dimensions as a classical trireme. It could be put up in the middle of a public square, or some such place, with jets of water playing all round it, to add to the beauty of the capital. You understand that in constructing these two fountains the architects must not be content with their own researches; they must conform to the views of learned men and antiquarians, so that the elephant and the galley may give exact reproductions of the way in which they were used by the ancients.

My intention is to make use of the water from the Ourcq to embellish the Tuileries garden with streams and cascades, and the Champs-Elysées and its surroundings with big sheets of water, as large as the Tuileries garden, on which we can have boats of every variety.

[CORRESP., xviii, 14599.]

## 172

## THE RISING GENERATION

### TO COUNT FOUCHÉ, MINISTER OF POLICE

BENAVENTE, *December* 31, 1808.

I am informed that some of the *émgré* families are refusing to let their children enlist, and are keeping them in undesirable and culpable idleness. There is no denying that the rich old families which do not owe their origin to my regime are definitely opposed to it. I want you to draw up a list of ten of the leading families in each Department, and fifty in Paris, showing the age, income, and profession of each of their members. I intend to issue a decree by which all the young people belonging to these families between the ages of 16 and 18 shall be sent to the Military School at Saint-Cyr. If any one objects, there is no answer to make, except that I wish it so. That generation must not be allowed to suffer for the petty hatreds and passions of this. . . .

[LECESTRE, i, 386. 'I wish it so.' Napoleon uses the old royal phrase, *mon bon plaisir.*]

## 173

## CANDLEMAS

### TO COUNT DE CHAMPAGNY, MINISTER FOR FOREIGN AFFAIRS

BENAVENTE, *January* 1, 1809.

It is the Pope's custom to present candles to the various powers. You are to write to my agent at Rome, saying that I refuse to have any. The King of Spain doesn't want them any more than I do. Write to Naples and Holland saying that they are to refuse them too. It would be improper to accept them, because the Pope had the insolence not to give any last year. This is how I want the affair conducted. My *chargé d'affaires* will make it known that on Candlemas day I am accepting candles blessed by my *curé*, and that the value of such things does not depend upon purple and power. There are probably Popes in Hell, as well as parsons, so that a candle blessed by my *curé* is just as likely to be holy as one blessed by the Pope. I refuse to accept the Pope's presentation candles, and all the princes in my family are to do the same as I do.

[CORRESP., xviii, 14633.]

# 174

# THEN AND NOW

## TO COUNT FOUCHÉ, MINISTER OF POLICE

VALLADOLID, *JANUARY* 13, 1809.

Now that we are in 1809, I think it would be useful to have some articles written, in good style, contrasting the misfortunes from which France was suffering in 1709 with the prosperous state of the Empire in 1809. The comparison should be worked out under several heads – territory and population, internal welfare, international prestige, finance, etc. You have got men competent to write 5 or 6 good articles on this very important subject, and to give public opinion a lead in the right direction. Louis XIV spent his time building Versailles, and a number of hunting-lodges. We spend our time improving Paris, from its water-supply to its palaces, from its markets to the Temple of Victory, and the Stock Exchange. Everything wanted doing, and everything is being done.

Starting from that point, one could go on to speak of the perfection and simplicity that we have given to our institutions, and the tranquil flow of ideas that characterises 1809. In 1709 the edict of Nantes had been revoked, and the Protestants were being persecuted; Marshal Villars was wasting his generalship on civil war in the Cèvennes, and Père Lachaise tyrannised over the conscience of the old King. In 1809 the altars have been set up again, and we tolerate differences in religion. Under the head of morals, it could be pointed out that bishops no longer frequent houses of ill repute, or the ante-chambers of the rich, but stay at home in their dioceses. There is material for some splendid articles here. But we don't want to undertake a long work that would never be finished. We might have an article once a month, and all of them under the same title, '1709 and 1809.'

[CORRESP., xviii, 14695. The Edict of Nantes was revoked by Louis XIV in 1685. In 1703, Marshal Villars was recalled from a successful campaign in Germany to put down a rising of the Camisards in the Cevennes. The Jesuit Père La Chaise was Louis XIV's confessor from 1674 to 1709.]

# 175

# MOORE'S RETREAT

## TO REAR-ADMIRAL COUNT DECRÈS, MINISTER OF MARINE

PARIS, *JANUARY* 29, 1809.

It is my intention that you shall give orders for the firing of a salvo of 30 guns on all coasts where there are British cruisers, and particularly in the neighbourhood of Boulogne, to celebrate our victory over the English, and their expulsion from Spain. You are also to order flags to be flown in the manner sailors usually employ on such occasions. Repeat these orders on the Mediterranean coast, and to all my fleets. Make a short announcement to the effect that an army of 36 – 40,000 English, under the command of Generals Moore and Baird, reinforced by a Spanish army, has been pursued with the sword in its back for 50 leagues; that we have killed 2,000 of their men, and captured 7,000, with their field-hospitals and baggage-train; that they houghed more than 6,000 of their own horses; and that they were forced to desert the Spaniards under La Romana, who have perished to a man.

[CORRESP., xviii, 14757. Sir John Moore, after an advance towards Madrid, had to retreat with 20,000 men to Corunna. Napoleon started in pursuit with 25,000 men, on December 22. On January 1, as the result of letters from Paris, he handed over the command to Soult and Ney, and soon after left for France. On January 17 the British forces embarked at Corunna with a loss of 6,000 men. La Romana's forces were only dispersed: within 2 months the Spaniards had 100,000 men in the field.]

# 176

## PEW RENTS

### TO COUNT MARET, MINISTER SECRETARY OF STATE

PARIS, *FEBRUARY* 17, 1809.

M. Maret is to refer the enclosed Charge to a Committee consisting of State-Minister Regnaud and State-Counsellors Treilhard and Portalis, with instructions to let me have a report on it at tomorrow's meeting of the State Council.

(1) Have the bishops any right to publish Charges without rhyme or reason, whenever they like, and to criticise the Government policy, apropos of some question about eating eggs in Lent?

(2) Have they any right to levy taxes in this country, and to abuse the credulity and confidence of the common people by selling them dispensations from fasting, cash down?

(3) Have they any right to take advantage of conscientious scruples they themselves evoke, in order to make a profit out of dispensations, and even to take money out of the Empire, and send it to Rome?

(4) Have they any right to sell sittings to the highest bidder, so that poor people cannot go to Church? Ought chairs to be charged for and places priced like seats at a theatre?

The Committee will draft a decree to remedy these abuses, and will present it to me tomorrow at the State Council. My intention is that taxes shall not be raised by any authority but that of the law; a tax levied on conscience is as real as a tax levied on land. My intention is that there shall be no charge for entrance into a church-all my subjects have a right to be there; that dispensations from fasting shall be obtainable free of charge; that marriage licences shall cost nothing; that, in order to make these measures effective, all payments under the head of alms shall be properly audited, either by the Church-wardens or by the Prefect; and finally, that no Charges shall be given except upon the initiative of the Minister of Public Worship, and none published unless previously approved by him. Anyone opposing these measures will be liable to punishment.

[CORRESP., xviii, 14785.]

# 177

# INTERCESSION

### TO M. BIGOT DE PRÉAMENEU,
### MINISTER OF PUBLIC WORSHIP

PARIS, *MARCH* 3, 1809.

Inform me why the Archbishop of Aix has ordered nine days' intercession for the illness of Queen Louise, and why the general public should be told to pray for anyone without the permission of the Government.

[LECESTRE, i, 417. Queen Louise is the ex-Queen of Spain, at this time living in Provence.]

# 178

# PAPAL HISTORY

### TO EUGÈNE NAPOLÉON, VICEROY OF ITALY

PARIS, *MARCH* 3, 1809.

Cesarotti has left a history of the Papacy. See what this work is like, and if its purpose is to make known the harm the Popes have done to religion and to Christianity, have it printed at once.

[CORRESP., xviii, 14842. Melchiore Cesarotti, translator of Ossian, and admirer of Napoleon, died November 3, 1808. His works include *I primi Pontifice* in 6 vols.]

# 179

# SARAGOSSA

### TO JOSEPH

RAMBOUILLET, *MARCH* 11, 1809.

I have been reading an article in the *Madrid Gazette* describing the capture of Saragossa. The writer praises the defenders of the town – no doubt in order to encourage those of Valencia and Seville. A singular policy indeed! I'll wager there's not a Frenchman who doesn't utterly despise the defenders of Saragossa. People who allow themselves to say such things are more dangerous to us than the rebels themselves. I'm quite sure O'Farill didn't mean any harm by it; but it is the second time that this has happened. In an earlier proclamation he referred to Saguntum – a most unsuitable comparison.

[JOSEPH, vi, 73. Saragossa, garrisoned by Palafox and remnants of the Spanish army defeated in 1808, held out against 45,000 French till February 21; 50,000 of its inhabitants fell in its defence. Saguntum, near Valencia, was besieged by Hannibal in 219 B.C., and made a heroic resistance for eight months. General Gonzalo O'Farill had been Spanish Minister in Prussia (1804) and Commander of a Spanish force in Italy (1805 – 7).]

# 180

# GAMBLING SALOONS

## TO ÉLISA, GRAND DUCHESS OF TUSCANY

PARIS, *April* 6, 1809.

My sister; take care that no one starts any kind of gambling-saloon at Florence. I don't allow them at Turin, or anywhere in the Empire. They set a bad example, and ruin family life. The only place where I tolerate them is Paris; partly because in this huge city it would be impossible to suppress them; and partly because they are made use of by the police. But my intention is that they shall not exist in any other part of my Empire.

[CORRESP., xviii, 15024. Tuscany, under the title of the Kingdom of Etruria, was given to Napoleon's sister, Elisa, early in 1809.]

# 181

# TEMPORAL POWER

## TO COUNT DE CHAMPAGNY,
## MINISTER FOR FOREIGN AFFAIRS

SCHÖNBRUNN, *May* 17, 1809.

The Emperor intends to communicate the enclosed decrees made by His Majesty, on the subject of the Papal States, to the Senate between June 5 and 10, accompanied by a report from the Minister for Foreign Affairs.

His Majesty wishes this report to develop the motives laid down in the preamble; to prove that, when Charlemagne made the Popes temporal sovereigns, he meant them to remain vassals of the Empire; that nowadays, far from regarding themselves as vassals of the Empire, they refuse to belong to it at all; that the motive of Charlemagne's generosity to the Popes was the good of Christianity, and that now they are becoming allies of the Protestants, and of the enemies of Christ; and that one of the minor disadvantages resulting from this disposition is the sight of the head of the Catholic religion negotiating with Protestants, whereas according to the laws of the church, he ought to avoid them and excommunicate them (there is a prayer to that effect in use at Rome).

The French armies at Naples and in north Italy are cut off from each other by the Papal States. His Majesty's first idea was to leave the Pope his temporal power, as Charlemagne did; whilst requiring him, as a sovereign, and in the interests of the whole peninsula, to contract an offensive and defensive alliance with the Kingdoms of Naples and Italy. The Pope refused. This meant that His Majesty would have to stand by whilst the English placed themselves between the armies of Naples and Italy, cut their communications, and made Rome the headquarters of their conspiracies, and an asylum for the brigands whom His Majesty's enemies organise (if they do not actually disgorge them) on Neapolitan territory. Under these circumstances the only possible course was to occupy Rome with troops.

This measure, though indispensable, excited endless protests and lasting enmity on the part of the Head of religion against the most powerful prince in Christendom. But it was not as the Head of religion that the Pope set himself up against measures of precaution on the part of a Catholic nation; it was as a temporal sovereign; and before long it was seen that, influenced by enemies of the Roman church, the spiritual power was supporting the temporal power. This became a source of anxiety and dissension in the very heart of His Majesty's vast domains.

There is only one way in which His Majesty can put an end to debates so contrary to the welfare of religion and of the Empire; and that is to revoke the Donation of Charlemagne, and to reduce the Popes to their proper rank, by safeguarding the spiritual power from the passions that control the temporal power. Jesus Christ, though born of the seed of David, refused to be a king. For centuries none of the founders of our religion were kings. There is no learned doctor and no candid historian who does not agree that the temporal power of the Popes is fatal to religion. If for so many years the internal history of France was marked by religious dissension, the cause lay, not in the spiritual, but in the temporal claims of the Papacy. If great nations broke away from the church, the cause still lay in Rome's abuse of her power. When Julius sent his armies to cut off Charles VIII's retreat, he did so in the interests of the Pope, not as pontiff but as prince. It was this confusion of the two powers, this support that each gave the other to forward their common usurpations, which forced our ancestors to establish the liberties of the Gallican church, and which obliges us to separate the two powers.

The method commonly employed in the last century to bring the Popes to reason was to occupy Avignon. At Rome the interests of the Church – interests which ought to be beyond change, or any worldly consideration – were constantly sacrificed for the sake of temporal gains. The influence of the Pope, as Head of Christendom, ought to be equal in all parts of the Christian world; though it ought to vary according to circumstances, and the policies of the various states. Spiritual affairs should never be hampered by personal interest. But how can it be otherwise, when the interests of the Pope as sovereign and the Pope as pontiff disagree? Jesus Christ said 'My Kingdom is not of this world'; and by that doctrine he condemned for ever any intermingling of religious interests and worldly affairs.

It is as much for the welfare of religion as it is for that of the French, German, and Italian peoples, that His Majesty should put an end to this farce of the Temporal Power, this feeble relic of the pretensions of people such as Gregory, etc., who claimed to rule over kings, to confer crowns, and to direct affairs on earth as well as affairs in heaven. It is all very well for the Popes, in the absence of Councils, to manage matters ecclesiastical, so long as they don't interfere with the liberties of the Gallican church – but they should have nothing to do with armies, or with the policing of states. If they are the successors of Jesus Christ, they cannot exercise any rule but that which they hold from. him; and his Kingdom was not of this world.

Unless His Majesty takes this step – and no one else is strong enough to do so – Europe will be left to harvest a whole

crop of discords and debate. Posterity will praise him for restoring Catholic worship and the Catholic altars; but it would
equally blame him, were he to abandon Europe – that is, the
great bulk of Christendom – to the influence of this fantastic
confusion of powers, fatal both to religion and to the peace of
the Empire. It is an obstacle which can be overcome only by
separating the temporal and spiritual authorities, and by declaring the incorporation of the Papal States in the French Empire.

[CORRESP., xix, 15218. Two months later Pius VII was arrested by General Radet, taken from Rome to Grenoble, and subsequently interned at
Savona, *v.* No. 216.]

# 182

## FREEDOM OF THE SEAS

### TO GENERAL ARMSTRONG,
### MINISTER OF THE UNITED STATES OF AMERICA

SCHÖNBRUNN, *MAY* 18, 1809.

M. de Champagny, the Minister for Foreign Affairs, has
submitted to H.M. the Emperor and King various letters from
His Excellency the Minister of the United States of America.
He has been instructed to make the following answer.

The seas belong to all nations. Every vessel, so long as it
sails under some national flag, and is recognised and
acknowledged by that nation, ought to be as free on the high
seas as in its own home ports. The flag flown at the mast – head
of a merchantman should be as fully respected as the flag that
flies on a village church-tower.

In the event of war between two maritime powers, neutrals
ought not to submit to laws passed by either side. It should be
understood that every ship is protected by its flag, and that any
power violating it thereby declares war on the power to which
it belongs. To insult a merchant vessel carrying the flag of
another power is equivalent to invading a village or colony
belonging to that power. His Majesty hereby declares that he
regards the ships of all nations as floating colonies, and as part
of their national territory. It follows from this principle that the
sovereignty and independence of any nation can claim protection from neighbouring powers. If a French citizen were to be

insulted in an American port or colony, the government of the United States would not disclaim responsibility. Similarly the government of the United States ought to be held responsible for any violation of French property on board an American vessel, or floating colony. Otherwise, this government proving itself unable to guarantee the integrity of its rights, and the liberty of its flag, His Majesty is bound to consider American vessels as denationalised, and no longer belonging to the United States, and therefore as liable to examination, the imposition of dues, and other arbitrary acts, without any violation of national rights.

Nevertheless, as soon as the government of the United States gives orders that its merchant vessels are to be armed, so as to resist England's unfair attacks, and to uphold American law and sovereignty against England's refusal to recognise the great principle that the goods are covered by the flag, and against her unjustifiable claim to impose her law upon neutral shipping, His Majesty will be ready to recognise and treat the United States as a neutral power.

[CORRESP., xix, 15227. During the winter of 1807 – 8 the British Government issued a number of Orders in Council designed to pass neutral shipping through British ports, and to use it for exporting British goods to the Continent; whilst it reimposed the right of searching neutral vessels. On December 23, 1807, the United States passed an Embargo Act, with the professed intention of upholding 'freedom of the seas.' But in February, 1809, this had to be rescinded. General John Armstrong was American ambassador to France, 1804 – 10.]

# 183

# TRAVELLING LIBRARY

## TO M. BARBIER

SCHÖNBRUNN, *JUNE* 12, 1809.

The Emperor feels every day the need of having a travelling library of historical works. His Majesty would like to make up the number of volumes in this library to 3,000, and they should all be of 18° size, like those of the Dauphin's 18° collection, with 4 – 500 pages to the volume, and printed in good Didot type on thin vellum paper. The 12° size takes up too much room; besides, nearly all the books printed in that size are in poor editions. The 3,000 volumes would be packed in 30 cases, containing 3 rows of 33 volumes each. The collection would have a general title, and a consecutive system of numbering, independent of the titles of the separate works. It could be divided into 5 or 6 groups: –

(1) Chronology and universal history.

(2) Ancient history: (a) original authorities, and (b) modern works.

(3) History of the Medieval Empire: (a) original authorities, and (b) modern works.

(4) History in general, and in particular – e.g. Voltaire's *Essai*.

(5) Modern history of the European States: – France, Italy, etc.

The collection should include Strabo, Danville's maps of the ancient world, the Bible, and some history of the Church.

This is only an outline of 5 or 6 groups, which would have to be examined, and carefully filled up.

A certain number of literary men, people of taste, would be commissioned to review these editions, correct them, and suppress everything useless in them, such as editorial notes, etc., and all quotations in Greek or Latin, keeping only the French translation; but a few Italian works, of which no translation exists, could be left in the original language.

The Emperor begs M. Barbier to draw up a plan for this library, and to let him know what is the best and cheapest way of producing these 3,000 volumes.

When the 3,000 volumes of history are ready, they could be followed by 3,000 more on Natural History, Travels, Literature, etc. It would be easy enough to collect most of them, for plenty of these works are published in 18° size.

M. Barbier is also requested to send a list of these works, with clear and detailed notes on the whole proposal, and as to the literary men who might be set to do the work, together with some idea as to the time, expense, etc., involved.

[FAIN, *Memoirs*, 71. cf. No. 165.]

## 184

## WAGRAM

### TO THE EMPRESS JOSÉPHINE

EBERSDORF, *JULY* 7, 1809, 5 A.M.

I am sending you a line with the good news of the victories of Enzersdorf, which I won on the 5th, and of Wagram, which I won on the 6th.

The enemy is flying in disorder, and everything is proceeding according to plan.

Eugène is well.

Prince Aldobrandini has been wounded, but only slightly. Bessières was hit by a bullet in the fleshy part of the thigh: the wound is a trifling one. La Salle has been killed. My losses are high; but the victory is decisive and complete.

We have taken more than 100 guns, 12 flags, and a number of prisoners.

I am sun-burnt.

Good-bye, my dear. I send you my love. Many kind regards to Hortense.

[CORRESP., xix, 15491.]

## 185

## ENCYCLICAL

### TO THE FRENCH BISHOPS

IMPERIAL CAMP AT ZNAYM, *JULY* 13, 1809.

The victories of Enzersdorf and Wagram, in which the God of Hosts so evidently protected the French arms, ought to excite the liveliest gratitude in the hearts of Our people. It is therefore Our intention that upon the receipt of these present you should co-operate with the proper authorities to assemble Our people in the churches, and to address heaven with acts of thanksgiving, and prayers agreeable to the sentiments which We feel.

Our Lord Jesus Christ, though born of the seed of David, wished for no temporal rule; on the contrary, he enjoined obedience to Caesar in the regulation of worldly affairs. He was inspired with one great aim, and one only – the redemption and salvation of souls. As We inherit Caesar's power, so We are resolved to maintain the independence of Our throne, and the integrity of Our rights. We shall persevere in the great work of re-establishing religion. We shall surround the ministers of religion with the favour which We alone can give them. We shall listen to their voice in everything bearing on the spiritual life, and the regulation of the conscience.

Amidst the cares of the camp, amidst the alarms and anxieties of war, it has given Us special pleasure to acquaint you with these Our feelings, in order that We may bring into discredit those works of weakness and ignorance, of mischief or of madness, by which attempts are being made to sow trouble and disorder in Our provinces. We shall not be turned aside from the great goal towards which We are travelling, and which We have already in part happily attained – the re-establishment of the altars of Our religion – by the attempt to make Us believe that its principles are incompatible with the independence of thrones or of nations, as has been asserted by the Greeks, the English, the Protestants, and the Calvinists. God has enlightened Us sufficiently to avoid such errors: such fears find no place in Our heart, or in the hearts of Our subjects. We know that those who would make the eternal interests of the conscience and spiritual affairs depend upon a temporal and perishable order are alien alike to the charity, mind, and religion of him who said, 'My kingdom is not of this world.'

[CORRESP., xix, 15518.]

# 186
# AT THE FRONT
## TO JÉRÔME NAPOLÉON, KING OF WESTPHALIA

SCHÖNBRUNN, *July* 17, 1809.

I have seen an Army Order of yours which makes you the laughing-stock of Germany, Austria, and France. Have you no friend at your side to tell you a few home truths? You are a king, and the Emperor's brother; but those are no qualifications for war. In war one must begin as a soldier, continue as a soldier, and end as a soldier. No ministers, no foreign attachés, no ceremonial. War means bivouacing at the head of the army, spending days and nights on horseback, and marching with the advance guard, to get the news-otherwise one had better stay behind in the women's quarters.

You go to war like a Persian Satrap. Good God! did I teach you such methods? – I, who, with an army of 200,000 men, march at the head of my skirmishers, and do not even let Champagny come with me, but leave him behind at Munich or Vienna?

What has been the result? Everyone complains of you. Kienmayer, with his 20,000 men, despises you, and your absurd pretensions: he has concealed his movements from you, and fallen upon Junot. This would never have happened if you had been with your advance guard, and had given your orders from that position. Then you would have known what he was doing, and could have pursued him, either along his line of retreat, or by way of Bohemia. You have plenty of ambition, some intelligence, and a few good qualities; but they are spoilt by silliness, and gross conceit; and you have no knowledge of the world. Meanwhile, unless an armistice has been declared, Kienmayer will have put Junot out of action, and turned upon you.

Stop making a fool of yourself. Send the foreign attachés back to Cassel. Do without your procession of luggage – carts: cut down your dinners to one table. Go to War like any young soldier who wants to win honour and glory. Try to deserve the rank you have reached, and the esteem of France and Europe, who are watching everything you do. And, for Heaven's sake, have the sense to write and speak as becomes your rank!

[LECESTRE, i, 479. Baron von Kienmayer, commanding the Austrian troops in Saxony, defeated Junot near Gefrees on July 8: Jerome escaped defeat by abandoning Dresden and retiring to Cassel.]


# 187

# FLUSHING AND TALAVERA

## TO COUNT FOUCHÉ, MINISTER OF POLICE

SCHÖNBRUNN, *August* 22, 1809.

I have received your letter of the 16th. You say that you are afraid Flushing may be bombarded into surrender. You needn't be alarmed. Flushing is impregnable, so long as its food holds out; and it has enough for 6 months. It is impregnable, because to reach it one must cross a moat filled with water; whilst as a last resort the dykes can be cut, and the whole island inundated. If Flushing falls within 6 months, every general, colonel, and officer defending the place ought to be arrested and put on trial. I don't believe that Rammekens will be taken either. I don't know the fort; but as the dykes can be cut in case of need, it ought not to fall. Tell everyone you write to, and everyone you meet, that Flushing can't be taken, short of cowardice on the part of its officers. Besides, I am confident that it won't be, and that the English will withdraw without capturing it. I haven't the slightest fear on that score. Bombs are no use, absolutely none. They will demolish a few houses, but that has never caused a town to surrender.

Whilst the English are wasting their time on the Scheldt, in Spain Lord Wellesley has been beaten, surrounded, and utterly routed. He is trying to save himself by headlong flight in the middle of the hot season. When he retired from Talavera, he surrendered to the care of the Duke of Belluno 5,000 sick and wounded English, whom he was forced to leave behind him. At last English blood is being shed! It is the best omen that peace is at length approaching. Undoubtedly if matters had been better managed in Spain, not a single Englishman would have escaped. But anyhow they have been beaten – 6,000 killed, 8,000 taken prisoners. Make these ideas the subject of articles in the papers; point out the folly of ministers who expose 30,000 English, in the heart of Spain, to the attacks of 120,000 French – the finest troops in the world, whilst at the same time they send 20,000 more to run their heads against a stone wall in the Dutch marshes, where their efforts have no effect but to excite the zeal of the national guards. Make people see the stupidity of this policy of scattering their forces. To pack in small parcels has always been the hall-mark of a fool.

[LECESTRE, i, 513. Flushing had already fallen (August 15). But otherwise the Walcheren expedition was a failure, and the survivors of the 40,000 men landed in July, 1809, were withdrawn. At Talavera 17,000 British troops, with little help from 35,000 Spaniards, forced 30,000 French to retire with a loss of 7,000 men. The British losses were 5,000.]

## 188

# TALAVERA: SECOND THOUGHTS

## TO GENERAL CLARKE

SCHÖNBRUNN, *AUGUST* 25, 1809.

...You will see that, according to the despatches of Welles-ley, the English General, we lost 20 guns and 3 flags at Talav-era. Inform the King of my surprise, and General Jourdan of my displeasure, that, instead of being told the real state of affairs, I am sent republican romances, the kind of history they write for schoolboys. Tell them I want to know what gunners abandoned their pieces, and which infantry divisions let the enemy capture their flags. Allow the King to infer from your letter that I was sorry to see the Order of the Day, in which he told the men that they had won the battle: it's fatal to the troops. And tell him that I must have true information, with the number of men killed and wounded in each corps, the number of guns and flags lost, etc. They start engagements in Spain without preparation, or knowledge of war; and on the day of battle they carry on with-out plan, or combination, or energy. Write to General Sebas-tiani, saying that the King has sent me his report; that it is not the kind of report any soldier should make, when giving an account of what has happened, and of the present situation; that it seems to me a highly coloured version; that I should have liked him to say what he really thinks, and to give a true and detailed description of the affair; in a word, I ought to be told the truth, – it is essential for the efficiency of the army. Make them realise, one and all, how much it discredits the Govern-ment to conceal information which can be picked up from every soldier who writes home from the front, and who is tempted by such concealment to believe all the enemy's false reports.

[JOSEPH, vi, 375.]

## 189

# PAPER MONEY WAR

## TO COUNT FOUCHÉ, MINISTER OF POLICE

SCHÖNBRUNN, *SEPTEMBER* 6, 1809.

Maret is sending you specimens of all the different kinds

of bank-note current here. I enclose a decree dealing with this matter. I want you to organise the printing of these bank-notes in all denominations up to a total sum of 100 millions. You will require a press capable of turning out 10 millions a month. It is by means of paper money that the House of Austria has financed the war against me, and it might do so again. That being so, it must be my policy in peace-time as well as in time of war to depreciate this paper issue, and to force Austria back onto a metal currency. That will inevitably compel her to reduce her army, and to cut down the mad expenditure by which she has compromised the safety of my states. I want this operation carried out secretly, and with an air of mystery; though my object is much more a political one than anything that might be gained by financial speculation. It is in fact an object of the first importance. There is no hope of peace in Europe so long as Austria can obtain loans of 3 or 400 millions on the security of her paper money.

Send me an intelligent and tactful agent, who can collect on the spot, while I am still here, all the information necessary to try this experiment on the big scale which I intend, and which will make it so effective.

[LECESTRE, i, 520.]

# 190

# MONKS

## TO COUNT GAUDIN, MINISTER OF FINANCE

SCHÖNBRUNN, *September* 26, 1809.

I have received your report of the 12th about the way to deal with the monks in the states of Rome. This is my idea, for Rome as well as for Piedmont, Parma, and Tuscany – to suppress all monks indiscriminately, and to order that, as from the day of publication of the forthcoming decree, they shall be obliged to quit their habits and their houses – begging friars, public teachers, all of them, to whatever class they belong, so that not a single monk remains either in Italy or in France. Their houses and goods must be sold, leaving only the monks of Mont Cenis, Mont Genèvre, and Mont Saint-Bernard, and those on the Appennines, in the Carthusian monastery at Florence, and in a few other privileged places.

Draft a decree on these lines for Tuscany, Parma, and Piedmont, so that I may deal with the question here at the same time as the other work that I am going to take in hand in Paris. And there's an end of the whole question. I never want to see a monk's habit or a monastery again. Halfhearted measures only strengthen their position. Unless we destroy these ridiculous institutions at one blow, we shall see them springing up again. I would not send the monks home, but attach them to parish priests, chapters, and collegiate establishments, so that they may have work to do in the church.

But these comprehensive changes must be part of my forthcoming work at Paris, when peace has been made, and when I have strong garrisons in Florence, Parma, and Rome. Until then, nothing can be done; except that the Consulta can use police orders to send back foreign monks to France, Germany, Spain, and Naples, and so get rid of them from Rome; but this must be done by special action in each case, not under a general rule. I don't think there is anything else to do, except to take every precaution for the proper supervision of the monks, and to wait for the conclusion of peace.

[CORRESP., xix, 15863.]

# 191

# SOULT IN DISGRACE

## TO MARSHAL SOULT, DUKE OF DALMATIA, COMMANDING THE ARMY IN PORTUGAL

SCHÖNBRUNN, *SEPTEMBER* 26, 1809.

I am displeased with your conduct. The cause of my displeasure is the following paragraph in the circular issued by your Chief of Staff: 'The Duke of Dalmatia would be asked to take the reins of government, to represent the sovereign, and to invest himself with all the attributes of supreme authority; the people promising with an oath to be faithful to him, and to support and defend him at the cost of their lives and fortunes against every opponent, even against the insurgents in other provinces, until the submission of the whole Kingdom. . . .' If you had claimed supreme power for yourself *proprio motu*, it

would have been such a crime as to oblige me to consider you
guilty of *lèse-majesté*, and of a culpable attack on my authority. How could you have forgotten that the power you exercised
over the Portuguese sprang from the command I entrusted to
you, and not from the play of passions and intrigue? How could
a man of your ability have supposed that I should ever allow
you to exercise any authority not derived from me? Your action
shows a forgetfulness of principles, and a failure to realise my
character, or the point of view of a proud nation, which I cannot reconcile with my opinion of you. It is due to false moves
of this kind that discontent has increased, and that you have
been supposed to be working, not for me, or for France, but for
yourself. You have undermined your own authority; for it
would be difficult to say, after this circular of yours, whether
any Frenchman could be blamed for ceasing to obey your
orders. . . .

In spite of all this, after hesitating for a long time as to what
course I should adopt, my affection for you, and the memory of
your services to me at Austerlitz, and on other occasions, have
decided my mind. I shall overlook what has happened; I hope it
will be a warning to you; and I entrust you with a major-gener-
alship in my Spanish army. As the King has no experience of
war, I wish you to be responsible for what happens until I
arrive. I want to enter Lisbon myself as soon as possible.

[CORRESP., xix, 15871. This refers to Soult's occupation of Oporto, where
he assumed 'quasi-regal state' and 'dreamed of becoming 'King of Northern
Lusitania.' ' (*Cambridge Modern History*, ix, 450.)]

## 192

# IMPERIAL TITLES

### NOTE, ON THE PROPOSED INSCRIPTIONS FOR THE
### ARC DE TRIOMPHE

SCHÖNBRUNN, *OCTOBER* 3, 1809.

The Institute proposes to give the Emperor the titles of
*Augustus* and *Germanicus*. Augustus only fought one battle –
Actium. Germanicus may have appealed to the Romans
through his misfortunes; but the only famous thing he did was
to write some very mediocre memoirs.

I can see nothing to envy in what we know about the

Roman Emperors. It ought to be one of the principal endeavours of the Institute, and of men of letters generally, to show what a difference there is between their history and ours. What a terrible memory for future generations was that of Tiberius, of Caligula, of Nero, of Domitian, and of all those princes who ruled by no laws of legitimacy, or rules of succession, and who, for what reasons it is needless to specify, committed so many crimes, and burdened Rome with such a weight of misfortunes!

The only man who distinguished himself by his character, and by many illustrious deeds – and he was not an Emperor – was Caesar. If the Emperor desired any title, it would be that of *Caesar*. But the name has been dishonoured (if that is possible) by so many petty, princes that it is no longer associated with the memory of the great Caesar, but with that of a mob of German princelings, as feeble as they were ignorant, not one of whom is familiar to the present generation.

The Emperor's title is *Emperor of the French*. He does not want any name carrying alien associations – neither *Augustus* nor *Germanicus*, nor *Caesar.*

The inscriptions ought to be written in French. The Romans sometimes used Greek for their inscriptions but that was only a relic of the Greek influence upon Roman arts and sciences. French is the most cultivated of all modern tongues: it is more widely spread, and more exactly known, than the dead languages. Nobody, then, wants any other language to be used for these inscriptions.

[CORRESP., xix, 15894. Germanicus Caesar, nephew of the Emperor Tiberius, helped him in his wars against the Germans (A.D. 11 – 12). His subsequent successes in Germany made him a popular hero, but roused Tiberius's jealousy: he was transferred to the East, and died there in A.D. 19, perhaps poisoned by order of Piso, the Governor of Syria.]

# 193

# MISSIONARIES

## TO CARDINAL FESCH, ARCHBISHOP OF LYON

SCHÖNBRUNN, *October* 8, 1809.

I have received your letter of September 30. I never balance the relative value of spiritual and temporal interests. If the Foreign Missions think it to their advantage to put themselves under English protection, I shall be glad to see them do so, for England is in a better position to protect their holy endeavours than I am. Let them put aside all thoughts of France, and fix their eyes on their heavenly fatherland.

As regards Home Missions, I have been told that they do harm. In any case, my parochial clergy are too fine a set of men for me to need these fanatics, about whose principles I know nothing. No cause is dearer to me than the interests of my people. For their sake I have resolved to prohibit these vagrant missions in my provinces; all the more so, since my states, widened, as they have been, by the succour of divine Providence, include churches that hold various views as to their relations with the spiritual authority, and because some of these missionaries have been educated at Rome in anti-Gallican principles, and derive their ideas of duty from the lessons on pride and the maxims of usurpation that are current in the Roman curia. My decision on this point is irrevocable: it remains for my clergy to conform to it. I don't share the fear you hint at because it is the duty of my clergy to obey me, and because, the first day they tried to stray from the path of duty, the Holy Spirit would cease to be with them.

[CORRESP., xix, 15918.]

# 194

# BAVARIAN TROOPS

## TO GENERAL DE WREDE, COMMANDER IN CHIEF OF THE BAVARIAN TROOPS

SCHÖNBRUNN, *OCTOBER* 8, 1809.

I am displeased with the Bavarian troops. Instead of fighting, they get up charges and plots against their commander. I have just brought General Stengel before a court of inquiry for evacuating Gölling. Why didn't he die there? No one has any right to evacuate a position without orders from the Commander-in-chief. The Bavarian troops have become demoralised. Show my letter to Deroy, and tell me whether the Bavarians want to win my good or my bad opinion. When troops are demoralised, it is for their Commanders and officers to restore their morale, or to die in the attempt. There have been instances of cowardice, such as allowing oneself to be taken prisoner in the passes, rather than secure the retreat, which for the honour of the Bavarian army ought to be denounced and punished.

At the front there is no such person as a prince. Possibly the Prince Royal has good cause to complain of the Duke of Dantzig; but that is not a question of military honour. His duty was to march on the enemy, who had insulted the Bavarian flag, and attacked him outside Saltzburg. I had thoughts of addressing an Order to your army; but it would have remained on record against you, and I prefer to write privately to you, for I have a regard for your ability and courage. Speak to your comrades, see that they are not disgraced. I will have no one objecting to me with 'if,' or 'but,' or 'because.' I have been a soldier all my life. You must either conquer or die. I could wish that, at the first sign of attack, the Prince had visited his outposts, and restored the morale of his division. Make such use of this letter as you think fit. I know that you are as fond of the Prince as I am.

[LECESTRE, i, 536. The reference is to the failure of the Franco-Bavarian troops to suppress Hofer's rebellion in the Tyrol in the summer and autumn of 1809. The Bavarians were under Wrede and Deroy.]

# 195

# ALL'S FAIR IN WAR

## TO GENERAL CLARKE, COUNT OF HUNEBOURG, MINISTER FOR WAR

SCHÖNBRUNN, *October* 10, 1809.

Please write to the King of Spain, and make him understand that nothing is more contrary to military usage than to publish the strength of one's army, either in Orders and Proclamations, or in the Gazette; that, supposing there were any reason for talking of one's forces, one ought to exaggerate them, and to make them appear redoubtable by doubling or trebling their number; whereas, in speaking of the enemy, one ought to represent his numbers as a half or a third of what they really are – for everything is moral in war; that the King abandoned this principle when he said that he only had 40,000 men, and published the fact that the enemy had 120,000; that it is merely discouraging the French troops to tell them that the enemy are in immense numbers, whilst it gives the enemy a poor opinion of the French if they are represented as being very few; (in a word) that by publishing his weakness all over Spain he is giving the enemy a moral advantage, and throwing away his own; for it is only human nature to believe that in the long run the smaller force will be beaten by the bigger.

The most experienced soldiers take care, on the day of battle, to estimate the number of men in the enemy army, and natural instinct generally leads them to over-estimate the number of those they can see. But if one is so unwise as to let such ideas get about, or to give currency to exaggerated estimates of the enemy's forces, the trouble of it is that every cavalry colonel who goes on a reconnaissance sees an army-corps, and every scout-captain half a dozen battalions. . . . I repeat it: in war, the morale and opinions of the army are more than half the battle. Great commanders always take care to give it out that their own troops are in overwhelming numbers, and to induce the enemy to believe it, whilst to their own army they represent the enemy as hopelessly inferior. It is the first time I have ever known a general understate the number of his own men and overstate that of the enemy.

[CORRESP., xix, 15933.]

# 196

# ATTEMPTED ASSASSINATION

## TO COUNT FOUCHÉ, MINISTER OF POLICE

SCHÖNBRUNN, *October* 12, 1809.

Today, during parade, a young man of 17, the son of a Lutheran minister at Erfurt, tried to approach me. He was arrested by the officers: suspicion was excited by his appearance of anxiety: he was searched, and was found to be in possession of a dagger. I had him brought before me, and the wretched young fellow, who seemed to be quite well educated, told me that he intended to assassinate me in order to rid Austria of the presence of the French. I found no traces of religious or political fanaticism in him. He didn't seem to understand that Brutus was a murderer. The fit of exaltation into which he had worked himself prevented my discovering any more. He will be questioned when he is cold and hungry, but possibly nothing will come of it. He will be tried by a military court.

I wanted to tell you of this incident, so that it may not be regarded as more serious than it appears to be. I hope it will not get about: if there were any question of that, it would be necessary to have the fellow certified as insane. Unless you hear it talked about, keep the matter strictly to yourself. The incident caused no scandal on parade; I never even noticed it myself.

P.S. – I repeat it again, and you must clearly understand: not a word is to be said about this affair.

[CORRESP., xix, 15935. Friedrich Staps was the son of a Naumburg pastor. He was tried by a military court, and shot on the 16th.]

## 197

# CHURCH POLICY

### CIRCULAR LETTER TO THE BISHOPS

FONTAINEBLEAU, *NOVEMBER* 6, 1809.

...We consider it necessary for the good of Our peoples and the political interests of Our Crown to govern directly that part of the Empire which Charlemagne, Our august predecessor, thought fit to entrust to the bishops of Rome as fiefs held for the promotion of the faith, and not of heresy.

We hold Our throne from God, and We are accountable to him alone for Our actions. Whatever We have done, We have done both for the glory and welfare of Our peoples and in the best interests of religion – religion, which owes its lasting power to the simplicity, charity, and truth of the faith, and not to institutions foreign to it, which Jesus Christ could have established, but refused to do so.

When, on the battlefield of Marengo, We resolved to erect the altars that Our fathers overthrew, We had no intention of recognising those monstrous claims, those claims contrary to all the principles of religion, which have given its enemies a handle for calumny, engendered so many evils, and caused the shedding of so much blood – those claims which were made by such men as Gregory VII and Julius II. Our intention was to re-establish the doctrine that the School of Paris, the Sorbonne, and the French clergy took as the basis of their teaching, notably in the Declarations of 1682. This is the doctrine that We received from our ancestors, that We intended to re-establish, and that We wish to maintain.

We shall look with pity upon those who, imbued with false teaching, fail to recognise Jesus Christ's command to 'render unto Cæsar the things that are Cæsar's,' and his refusal to let conscience and spiritual interests be determined by worldly considerations. What a man has done, a man can undo; what God has done is immutable.

[LECESTRE, i, 544. Napoleon struck out this passage in revision.]

# 198

# MISS PATERSON

## TO THE MINISTER FOR FOREIGN AFFAIRS

PARIS, *December* 9, 1809.

Write to General Thureau to the effect that I authorise him to allow Mlle Paterson all the funds she needs for her support, whilst reserving the right to settle her future out of hand. Tell him that I have no concern in the matter except my personal interest in this young lady; but that, if she were to misconduct herself so far as to marry an Englishman, my interest in her affairs would end, and I should consider that she had renounced the views which she expressed in her letter, and which were the sole origin of my interest in her.

[DUCASSE, 126. Cf. No. 89. The Pope had refused to dissolve her marriage with Jérôme. Napoleon thereupon did so by an Imperial edict.]

# 199

# DIVORCE

## TO THE EMPRESS JOSÉPHINE (AT LA MALMAISON)

TRIANON, *December* 19, 1809, 7 P.M.

I have received your letter, dear. Savary tells me that you are always crying. That is a pity. I hope you have been able to go for a walk today. I sent you some game from my hunt. I will come and see you when you tell me that you are being sensible, and that your courage is winning the day.

Tomorrow I am busy with the ministers all day.

Good-bye, my dear; I am unhappy today too. I want to hear that you are satisfied, and to know that you are recovering your balance. Sleep well.

[CORRESP., xx, 16068. Divorce had been thought of for some years. On November 30, 1809, Napoleon told Josephine the Deed of Separation must be signed on December 15. This was done, and on the 16th she left the Tuileries for the last time.]

# 200

## ANNEXATION OF HOLLAND

### TO LOUIS NAPOLÉON, KING OF HOLLAND

TRIANON, *December* 21, 1809.

I am in receipt of Your Majesty's letter. Your Majesty wishes me to make known my intentions as to Holland. I will do so frankly.

When Your Majesty ascended the throne of Holland, part of the Dutch people desired reunion with France. The respect for this brave nation which I had derived from my knowledge of its history led me to wish that it should retain its name and its independence. I therefore drew up with my own hand the constitution which was to be the basis of Your Majesty's throne, and I placed you upon it. I hoped that, as you had shared my education, so you would show that affection for France which the nation has a right to expect of all its sons, and particularly of its princes. I hoped that, schooled in my policy, you would realise that Holland, once conquered by my peoples, must rely, for its independence, upon their generosity; that with no resources, no allies, and no army, Holland could and inevitably would be conquered, the moment it set itself in direct opposition to France; that your policy must therefore be the same as mine, and that Holland was bound by treaty to France. I therefore hoped that, in placing upon the Dutch throne a prince of my own blood, I had found the happy mean which harmonised the interests of the two states, and united them in a common policy, and a common hatred of England; and I was proud of having given Holland the settlement that suited her case, as I had already done, by my Act of Mediation, in Switzerland.

But it was not long before I perceived that I was nursing a vain illusion. All my hopes have been deceived. The moment Your Majesty ascended the throne of Holland, you forgot that you were a Frenchman; ever since, you have tortured your sensitive conscience, and stretched your reason to breaking-point, in the endeavour to persuade yourself that you are a Dutchman. Those Dutchmen who were sympathetic to France have been persecuted and passed over; promotion has come to those who were in the service of England. Frenchmen, from officers to private soldiers, have been slighted and dismissed, and I have had the mortification of seeing the French name in Holland, under a prince of my own blood, exposed to every kind of affront. True, I have learnt to hold the honour and reputation of that name so near my heart, and to carry them so high on the bayonets of my soldiers, that it is beyond the power of Holland, or of any individual in the world, to cast a slur upon them, unavenged.

Your Majesty's public speeches are full of deplorable tendencies. France only appears there in parenthesis. Instead of setting an example of forgetting the past, they constantly recall it, thereby fostering the hidden animosities and passions of the enemies of France. After all, what have the Dutch to complain of? Were they not conquered by our arms? Do they not owe their independence to the chivalry of my peoples? Ought they not to bless the generosity of France, which has consistently opened its canals and its customs-houses to their commerce?- France, which has derived nothing from its conquest, save the duty of protecting the conquered – France, which, from that day to this, has made no use of its power but to consolidate Dutch independence? What justification, then, is there for Your Majesty's line of conduct, which is at once insulting to the French nation, and offensive to myself? Do not mistake me. I stand by my predecessors. I identify myself with all French history, from Clovis to the Committee of Public Safety. Any reflexion upon the governments that preceded me, however light-hearted, I take as a personal insult to myself. I am aware that it has become the fashion, in certain circles, to cry me up, and to cry France down. But he who loves not France cannot love me; and he who speaks evil of my peoples, I regard as my greatest enemy.

Had I no other cause of complaint than the disrepute into

which the French name has fallen in Holland, my royal right
would authorise me to declare war on a neighbouring sovereign
in whose state insults are permitted against my peoples. I have
taken no such step. But Your Majesty has a mistaken idea of my
character, based on false notions of my kindness, and of my
feelings towards you. You have broken all the treaties you made
with me. You have disarmed your fleets, dismissed your sailors,
and disorganised your armies; so that Holland finds herself
without armed forces on land or sea – as though merchants,
clerks, and stores of merchandise could make a great power! A
wealthy society – perhaps: but every king has money, and ships,
and the means of recruitment.

That, however, is not the whole count. Your Majesty took
advantage of my momentary embarrassment on the continent to
allow a resumption of relations between Holland and England,
and to violate the rules of the blockade, the only means by
which the latter power can be effectively damaged. I showed
my displeasure at this conduct by forbidding your presence in
France; and I made you realise that, without any recourse to
arms, I could put you in an even more critical position than if I
had declared war, by closing the Rhine, Weser, Scheldt, and
Meuse to Dutch trade, and thus destroying you by isolation.
This move caused a sensation in Holland: Your Majesty
appealed to my generosity and my feelings as a brother, and
promised to alter your behaviour. I thought the warning would
be sufficient, and removed the blockade. But soon Your
Majesty returned to your old policy: – I was at Vienna then, and
had a weight of war on my hands. Any American ship refused
at a French port, and presenting itself at a Dutch one, Your
Majesty allowed in. Once more I was obliged to close my customs against Dutch trade. One could hardly make a declaration
of hostilities in more authentic terms: to all intents and purposes we were at war.

In my speech to the Legislative Body I hinted at my dislike
of this situation; and I shall not conceal from you that it is my
intention to reunite Holland to France territorially: that is the
most dangerous blow I can aim at England, and it frees me from
the insults that the ringleaders of your Cabinet are constantly
heaping on me. The long and short of it is, that the estuary of
the Rhine and Meuse ought to belong to me. It is a fundamen-
tal principle in France that our natural frontier westwards is the valley route of the Rhine. Your Majesty writes to me in your letter of

the 17th that you are sure you can prevent any commerce between Holland and England: that you can provide funds, fleets, and armies; that you will reaffirm the principles of the constitution by refusing privileges to the nobility, and by getting rid of the marshals – a caricature of a rank, and quite incongruous in a second-class power; and finally, that you will confiscate the stores of colonial merchandise, and all goods that have come in American vessels, which ought never to have been admitted to your ports. My belief is that Your Majesty is making promises which you cannot fulfil, and that the reunion of Holland to France is only deferred. I admit that I have now nothing to gain by reuniting to France the districts on the right bank of the Rhine, any more than the Grand Duchy of Berg, or the Hanseatic towns. I can therefore leave Holland the right bank of the Rhine, and I am ready to cancel the customs embargo already ordered, whenever the treaties, in their present or in any revised form, are duly observed.

Here are my conditions:

(i) Prohibition of all commerce or communication with England.

(ii) Provision of a fleet of 14 ships of the line, 7 frigates, and 7 brigs or corvettes, all fully armed and equipped.

(iii) A land army of 25,000 men.

(iv) Suppression of the marshals.

(v) Abolition of all sham privileges of nobility, contrary to the constitution given and guaranteed by me.

Your Majesty may negotiate on this basis with the Duc de Cadore, through the agency of your minister. But I assure you that the first time a packet boat or vessel of any kind is admitted into a Dutch port, I shall re-establish the customs blockade, and that the first time any insult is offered to my flag, I shall arrest by force of arms the Dutch officer who allows himself to insult my eagle, and hang him at the masthead. Your Majesty will find in me a brother, if I find in you a Frenchman. But if you forget the feelings that attach us both to our fatherland, you must not take it ill of me if I also forget those by which nature has attached us to one another.

To sum up: the reunion of Holland to France is in the best interests alike of France, Holland, and the continent, for nothing will do England so much harm. This reunion may be brought about either by agreement or by force. I have enough grievances against Holland to justify a declaration of war.

Nevertheless I intend to put no difficulties in the way of an arrangement under which I shall get the Rhine frontier, and Holland will undertake to carry out the above stipulations.

[LECESTRE, i, 555. Louis was at this time in Paris: he returned to Holland in April, 1810 and for a time conformed to Napoleon's demands, but on July 1 abdicated and left the country. On July 9 it was annexed to France.]

## 201

# CONTINENTAL BLOCKADE

### TO M. DE CHAMPAGNY, DUKE OF CADORE, MINISTER FOR FOREIGN AFFAIRS

PARIS, *JANUARY* 10, 1810.

I enclose a report from the Minister of Finance, and another from the Minister for Home Affairs, upon the important subject of our present relations with America. I want you to make me a report on the history of our relations with the United States since the treaty of Mortefontaine, and to annex to it French translations of all the original documents mentioned by the two ministers. . . .

All the steps I have taken, as I have often remarked before, are mere acts of reprisal. I don't recognise any of the English claims with regard to the neutrals – what they call their maritime code. The English themselves have never pretended that I recognise it. Such a claim would have been pointless, since the code is entirely directed against France. At the same time the English claims have been no more admitted, or admitted only in part, by America and the northern powers. The maritime laws of England, previous to the last few years, were tyrannical, but not quite intolerable. But recently the English have completely altered the situation by arrogating to themselves the right to declare that all the ports of a country, and the whole coastline of an empire, are in a state of blockade. This means that, with respect to the blockaded country, England prohibits all commerce, and refuses to recognise any neutrals. I have said nothing of the influence England claimed to exercise over the neutrals: my Berlin decree was only a reply to the new extension she gave to the right of blockade; and even the Berlin decree cannot be considered as more than a maritime, certainly not as a continental blockade; witness the way in which it was carried out. I regard it simply as a kind of protest – as one act of violence answering another. It was really applied only to Hamburg, the Weser, and the continental coastline, and declarations were made to the neutrals to the effect that its operation would not be extended to the high seas. So far, little harm had been done; neutral ships still entered our ports. But the British Orders in Council necessitated my Milan decree, and thenceforward there were no neutrals. That decree had only one object, namely to protect myself and the neutrals against the intolerable right that England claimed to levy navigation dues upon the commerce and shipping of all nations – a claim which treated the high seas as I might treat the Seine, the Scheldt, or the Rhine. This meant an embargo on all commerce; and in opposing it, all thought of consequences had to be thrown to the winds. I was told today that the English are relaxing their regulations, and no longer impose a tax on shipping: let me know whether there is really an Order to this effect: even if there is not, let me know whether it is true in fact. Once I were sure that England is not going to levy navigation dues, I could relax my regulations in many respects.

I should not be unwilling to sign a treaty with America, by which she undertook (1) never, under any pretext, to allow England to levy dues on her commerce or shipping; (2) never to allow England to prevent her trading with France on the ground of a right of blockade, or any other pretext, it being understood that certain points might be blockaded, but not a whole empire; and (3) never to admit that, in order to reach France, her vessels must first call at some port in British territory. Granted these three conditions, I should be willing to declare, on my side, (1) that my warships and privateers will not exercise the right of search with respect to American ships, except so far as is necessary to make sure that they are really American, and do not belong to an enemy nation, (2) that American ships will be received in my ports, and will not be expected to pay more than the ordinary dues, always provided that they come direct from the United States, from another French port, from a country allied to France, or from a neutral; for I refuse to admit American ships coming from English ports. . . .

[CORRESP., xx, 16127. Cf. No. 182. The Non-Intercourse Act of March, 1809, limited the prohibition of American trade (by the Embargo Act of 1807) to England and France, but enforced it more strictly. This was Napoleon's first reaction to it. For the sequel, *v*. No. 209.]

## 202

# RIVAL BRIDES

### TO M. DE CHAMPAGNY, DUKE OF CADORE,
### MINISTER FOR FOREIGN AFFAIRS

PARIS, *FEBRUARY* 6, 1810.

Despatch a messenger before 6 o'clock this evening to the Duke of Vicenza. Inform him that a council was held a few days ago, and that opinion was divided between the Russian and Austrian princesses; that it is the same in the country, especially on the ground of religion; for even the people who attach least importance to religion can't reconcile themselves to the idea of not seeing the Empress attend church functions at the Emperor's side; that the presence of a Russian 'pope' constitutes an even greater difficulty, and that the Emperor would be making a serious admission of inferiority if he agreed to recognise the presence of a 'pope' at the Tuileries. You are to add that these lines were already written when the messenger of the 21st arrived, and that you interrupted your letter to decipher the despatches he carried; that in these despatches the Emperor points out that Princess Anne is not yet regular in her monthly periods; that girls sometimes have to wait two years after the first signs of nubility before they are really fit to marry; and that it would upset the Emperor's plans if he had to wait 3 years for a child. But that is not all. The 10 days' time limit expired on the 16th, and on the 21st the Emperor was still without an answer. His Majesty cannot understand how it is that, when the Empress-Mother has given her consent, and Princess Catherine herself is inclined to the match, a definite answer cannot be given. These delays contrast unfavourably with the keen and dutiful attitude of Austria. His Majesty, having no time to lose, is holding a council tomorrow to end this state of uncertainty. There was, indeed, at Erfurt, some question of the Princess Anne, but His Majesty now regards himself as effectively released, not indeed from any formal undertaking (for there was none), but from an honourable understanding based on his friendship for the Emperor Alexander, by the failure, after a whole month's delay, to reply to a simple question, and by the inconsistency between Romanzof's remarks.

[CORRESP., xx, 16210. In 1807, two years before his separation from Josephine (*v.* No. 199), Napoleon had considered a list of marriageable princesses. At Erfurt, in 1808, he sounded the Tsar about marriage to his sister, Katherina Pavlova: but in April, 1809, the Empress Dowager, who disliked Napoleon, married her to the Duke of Holstein-Gottorp-Oldenburg. He then asked for her younger sister, Anna Pavlova, aged 14: but within a fortnight of this letter he is found offering his hand to Marie Louise of Austria, *v.* No. 204.]

## 203

## IMPERIAL BALLET

### TO M. DE RÉMUSAT, PREFECT OF THE PALACE

PARIS, *FEBRUARY* 13, 1810.

As the opera 'The Death of Abel' has been rehearsed, I consent to its being played. But it must be understood that in future no opera may be given without my order. If the old management have passed on my permission in writing to the new, it is all right, but not otherwise. The late management asked my approval not only when they accepted a work submitted to them, but also when they chose one for presentation. Generally speaking, I am opposed to staging any subject drawn from Holy Scripture: such things should be left to the Church. The Chamberlain responsible for public performances will at once notify authors to this effect, so that they may turn their attention to other subjects. The ballet 'Vertumnus and Pomona' is a cold and tasteless allegory. The ballet 'The Rape of the Sabine Women' is based on history: that is more what we want. Mythological and historical ballets may be given, but never allegorical ones. I wish to have four ballets produced this year. If M. Gardel is not capable of doing this, try to find another producer. In addition to 'The Death of Abel,' I should like a second historical ballet, but one more appropriate to modern conditions than 'The Rape of the Sabine Women.'

[LECESTRE, ii, 579. Pierre Gardel was ballet-master at the Opera, 1787 – 1828.]

## 204

# COURTSHIP

### TO THE ARCH-DUCHESS MARIE LOUISE OF AUSTRIA

RAMBOUILLET, FEBRUARY 23, 1810.

My cousin: the brilliant qualities with which it is adorned have inspired Us with the desire to serve and honour your person. Whilst addressing Ourselves to the Emperor your father, and begging him to entrust Us with Your Imperial Highness's happiness, may we hope that Y.I.H. will share the sentiments that prompt Us to take this step? May we flatter Ourselves that Y.I.H. will not be swayed solely by the duty of obedience to your parents? Whatever little partiality for Us Y.I.H. may feel, it is Our wish to cultivate with so much care, and to make it Our endeavour so constantly to please you in every way, that We are confident of succeeding some day in becoming acceptable to you. That is the goal at which We hope to arrive, and for the sake of which We beg Y.I.H. to favour Our suit.

[CORRESP., xx, 16288. Napoleon's Austrian marriage was talked of in the autumn of 1809, but up to January, 1810, Marie Louise had not been consulted. The marriage by proxy took place at Vienna on March 11.]

## 205

# MARRIAGE

### TO FRANCIS II, EMPEROR OF AUSTRIA

COMPIEGNE, MARCH 29, 1810.

My Brother and Father-in-law; Your Majesty's daughter has now been here two days. She fulfils all my expectations, and for two days now I have not failed to give her, and to receive from her, proofs of the tender sentiments which unite us. We suit one another perfectly. I shall make her happy, and I shall owe my own happiness to Your Majesty. Let me thank you, then, for the fine present you have given me, and may a father's heart rejoice in the assurance of a beloved child's happiness.

We leave tomorrow for Saint-Cloud, and we shall celebrate the ceremony of our marriage at the Tuileries on April 2nd. Your Majesty must never doubt my sentiments of esteem and

high consideration, least of all the tender affection with which I
have promised to regard you.

[CORRESP., xx, 16361. Napoleon went to meet Marie Louise at Courcelles
on March 28, rode in her carriage to Compiègne, and exercised his marital
rights the same night, without waiting for the civil and ecclesiastical marriage
ceremonies, which took place at Saint-Cloud and the Tuileries on April 1 – 2.]


206

THE 'BLACK CARDINALS'
TO COUNT BIGOT DE PRÉAMENEU,
MINISTER OF PUBLIC WORSHIP

PARIS, APRIL 5, 1810.
The Minister of Public Worship will send for the thirteen
cardinals who, without any excuse on the score of health, failed
to attend the ceremony of the religious marriage. He will have
them all brought together in his house, and he will inform them
as follows: – that after discussing in secret meetings whether
they ought to attend, and in spite of the fact that the majority
voted in favour of doing so, they failed to attend His Majesty's
religious marriage; that these assemblies should not have taken
place without His Majesty's leave, and were therefore acts of
rebellion; that, in the Pope's absence, they are null and void,
and have no jurisdiction; and that even if they had any, the
minority ought to obey the majority; that His Majesty sees in
this conduct of theirs the same rebellious spirit that they have
displayed for the last ten years – the same that obliged His
Majesty to occupy Rome, the same that led them to induce the
Pope to thunder out an excommunication which will seem as
laughable to posterity as it does at the present day; that hitherto His Majesty has despised their manoeuvres, and put a charitable interpretation on them, trying to persuade himself that
they had no ill intentions; but that this time they have gone too
far, and shown, both by their speeches at their secret meetings,
and by their criminal proceedings, that they are doing their best
to disturb the peace of the Empire, to scatter the germs of civil
war, and to sow discord among mankind; that it is high time
they remembered that His Majesty holds the sword with which
to strike down bad priests and traitors to the State; and that

whilst His Majesty postpones his decision as to their persons, he will at the same time deal with their status as cardinals and priests, for these qualities are deemed non-existent in persons falling under the blade of the law. Whether he considers he ought to put the cardinals on their trial, or whether he has other intentions – in either case, His Majesty has charged his minister to make the above communication to them, and no more. The general impression He wishes to be left by the speech is that, if they are brought to trial, there are no ecclesiastical courts in France, and there is nothing to prevent their being convicted – both trial and conviction emanating from the Imperial will. They must also understand that the reason why they are forbidden to dress as priests or cardinals is that they are already considered to be in detention under a charge.

[LECESTRE, ii, 601. Sixteen Cardinals failed to attend Napoleon's ecclesiastical marriage on April 2 – thirteen of these without excuse. He removed them from their functions and interned them for three years in various French towns.]

## 207

# LAST LETTER TO LOUIS

### TO LOUIS NAPOLÉON, KING OF HOLLAND

LILLE, *MAY* 23, 1810.

At the very moment when you are professing the best possible intentions, I hear that my ambassador's servants have been assaulted. My intention is that those who are guilty of this crime against myself shall be handed over to me, so that the punishment I inflict on them may serve as an example. M. Serurier has described the way in which you behaved at the interview with the ambassadors. After hearing his account, I want no Dutch ambassador here. Admiral Verhuell has orders to leave Paris within 24 hours. I am tired of protestations and fine phrases: it is time that I were told plainly whether you wish to be the bane of Holland, and to make your follies the ruin of the country. I will not have you sending a minister to Austria. I will not have you dismissing the Frenchmen in your service. I shall no longer keep an ambassador in Holland. The Secretary of the Legation, who is now there as chargé d'affaires, will communicate my wishes to you. I am not going to expose an ambassador to further insults of this kind: I shall only have a *chargé d'affaires*. It was the Russian ambassador, I suppose, whose master placed you on the throne, and it is natural enough that you should follow his advice? Don't write to me any more of your usual fine phrases. You have given me nothing else now for three years: and every moment proves how false they are.

P.S. – I will never write to you again as long as I live.

[LECESTRE, ii, 618. *v*. No. 200. The postscript is in Napoleon's own hand.]

# 208

# FOUCHÉ DISMISSED

## TO M. FOUCHÉ, DUKE OF OTRANTO

SAINT-CLOUD, *JUNE* 3, 1810.

I have received your letter of June 2. I am aware of all the services you have done me, and I believe in your attachment to my person, and your zeal in my service; nevertheless I should be failing in my duty to myself if I allowed you to remain in office. The position of Minister of Police demands absolute and entire confidence; and that confidence can no longer exist, since you have already, in certain important circumstances, endangered my peace, and that of the state, by conduct which is not excused in my eyes by the correctness of your motives.

Negotiations with England have begun. Conferences with Lord Wellesley have taken place. He knew that you were only speaking for yourself, when he ought to have believed that you were speaking for me. The result has been a complete upset of my international policy, and (if I were to overlook your conduct) a reflection upon my character which I cannot and will not endure.

Your singular conception of the duties of a Police Minister cannot be reconciled with the good of the state. Though I have no doubt of your attachment, or of your fidelity, yet I am obliged to be constantly on the watch: it tires me out, and I cannot be tied down to it. This supervision is necessitated by the number of things you do on your own responsibility, without finding out whether they square with my plans or intentions, or whether they may not be contrary to the whole trend of my policy.

I wanted to tell you myself my reasons for depriving you of the Ministry of Police. I can see no hope that you are likely to change your way of doing things, because, for some years past, neither signal examples nor repeated statements of my displeasure have produced any effect, and because you are so sure of the purity of your motives that you refuse to recognise that the path to Hell is paved with good intentions. In spite of all, my confidence in your talents and your fidelity is unimpaired, and I am only anxious to find an opportunity to prove the one, and to employ the others in my service.

[CORRESP., xx, 16529. Napoleon's suspicions of Fouché, who had long been intriguing against him, came to a head in April, when he was discovered carrying on private negotiations with England about the annexation of Holland. He was dismissed, and retired to his *senatorerie* of Provence.]

## 209

## AMERICA AND THE BLOCKADE

### TO M. DE CHAMPAGNY, DUKE OF CADORE,
### MINISTER FOR FOREIGN AFFAIRS

SAINT-CLOUD, *AUGUST* 2, 1810.

I send you the outline of a Note for M. Armstrong. The simpler it is the better.

*Proposed Note to the Minister of the United States*

Sir: I have submitted to His Majesty the Emperor and King the United States Gazette that you sent me, containing the Act of Congress of May 1. His Majesty could have wished that he were officially notified of Acts of the United States of possible interest to France. It was only unofficially and a long time afterwards that he knew of the Embargo and Non-Intercourse Acts. Grave inconveniences result, which would not be the case if your Excellency gave us official notice of such Acts.

His Majesty approved of the general embargo that the United States laid upon shipping, because, although this measure was contrary to the interests of France, it contained nothing prejudicial to her honour. As a result, France lost her colonies of Martinique, Guadeloupe, and Cayenne; but she did not complain about this, for she regarded it as a voluntary sacrifice to the principle that drove the Americans to impose the embargo, namely that it is better to close the sea against one's own ships than to recognise the right of another power to tyrannise over it.

Subsequently an Act of March 1 took off the embargo, and replaced it by a hostile measure. In this Act, which was not known in France till long afterwards, it was provided that every French vessel arriving in the United States should be confiscated. Upon this, law had to give way to reprisals. The proper and inevitable reply was the sequestration of all American vessels in French ports.

Now Congress takes another step. It rescinds the Act of March 1, opens American ports to French commerce, and undertakes to resist any power that refuses to recognise the rights of neutrals. In this new situation I am authorised to inform you that the Berlin and Milan decrees are rescinded, and that, as from November 1st next, they will cease to be effective, provided that, as a consequence of this step, the English withdraw their Orders in Council, and the new blockade principles that they have tried to establish; or, alternatively, that the United States, in conformity with the Act which you, Sir, have just communicated to me, force the English to respect their rights.

It is with peculiar gratification that I acquaint you with this resolve on the part of the Emperor. His Majesty loves the Americans, and regards their commercial prosperity as favourable to his policy. The independence of America is one of France's chief titles to fame; at a later date the Emperor took pleasure in aggrandising the United States; and whatever the circumstances, he will always consider anything that increases the prosperity of that country, and ensures its happiness, as associated with his interests and his dearest affections.

[CORRESP., xxi, 16743. Cf. No.182. For the Non-Intercourse Act of March 1, v. No. 201. In May, Napoleon had published the Rambouillet decree, ordering the seizure and sale of all American ships. Soon afterwards he heard of the temporary lifting of the American embargo by a law of May 1.]

## 210

## 'FRANCE FIRST'

### TO PRINCE EUGÈNE, VICEROY OF ITALY

SAINT-CLOUD, *AUGUST* 23, 1810.

I have received your letter of August 14. All the raw silk from the Kingdom of Italy goes to England, for there are no silk factories in Germany. It is therefore quite natural that I should wish to divert it from this route to the advantage of my French manufacturers: otherwise my silk factories, one of the chief supports of French commerce, would suffer substantial losses. I cannot agree with your observations. My principle is *France first*. You must never lose sight of the fact that, if English commerce is supreme on the high seas, it is due to her sea power: it is therefore to be expected that, as France is the strongest land power, she should claim commercial supremacy on the continent: it is indeed our only hope. And isn't it better for Italy to come to the help of France, in such an important matter as this, than to be covered with Customs Houses? For it would be short-sighted not to recognise that Italy owes her independence to France; that it was won by French blood and French victories; that it must not be misused; and that nothing could be more unreasonable than to start calculating what commercial advantages France gets out of it.

Piedmont and Parma produce silk too; and there also I have prohibited its export to any country except France. Why should Piedmont be treated in one way, and the Kingdom of Italy in another? If any discrimination were made, it should be in favour of Piedmont; for, whilst the Venetians fought against France, the Piedmontese came to her aid, taking sides against their own king. But never mind about all that. I understand Italian affairs better than anyone else. It is no use for Italy to make plans that leave French prosperity out of account; she must face the fact that the interests of the two countries hang together. Above all, she must be careful not to give France any reason for annexing her; for if it paid France to do this, who could stop her? So make this your motto too – *France first*.

If I were to lose a great battle, a million men – nay, two million men of my old France would flock to my banners, and every purse in the country would be opened for me; but my Kingdom of Italy would desert me. I find it odd, then, that there

should be any unwillingness to help the French manufacturers
in what is only another way of damaging the English. There is
plenty of silk in the Three Legations, plenty in the district of
Novara. What has Italy done to deserve these additions of
700,000 and 400,000 souls? How can she expect me to let these
annexations result in opposition to my will? French commodi-
ties pay half dues on entering Italy; they ought not to pay anything at all. . . .

[CORRESP., xxi, 16824. Between 1806 (the Berlin decree) and 1810, the
value of silk exports from Italy had sunk from 14½ to 10 million livres. The
result of Napoleon's measures to concentrate these exports on France was that
their amount fell from 522 kilos in 1810 to 259 kilos in 1811 (first six months
in both cases). And the figures for 1812 show that the exports to Germany and
Switzerland (which Napoleon regards as bound for England) still exceeded
those to France.]


# 211

# PRISON REFORM

### NOTE FOR THE MINISTER FOR HOME AFFAIRS

SAINT-CLOUD, SEPTEMBER 5 1810.

The Emperor desires the Minister for Home Affairs to set
to work with all possible energy on the prisons. The subject has
been under debate so long that those who are engaged upon it
ought to have their ideas cut and dried.

The Constituent Assembly laid down principles which won
general approval. What were its proposals? How much of its
scheme ought we to adopt? What parts ought we to modify or
to reject? Those are the points I want you to look into.

What we want to aim at, in general, is that the prisoners
should be healthy, and the prisons clean, and that those who
have been sentenced should be kept apart from those who have
only been charged. In carrying out these reforms it seems reasonable to adopt the same procedure as with the work-houses.
The Emperor will ear-mark for this purpose a large part of the
communal contributions to the Sinking Fund; and the balance
will come from the Departments.

The Emperor desires the Minister for Home Affairs to
submit a general report next Wednesday, together with a
detailed plan for the management of the prisons in one or in

a number of Departments.

[CORRESP., xxi, 16868.]

## 212

## DUTCH OPINION

TO PRINCE LEBRUN, ARCH-TREASURER OF THE EMPIRE,
LIEUTENANT-GENERAL OF THE EMPEROR IN HOLLAND

PARIS, *September* 25, 1810.

You speak to me of the grievances of the Amsterdam folk,
of their anxieties, and of their discontent. Do these Dutchmen
really take me for a Grand Pensionary Barnevelt? I can make
nothing of such talk. I shall do what suits the interests of my
Empire. I despise the clamour of madmen who think they know
my interests better than I know them myself. Really, one would
think you do not know me. At this rate you will soon have forgotten all about me. I did not take over the Government of Holland in order to consult the common people of Amsterdam, or
to do what other people want. The French nation has been wise
enough, at various times, to rely upon my judgment – you know
that as well as anyone. My hope is that the Dutch will come to
have the same opinion of me. When a contrary opinion is
expressed in your presence, you ought to use language befitting
my Lieutenant-General: 'The Emperor,' you should say, 'does
what is best for the welfare of his Empire; and when he has
made up his mind, he brooks no opposition.' The tall talk that
you think so convincing merely makes me sad – all the more so,
when I am living here in the midst of the most enlightened people in the country, and consulting their interests at every turn. I
hope this is the last time that such talk will be heard in your
presence.

[LECESTRE, ii, 684. After Louis' abdication, Holland was annexed to
France, and administered by Lebrun, formerly Third Consul, as Lieutenant-
General. John of Barnevelt, Dutch liberator from Spain, was executed for his
part in the Arminian controversy, 1619.]

## 213

# POCKET BATTLESIPS

## TO REAR-ADMIRAL COUNT DECRÈS
### MINISTER OF MARINE

FONTAINEBLEAU, *October* 12, 1810.

A vessel drawing 19$^{1}$/$_{2}$ feet can get out of the Texel. I want you to propound the following problem to 10 of the best engineers, beginning with Sané:

To produce designs for a vessel as powerfully armed as a 74-gunner, with a draught, when fully loaded, of 19$^{1}$/$_{2}$ feet, and capable of as high a speed as possible.

If there were any chance of getting a vessel as fast as our 74-gunners, all other considerations could go by the board.

(1) It will be enough if this ship can only carry 3 months' provisions instead of the usual 6, and 3 months' supply of water in place of 4$^{1}$/$_{2.}$

(2) If it is really necessary, the calibre of the guns can be changed to that of the English guns.

(3) Again, if it is really necessary, these ships can carry bronze guns, which weigh much less.

You are to submit the engineers' report to me personally.

[CORRESP., xxi, 17034. The Texel is the north-western outlet of the Zuyder Zee.]

## 214

# RUSSIA AND THE BLOCKADE

## TOM. DE CHAMPAGNY, DUKE OF CADORE,
### MINISTER FOR FOREIGN AFFAIRS

FONTAINEBLEAU, *November* 4, 1810.

Draft an answer that I can send to M. Kourakine. It must be very polite, and very mild, but must not fail to contain certain home truths that it is good for Russia to hear. You are to say that I have seen his note; that I have derived lively satisfaction from the assurance he gives me that the Emperor of Russia is resolved to do all the harm he can to English commerce; that it depends upon Russia whether peace is concluded, or the war goes on; that, if she makes a serious effort to stop the trade in colonial goods, England will make peace before the year is out; but that, to speak plainly, Russian policy has hitherto followed a directly opposite line. The one and sufficient proof of this is that the colonial goods shown at the last Leipzig fair were brought there by 700 carts that came from Russia; that nowadays the whole trade in colonial goods is carried on by Russia; and that the 1,200 vessels which the English convoyed up the Baltic with 20 warships, disguised under the Swedish, Portuguese, Spanish, and American flags, unloaded part of their cargoes in Russian ports. You are therefore to say that, if Russia wants peace with England, she has the means within her grasp: she has only to confiscate all the vessels arriving under British convoy, and to join France in requiring Sweden to confiscate the immense quantities of merchandise that the English have discharged at Göteborg under all kinds of flags. As to the objection that, though willing to make war on England, we don't want to make war on neutrals, you should point out that this idea is based on a fallacy; that the English dislike and disallow neutrality; that they refuse to let American ships sail, unless they carry British goods, and trade on Britain's account; that all the certificates signed by French consuls, and the other papers carried by these ships, are forged; that in fact there are no neutrals nowadays, because the English won't allow it, and stop every ship not carrying for themselves; and that thus all vessels arriving at a Russian port with so-called American papers really come from England. Tell him that these facts are too obvious to be ignored; that it lies with Russia whether we have peace or war, and that she is as deeply concerned as France in the issue; that if we are prepared to close the continent against the English, there will be peace; but that there can be none, so long as we consent to regard all the ships arriving with papers signed by French consuls and the like as trading in any other interests than those of England; and that, so long as English and Colonial goods enter Prussia and Germany by way of Russia, and have to be stopped on the frontiers, it is quite clear that Russia is making no proper effort to do harm to England.

[CORRESP., xxi, 17099. In October a large convoy of 'neutral' ships carrying British goods entered the Baltic. As a result of Napoleon's threats, many of them were seized by Prussia, Sweden, and Russia. But an *ukase* of December 31 admitted Colonial goods to Russian ports, and during 1811 the Tsar gradually abandoned the blockade.]

## 215

# GALLICANISM

## TO COUNT BIGOT DE PRÉAMENEU,
## MINISTER OF PUBLIC WORSHIP

PARIS, *JANUARY* 5, 1811.

I am sending you a memoir which has been submitted to me. Tell me what you think of the idea of sounding the bishops before calling a National Council. It seems to me that it would be a good plan for you to draw up a statement on the question, and to ask the opinion of certain bishops about it. This statement should deal with the Pope's refusal to give canonical institution, his bull of excommunication, his departure from Rome, the freedom that he enjoyed at Savona, and the way he abused it, the letters he wrote to Cardinal Fesch (copies of these should be annexed), showing his irritable and outrageous temper, and his letters to Cardinal Maury, and to the *Grande Vicaire* of Astros. The first persons to be asked their opinion should be the archbishops of Paris, Lyon, Tours, Malines, Toulouse, Turin, and Bordeaux; then some of the bishops – the strongest of them: the rest could be consulted later. Ask them to send you within a week reasoned replies to the following questions:

*1st question.* – Has the Pope any right to excommunicate ruling sovereigns and their ministers for temporal reasons? What steps ought to be taken to deal with this excommunication, the news of which has been broadcast by malevolent persons, and has given rise to rumours in the country? What attitude can be adopted? What do the rules of the Gallican church prescribe?

*2nd question.* – The Pope has violated the Concordat by refusing to give canonical institution to all bishops nominated by the government. The Emperor will not expose the dignity of his crown to insults of this kind. In these circumstances, what means does church history suggest for securing the canonical institution of bishops?

*3rd question.* – When His Majesty, with the best intentions, agreed that the bishops he had nominated should administer their dioceses as *vicaires capitulaires*, had the Pope any right to forbid the Chapters to bestow the necessary powers upon them, to carry on a clandestine correspondence in this country, to preach rebellion against authority, and to substitute his arbitrary will for the privileges of the Chapters?

*4th question.* – Finally, what is it best to do, under the circumstances, to bring to an end a state of vacillation so prejudicial to the liberty of the nation, the dignity of the throne, and the good of the church – a church which suffers from the sovereign's anticipation of trouble due to the greedy and ill-tempered attitude of the Pope?

[CORRESP., xxi, 17268. In order to end his struggle with the Pope, Napoleon, in June, 1811, summoned a Council of bishops with a view to founding an independent 'Gallican Church.' For the sequel, *v.* No. 218.]


# 216

# BABYLONISH CAPTIVITY

## TO PRINCE BORGHESE, GOVERNOR-GENERAL OF THE TRANSALPINE DEPARTMENTS

PARIS, *JANUARY* 6, 1811.

The Pope has taken advantage of the liberty I allowed him at Savona to sow rebellion and disorder amongst my subjects.

I had done no more than arrange that [until the important question of canonical institution is decided] the bishops I had nominated should function as *vicaires capitulaires* in the name of their Chapters: this is in accordance with church tradition, and follows the precedent laid down by Louis XIV and other European sovereigns. Nevertheless the Pope [inspired by a characteristic love of disorder] has been obstinate and treacherous enough to send to the Chapters at Paris, Florence, and Asti briefs contrary to the laws of the Empire [and of the rest of Europe, since the various sovereigns felt the need of protecting themselves against the moody manoeuvres of the Popes, and therefore prohibited any such communications without their permission. The Pope is all the more to blame in this matter, because even ultramontane opinion denies his right to influence a Chapter's decisions during the vacancy of a see. More particularly is it an attack upon the liberties of the Gallican Church].

As I intend to safeguard my subjects against the insane anger of this ignorant and irascible old man, I order you to inform him here and now that he is forbidden to hold communication with any church, or with any of my subjects: and that any infringement of this rule on either side will be punished.

You are to remove from the Pope's household any suspicious individuals, leaving only those who are necessary for his service; and you are to allow him no visitors, whoever they may be. Take steps to increase the garrison at Savona. Confiscate all the Pope's papers, books, and documents, and have them sent to Paris. If the Pope behaves unreasonably, shut him up in the citadel at Savona: but be sure to supply it beforehand with food, and all other necessaries.

Take steps to carry out these orders. It will be the business of the Prefect or of some other official to notify the Pope [in writing], and to inform him [that I no longer recognise him as Pope, and] that a person who preaches rebellion, and whose soul is full of the gall of bitterness, can no longer express the will of the Church.

You realise the importance of these measures. I have sent to Savona an officer of the gendarmerie; and you can easily get 300 or so veteran gendarmes from the Legion to carry out these orders. [There must be no more half-measures.] Since nothing will make the Pope see sense, he must be shown that I am strong enough to depose a Pope, as my predecessors have done before me.

The business of dealing with the Pope's papers needs tact. You must not leave him any paper, pens, ink, or writing materials. Let him have a few French servants; but remove any who are untrustworthy. You can refuse admission to members of his suite at your discretion.

[LECESTRE, ii, 747. The Pope had now been eighteen months virtually in prison, but still refused investiture to the bishops nominated by Napoleon. The bracketed passages were struck out in revision.]


# 217

# EX-SERVICE MEN

## TO GENERAL COUNT ANDRÉOSSY, PRESIDENT OF THE WAR COMMITTEE OF THE STATE COUNCIL

PARIS, *JANUARY* 27, 1811.

Call a meeting of the War Committee, and draft a measure to provide for discharged and wounded soldiers, by giving them preference in appointments to such administrative posts in the Forestry, Post Office, Tobacco, Taxation, and in fact all departments, as can profitably be held by discharged officers and men. It is unfair, and contrary to my intention, to give such posts to people who have done nothing. I rely upon the zeal and intelligence of the Committee to propose a suitable scheme.

[CORRESP., xxi, 17301.]


# 218

# GALLICAN CHURCH

## TO THE ECCLESIASTICAL COMMITTEE

PARIS, *MARCH* 16, 1811.

I have received and read with close attention your letter of March 5. You tell me that the clergy of France, steeped in the holy doctrine of the Gospel, would regard with indignation any attack upon the authority of the pontiff.

The Pope has attacked my authority, by excommunicating my ministers, my armies, and almost all my empire, and that merely in defence of his temporal claims. Nevertheless, in the present state of the Catholic Church, in which the teaching of those who sacrifice the bishops to the wishes and interests of the Roman Curia has won the day, what means are there by which I can secure my throne from such attacks? Is there any canonical procedure for punishing a Pope who preaches sedition and civil war?

The Pope has not merely attacked my authority: he has attacked the authority and welfare of the churches within the Empire, not only by allowing the destruction of the German Church, and by refusing to institute my bishops, but also by his subsequent instructions to the Chapters not to bestow the powers of *vicaires capitulaires* upon the persons I had nominated to their sees.

Before that, he had done all he could to impair the affection and obedience of my subjects, by instituting on his own authority the Archbishop of Malines, and by making no mention of my wishes when he instituted the bishop of Montauban.

Bulls and letters, printed by the Pope's orders, have been distributed all over Christendom. It is no credit to the Pope if such crimes as those of Clément, Ravaillac, and Damiens have not been repeated. If he could have his way, I should be deserted, as Philip the Tall was, by my subjects and my soldiers. I can only conclude that, if the thunders of Rome have had so little effect, I owe it to the enlightenment of the age, or perhaps to the depreciation of religion in the public mind all over Europe.

I am aware that one should render unto God the things that are God's. But the Pope is not God. When one sees the Papacy constantly disturbing Christendom, and turning it upside down, in the interests of the petty state of Rome – a sovereignty no bigger than a duchy, one can only deplore the condition of the Catholic Church, compromised for such miserable ends.

The present age takes us back to the times of Charlemagne. All the kingdoms, principalities, and duchies which formed themselves into republics out of the fragments of his empire have been regenerated under our laws. The church of my Empire is the church of the West, if not the church of universal Christendom.

I have made up my mind to call a Western Council, to which I shall summon the bishops of Italy and Germany, and which will draw up regulations, as desired by a great number of bishops, for a general system of discipline, so that my Empire may be one in morals as it is one in faith.

I wish to be informed:

(1) What is the procedure for summoning this Council.

(2) What subjects it should deal with, in order to bring to an end once for all these scandalous contests between the spiritual and temporal powers, which are so fatal to religion – for they alone are responsible for the schism of the Greek Church; the English Churches, and those of the Northern Powers, and to find means to protect my Empire from the hostility and hatred of the Roman Curia, which will otherwise persecute my descendants, as it did those of Charlemagne, until it has driven the Empire into schism, expelled the French from Italy, and reestablished the temporal sovereignty of the Popes – a sovereignty that cannot exist henceforward without the destruction of the Empire. The Concordat I should prefer to regard as no longer existent, and I cannot accept the modified form in which you submit it. A reciprocal contract is null and void as soon as it is broken by either of the parties to it. The Pope has violated the Concordat for the last 4 years, just as he previously broke the contract that he made with my Kingdom of Italy, to the deep

indignation of my Italian church.

Under these circumstances, the clause providing for the institution of bishops by the metropolitans, if the Pope fails to act, does not guarantee my successors against further possible quarrels with the Papal See.

[CORRESP., xxi, 17478. After two abortive Ecclesiastical Commissions in 1809 and January, 1811 (*v.* No. 215), Napoleon summoned a third Council of French and Italian bishops on June 17, 1811, in order to coerce the Pope. This too refused his suggestions, and was dissolved. Philip 'the Tall' (*le Long*) was King of France 1316 – 22. Clément, Ravaillac, and Damiens, were the assasins of Henri III, Henri IV and Louis XV.]

# 219

# BEET-SUGAR

## NOTE FOR THE MINISTER FOR HOME AFFAIRS

PARIS, *MARCH* 18, 1811.

The Minister for Home Affairs is to make a report, to be sent to the State Council, explaining the advantages of manufacturing sugar from beet. He will suggest all the steps that should be taken to encourage the cultivation of sugar-beet, either by showing that, even if the customs duty on colonial goods is changeable, it will not be changed for the next 5 years, or by anticipating the time when it may be possible to prohibit all imports of sugar from the colonies, or by suggesting some other means of attaining the same end.

The Minister will report tomorrow on a convenient place for making a large scale experiment, and for establishing a school of instruction in the manufacture of beet-sugar. This institution could probably be established at the Rambouillet farm, where some useful tests have already been made. It would be a good thing to send for the director of the farm, and to ask his advice.

Finally, the Minister is to submit, before next Sunday, the draft of a circular to the Prefects, explaining the government policy. In this circular he will give notice of the intention to maintain the tariffs on colonial goods, and even to prohibit entirely the importation of foreign sugar. He will assign to each Department its share of the 70,000 *arpents* to be given up to beet cultivation in order to provide all the sugar needed for

French consumption. He will enlist the Prefects' support in encouraging land-owners to take up the cultivation of beet, and will show them, on land set aside for this purpose, what they have to do. He will persuade farmers in the tobacco-growing Departments that it is profitable to grow beet instead. He will give them to understand, in general terms, that the cultivation of beet improves the ground, and that the waste products of the sugar-factory make an excellent food for cattle. He will show what outlay produces what returns, and how beet-cultivation, even on a small scale, can deprive foreigners of the kind of tribute they now get from France. A well-written circular on these lines will prove quite clearly the incalculable advantages of a scheme which we want to commend to all sensible men.

[CORRESP., xxi, 17485. This letter was followed a week later by a decree setting aside 80,000 acres for the planting of beet, and founding 6 schools for teaching the manufacture of beet-sugar.]

# 220

## SON AND HEIR

### TO THE EMPRESS JOSÉPHINE

PARIS, *MARCH* 22, 1811.

My dear, I have received your letter; thank you for it. My son is a big healthy child. I trust he will do well. He has my chest, my mouth, and my eyes. I trust he will fulfil his destiny.

I am still very pleased with Eugène: he has never given me an hour's anxiety.

[CORRESP., xxi, 17499. Marie Louise's son, the 'King of Rome,' was born on March 20.]

# 221

## RUSSIA – PEACE OR WAR?

### TO FREDERICK, KING OF WÜRTTEMBERG

PARIS, *APRIL* 2, 1811

. . . I hope and believe, as Your Majesty does, that Russia will not declare war. But she has built 20 fortresses since the end of last year; at this moment she is forming 15 new regiments; the divisions from Finland and Sweden are marching towards the frontiers of the Grand Duchy; and so are 4 divisions of her army in Moldavia. It is deeds, not words, that show the real intentions of a government. Why withdraw troops so useful to Russia in her war with the Turks? Why create new regiments at a moment of penury, when they have no money, and a big war on hand, and no means of meeting expenses but by a paper currency? These are the plain facts. For the last 6 months, the Emperor Alexander has been fed on fables. They have persuaded him that I demanded the forces of the Confederation, and the details he gave on this point show that he is already listening to what our enemies say. The *ukase* on commerce – not that he could ever have carried it outshows that his whole attitude has changed; there is something about it friendly to England, and hostile to France; whereas at one time the Emperor was the only person in Russia who backed the alliance against England. . . .

I attach no importance to Your Majesty's relations with Russia, any more than I do to the attitude of the Imperial court. In the dealings of one great nation with another, facts say more than words, and public opinion holds the helm. The King of Prussia drifted into war while it was still at a distance; he would have stopped it, when he had lost the power to do so; and he wept before Jena, because he had a presentiment of what would happen. It was the same with the Emperor of Austria: he allowed the arming of the *landwehr,* and it was no sooner armed than it dragged him into war. I am inclined to think that the same thing will happen to the Emperor Alexander. He has already completely abandoned his point of view at Tilsit, and Russia is the source of all the talk about war. If the Emperor wants war, public opinion backs him up: if, without wanting war, he yet fails to stop the movement towards it, he will be dragged into it next year against his will; and war will come about, though I don't want it, neither does he, and though it is equally against the interests of France and of Russia. I have seen this happen so often before that my experience of the past reveals the future. It is all like a scene at the opera, with the English in the wings. If anything can save the situation, it will be the straightforward language I have used to Russia. . . .

Finally, Your Majesty cannot suppose that I, of all people, desire war. Why should I? To set Poland on its feet again? I could have done that after Tilsit, or after Vienna, or this very year! I am too good a tactician to have missed such easy opportunities. It was simply that I didn't want to do so. The fact is, I have the war in Spain and Portugal on my hands – a war which covers an area larger than France, and absorbs a quantity of men and material: I cannot possibly want another war. And yet I have raised 120,000 men this year, and shall be raising another 120,000 next year; I am forming new regiments, and remounting my cavalry and artillery; and all because I am suspicious of Russian intentions, and believe that she is working for an outbreak of war in 1812. My extraordinary expenditure this year amounts to 100 millions: does Your Majesty suppose I am doing it to amuse myself? But if I have no wish for war, and if I am still less anxious to play the part of a Polish Don Quixote, I have at least no right to ask that Russia should stand by her alliance; and I must be able to prevent her finishing the Turkish war (which will probably be this summer), and then coming to me and saying, 'I am throwing over our arrangement, and making peace with England.' The Emperor might just as well declare war on me. For, unless I am the first to break with Russia, the English will begin by turning her alliance into neutrality, and end by turning her neutrality into war. . ..

[CORRESP., xxii, 17553.]

# 222

## ROYAL BAPTISM

### TO THE COUNT OF MONTALIVET,
### MINISTER FOR HOME AFFAIRS

PARIS, *April* 13, 1811.

I have fixed June 2 for the baptism of the King of Rome. It will be celebrated in the metropolitan church of Nôtre Dame at Paris, where the Empress and I shall attend in state to take part in the ceremony, and to render thanks to God for the birth of our son. After the ceremony at Nôtre Dame I shall dine at the Town Hall of my good city of Paris, and watch a display of fireworks. The same day the *Te Deum* will be sung throughout the Empire. I desire all the fêtes and rejoicings to take place simultaneously, and according to the programme you have submitted to me; I therefore wish you to send instructions to the mayors of the communes, fixing the amount they are allowed to spend on these fêtes. Let me also have the list of the marriages that could be arranged for in all the principal towns, by providing dowries for poor and orphan girls, and by mating them with discharged soldiers. I want you also to invite the mayors of approved towns to the baptism; each mayor to be accompanied by two deputies chosen from the leading members of the General Council. Make each of them an allowance for travelling expenses, on a scale which will enable them to keep up a proper appearance during their stay in Paris, and to put their servants into the livery of the towns they represent.

[CORRESP., xxii, 17604.]

## 223

# WORK FOR THE UNEMPLOYED

### TO GENERAL LACUÉE, COUNT OF CESSAC, MINISTER IN CHARGE OF WAR ADMINISTRATION

SAINT-CLOUD, *MAY* 2, 1811.

There are a number of unemployed hat-makers, bonnet-makers, cobblers, tailors, and saddlers in Paris. I should like you to take steps to arrange for the manufacture of shoes at the rate of 500 a day, on the understanding that employment is given to 1,000 cobblers, and that no ready-made shoes are included in the number supplied: that will mean 15,000 pairs a month. You must take whatever precautions are necessary to ensure that the shoes are well made.

I should like to manufacture in the same way 250 shakos a day, about 30 saddles, and a certain number of complete outfits, care being taken that new workmen are always employed.

As there are still other workmen out of employment, see whether it would be feasible to manufacture 100 or so baggage-carts: but be sure that they are of good workmanship; and we ought to be able to get them as cheaply as at Sampigny.

[CORRESP., xxii, 17684.]

## 224

# PREFECT AND PUBLIC

## TO PRINCE LEBRUN, ARCH-TREASURER OF THE EMPIRE, THE EMPEROR'S LIEUTENANT-GENERAL IN HOLLAND

SAINT-CLOUD, *MAY* 3, 1811.

. . .The Prefect at Emden is a very weak man. I shall wait for the report that Count Réal is sending me before making up my mind about him. But my intention is that the 500 men composing the crowd which beat the Prefect shall all be removed to France, to work in my ports. Write in this sense to State-Counsellor Réal. I will stand no nonsense about this. The Prefect is my representative. Those who stood by while he was assaulted are all guilty. I suppose I ought to be grateful because the two towns let themselves be disarmed when the troops arrived? As for those of the offenders who got away, their houses must be burnt down, their families arrested, their property confiscated, and they themselves condemned to death by court martial for failing to appear. A number of the worst offenders are to be shot. Send a copy of this letter to State-Counsellor Réal. It needs bloodshed and chastisement to wash out such an insult to the government.

[LECESTRE, ii, 804.]


## 225

# IRELAND AGAIN

## TO GENERAL CLARKE, DUKE OF FELTRE, MINISTER FOR WAR

SAINT-CLOUD, *JULY* 4, 1811.

I want you to send for O'Connor and the other Irishmen in Paris, and to see if you can revive a party in Ireland. At the present moment I have 25 war-ships off the Scheldt, and 9 in the Texel. I am very much inclined to send an expedition of 3,000 men and 4,000 horses to Ireland in October, if I can be sure of finding support there, and if England goes on reducing her garrisons to send troops to Portugal. You can easily understand that my control of the Scheldt and Texel, coinciding with the English disarmament, provides an unique opportunity.

I will agree to any terms the Irish like. It is a matter of immense importance. I want to have a plan, and to know what I can expect from it, within a fortnight. There is nothing to prevent my sailing out of the Scheldt; and, as the British haven't a man in England, they will be forced to recall their troops from the Peninsula, which will take them 2 or 3 months. We shall have time to establish ourselves in the country before they arrive.

[CORRESP., xxii, 17875. Arthur O'Connor, a member of the 'United Irishmen,' was despatched from Scotland to France in 1803, and made a general by Napoleon in 1804.]

# 226

## SPIES PUNISHED

### TO GENERAL COUNT HULLIN, GOVERNOR OF THE CHÂTEAU DE VINCENNES

SAINT-CLOUD, *JULY* 25, 1811.

I have received the sentence passed on Cifenti and Sassi della Tosa. Have Cifenti executed – he is a wretched spy. In Sassi's case, I agree to a commutation of his sentence. But you are to have him taken to the place of execution, and you must not produce the reprieve until Cifenti has been executed, and it is Sassi's turn to mount the scaffold. I want him to see with his own eyes how a crime like his is punished.

[LECESTRE, ii, 841.]

# 227

## ENGLISH ASSASSINS

### NOTE FOR THE MINISTER FOR FOREIGN AFFAIRS

RAMBOUILLET, *AUGUST* 8, 1811.

I am sending M. the Duke of Bassano, for insertion in the papers, an article which says that the gang of assassins organised by Lord Wellesley and Mr. Perceval to get rid of the enemies of England has already made an attempt on the life of the

King of Denmark. Fortunately it failed. Publish the story, but don't mention that the assassin was a Swedish officer.

[BROTONNE, i, 871. Spencer Perceval was Prime Minister from 1809 to 1812: Lord Wellesley was Foreign Secretary.]

# 228

# WARDROBE

## TO GENERAL DUROC, DUKE OF FRIULI,
## GRAND MARSHAL OF THE PALACE

SAINT-CLOUD, *August* 19, 1811.

Inform Count Rémusat that he is to have nothing more to do with my Wardrobe, and that I have deprived him of the title of Master of the Wardrobe. You are to carry on his functions until I find a substitute for him. I send you this year's estimate for my Wardrobe that I have drawn up, and an order to Count Estève to pay the 16,000 francs I owe. I don't want to charge this sum to the annual account. The estimate needs no revision; it is the same as that which I drew up at the beginning of the year. The Treasurer will pay the 16,000 francs from my private purse.

Have an inventory made of my things: see that they are there, and check them off. I think one could still save something on the estimate. See that the tailor arranges to send in no bad work, and not to exceed his estimates. Whenever any new clothes are delivered, bring them to me yourself, so that I may see whether they fit me properly: if they do, I will have them. Regularise all this, so that, when I appoint a Master of the Wardrobe, he will find his duties cut and dried. I fancy Count Rémusat was not appointed by decree; but if he was, you are to submit a decree for his dismissal.

*Estimate for the Emperor's Wardrobe.*

FRANCS

*Uniforms and Great-coats.*

1 Grenadier's tail-coat on January 1st with
  epaulettes, etc.

1 Chasseur's tail-coat on April 1st with epaulettes
  etc.

at 360 each
=1,400

1 Grenadier's tail-coat on July 1st, with

epaulettes, etc.,
1 Chasseur's tail-coat on October 17, with
epaulettes, etc.
(Each tail-coat will have to last 3 years.)
 2 Hunting coats: one for riding, in the Saint-
Hubert style, the other for shooting, on
August 1st                                        860
       (These coats will have to last 3 years.)
1 Civilian coat on November 1st (to last 3 years.)   200
2 Frock-coats: one grey, and the other another colour.   400
    (They will be supplied on October 1st
    every year, and will have to last 3 years.)

*Waist-coats and Breeches.*
48 pairs of breeches and white waist-coats at
  80 francs                                    3,840
  (They are to be supplied every week, and must
         last 3 years.)

*Dressing-gowns, Pantaloons, and Vests.*
2 dressing-gowns, one quilted, on May 1st,
and one of swansdown, on October 1st               500
2 pairs of pantaloons, one quilted and one of
wool, supplied in the same way                     60
    (The dressing-gowns and pantaloons will have
        to last 3 years.)
48 flannel vests (one a week) at 30 francs         1,400
     (The vests will have to last 3 years.)

*Body-linen.*
4  dozen shirts (a dozen a week)                   2,880
4  dozen handkerchiefs (a dozen a week)            576
2  dozen cravats (one a fortnight.                 720
1  dozen black collars (one a month) which
  must last a year                           96
2  dozen towels (a dozen a fortnight)              200
6  Madras night-caps (one every 2 months)
  to last 3 years                            144
2  dozen pairs of silk stockings at 18 francs
  (one pair a fortnight)                     432
2  dozen pairs of socks (one pair a fortnight)     432
  (All this linen, except the black collars and

the night-caps, will have to last 6 years.)

*Footwear.*
24 pairs of shoes (one pair a fortnight, which
   must last 2 years)                         312
6 pairs of boots, to last 2 years         600

*Headwear.*
4 hats a year, supplied with the tail-coats
*Miscellaneous.*
Scents, slimming mixture, eau de Cologne,
   etc..
Washing the linen and silk stockings    Various
expenses.   Nothing to be spent without His
Majesty's approval

TOTAL. . . . . . .

[CORRESP., xxii, 18051.]

## 229

# A WIFE'S DUTY

### TO M. MARET, DUKE OF BASSANO,
### MINISTER FOR FOREIGN AFFAIRS

SAINT-CLOUD, *August* 24, 1811.
    Princess Stéphanie has no right to like Mannheim: it is her duty to be where her husband is. She has no right to prefer dining at 5: it is her duty to dine when her husband does. She ought to do what he wants and to be where he is, instead of running away from him. Far from encouraging the Princess in these petty acts of rebellion, Baron de Moustier ought to get her lady-in-waiting to give her my advice. The Princess ought to use all the care and coquettishness she can to please her husband, not the little she has displayed hitherto. It is her duty; it is also in her own interest. . . .

[CORRESP., xxii, 18078. For Princess Stephanie *v.* No. 113. C. E. Marquis de Moustier (1779 – 1830) was plenipotentiary at Württemberg, 1813 – 20.]

## 230

## HOSTAGES

### TO GENERAL SAVARY, DUKE OF ROVIGO,
### MINISTER OF POLICE

COMPIEGNE, *September* 12, 1811.

Have the wife of the pilot Gallet, who is in the English service, arrested, and write to him saying that, unless he either returns to France, or goes to live in a neutral country under conditions guaranteeing that he is not in English pay, she and her children will be put in prison, in solitary confinement, and fed on bread and water. Apply the same measure to the wives and families of all pilots in the English service. Present me with a decree to this effect, and have an inquiry made as to the pilots who are on board enemy ships.

[LECESTRE, ii, 873.]

## 231

## JOSÉPHINE'S EXTRAVAGANCE

### TO COUNT MOLLIEN, MINISTER OF THE
### PUBLIC TREASURY

WESEL, *November* 1, 1811.

The Crown Treasury has advanced a sum of several hundred thousand francs owed by M. Pierlot to the Empress Joséphine and Queen Hortense. Please let me know when the settlement of M. Pierlot's affairs will enable this amount to be repaid to the Crown Treasury.

It would be a good plan if you would privately send for the Empress Joséphine's steward, and make him understand that not a penny will be paid him except upon proof that he has no outstanding debts. I will stand no nonsense about this. The steward's own property must be the guarantee of his good faith. You will therefore notify him that, as from January 1st next, no payment will be made to you, or to the Crown Treasury, except upon his certification, secured upon his own property, that there are no debts.

I am informed that the expenditure on the Empress's household is hopelessly extravagant. See the steward about this. Find out what the position is as regards payments in cash. It is absurd that, in place of the saving of 2 millions that the Empress was to have made, there should still be debts unpaid. You should have no difficulty in getting the steward to tell you about all this, and in making him see that he himself might be in a very awkward situation.

Arrange for a personal interview with the Empress Joséphine. Make her understand that I hope her establishment will be managed more economically, and that, if it is not, she will incur my extreme displeasure. The Empress Louise has only 100,000 crowns; she pays her bills every week: and she goes without frocks, and stints herself in various ways, rather than run into debt.

It is therefore my intention that, as from January 1st next, not a penny more shall be paid on account of the Empress Joséphine's establishment, except upon a certificate from her steward saying that there are no debts. Look into the accounts for 1811, and the estimate of expenditure for 1812. The latter ought not to exceed 1 million. If too many horses are being kept, some must be got rid of. The Empress has children and grandchildren. She ought to be saving up, so as to be able to help them, instead of running up bills.

You must not make any more payments to Queen Hortense, either under the head of 'apanage' or of 'timber', without asking me first. Have a talk with her steward too.

Tell him her establishment must be properly managed; not only must there be no debts, but also all expenditure must be carefully regulated.

[LECESTRE, ii, 891.]

## 232

## ENGLISH PRISONERS

### TO GENERAL CLARKE, DUKE OF FELTRE

SAINT-CLOUD, *November* 12, 1811.

Whilst I was crossing the river at Givet, a detachment of English prisoners was at work repairing a pontoon bridge. I noticed particularly the keenness and activity of 8 or 10 of these men, who jumped into a small boat to help get the bridge into position. Order a list to be made of the 10 men who distinguished themselves most in this affair: see that each of them is given a new suit of clothes, 5 *napoléons,* and a passport for Morlaix, where they will be referred to the Transport Office, with an account of the reason for their liberation. Inform the Minister of Marine, whom this correspondence also concerns. There must be no favouritism: preference must be given to the men who behaved best. There is also at Morlaix an English minister who came to ask my leave for a 3 months' visit to England. Let him have it. He could be put in charge of the rest. Finally I am sending you a petition sent me under similar circumstances by an English woman: send me a report on what she wants.

[CORRESP., xxiii, 18250.]

## 233

# HOME OFFICE AGENDA
## TO THE COUNT OF MONTALIVET, MINISTER FOR HOME AFFAIRS

SAINT-CLOUD, *NOVEMBER* 15, 1811.

I am going to hold a Council for Home Affairs once a week from November to February – 14 meetings in all. The first subject to be dealt with will be questions of commerce and manufactures. Then we will take the different departments of your Ministry, in order. Three meetings can be devoted to the business of Roads and Bridges, and Public Works; three, at intervals of a fortnight, will deal with the balance-sheet of the city of Paris, and of towns with revenues of over a million a year, and with the auditing of deposit companies' accounts; two, also a fortnight apart, with mineral-water works, prisons, and workhouses; one, with departmental indebtedness, and the budgeting for the 1 per cent tax, both fixed and variable; that will leave other meetings to deal with new appointments to prefectures, and mayoralties of the approved towns, with mines, libraries, public education, sciences and arts, and the other subjects that fall under your department. Please let me have a report on the allocation and order of the subjects to be dealt with at these meetings. The accounts for 1810 – 1811 will be examined, so that, if the grants allowed are inadequate, they can be supplemented wherever necessary, taking each head in turn. After dealing with the accounts of each branch of the administration, we will consider the relevant legislation, and propose whatever charges may contribute towards ultimate perfection in every department. The minutes of these council-meetings, taken as a whole, should provide both a summary of the financial position, and a statement of the grounds for the changes and improvements carried out. The upshot of all these reports will be (1) a statement of the actual expenses for 1810, (2) an approximate statement of the expenses for 1811, and (3) the budget for 1812.

[CORRESP., xxiii, 18262.]

## 234

## CASINOS

### TO COUNT MOLLIEN,
### MINISTER OF THE PUBLIC TREASURY

SAINT-CLOUD, *NOVEMBER* 20, 1811.

I want you to make certain very confidential inquiries, and to see if you can't suggest some ideas to me for regulating the management of gambling. The body that has the contract for gambling in Paris appears to possess a 'bank' of from 11 to 1,200,000 francs. After meeting all expenses, and paying over 3 or 4 millions to the police account, it makes a profit estimated at 100 – 150 per cent, i.e. a return of 2 or 3 millions on a capital of 1,200,000 francs. It is reckoned, I believe, that the bankers' gross earnings are 7 or 8 millions. It seems to me utterly absurd to allow to a concern which has made an immense fortune an annual bonus of 1,800,000 francs. There was a time when a sum of 1,200,000 francs – now an everyday affair – would have been thought worth consideration.

It would be as well, then, to find out how the machinery of this gambling concern works, and to see if it couldn't be exploited by a company, either for the benefit of the hospitals, or to provide a reserve supply of grain for the city of Paris.

There is a man named Davelouis who has gone into the whole matter: it is worth hearing what he has to say, though you needn't believe all his assertions. He can tell you who are the people involved in the business. But you must proceed secretly and tactfully, because the police are very touchy on the subject, and regard gambling as a profitable undertaking that many of the minister's agents are willing to exploit for their benefit.

[CORRESP., xxiii, 18271.]

# 235

# COURT CIRCULAR

## TO GENERAL SAVARY, DUKE OF ROVIGO,
## MINISTER OF POLICE

PARIS, *DECEMBER* 17, 1811.

The Tuscan papers give detailed accounts of what the Grand Duchess is doing; and too often the Paris papers, naturally enough, copy them. You must instruct the director of police to prevent this rubbish being printed. The less the Grand Duchess is talked about, the better. It must at any rate be something worth talking about, and care must be taken that nothing indiscreet gets into the press. I read in a recent article that some French crew shouted 'Vive Élisa! Vive l'Empéreur!' What stuff! I shall hold the director of police personally responsible if anything so unsuitable appears again. The Grand Duchess may know nothing about this: but if the articles came from her secretaries, get someone in Paris to drop her a hint that she is making herself ridiculous. Europe doesn't care a hang what the Grand Duchess is doing. Sovereigns let the papers print their doings, not because they like it, but to prevent stupid rumours. The papers are allowed to say that the Emperor went hunting yesterday, and so forth, because, if the public did not hear him talked about, they would invent all kinds of rumours. Besides, it is a matter of great interest what Sovereigns are doing; but as to what Grand Duchesses are doing – who cares?

[LECESTRE, ii, 915. The Grand Duchess of Tuscany, since 1809, was Napoleon's eldest sister, Marie-Anne (Elise). Her husband, Felice Baciocchi (*v*. No. 109) remained Prince of Lucca and Piombino.]

## 236

# BOOKS ON RUSSIA

### TO M. BARBIER, THE EMPEROR'S LIBRARIAN

PARIS, *DECEMBER* 19, 1811.

Will M. Barbier please send me, for His Majesty, a few good books – those that are best worth consulting – on the topography of Russia, and especially of Lithuania – marshes, rivers, forests, roads, etc.?

By order of the Emperor,
Méneval.

His Majesty also wishes to have the most detailed account there is in French of Charles XII's campaigns in Poland and Russia. A few works on military operations in those parts would be equally useful.

[CORRESP., xxiii, 18348. Charles XII's Russian campaign of 1708 – 9 anticipated the line of Napoleon's march on Moscow, and ended, largely owing to a hard winter, in the disaster of Poltawa.]

## 237

# ESPIONAGE

### TO M. MARET, DUKE OF BASSANO, MINISTER FOR FOREIGN AFFAIRS

PARIS, *DECEMBER* 20, 1811.

Write in cypher to Baron Bignon and tell him that, in the event of war, I intend to attach him to my Headquarters' staff, and to put him at the head of the secret police, with the duties of spying in the enemy army, translating intercepted letters and documents, collecting prisoners' reports, etc.; that it is therefore necessary that he should begin today organising an efficient service of secret police; and that he ought to secure two Poles who speak Russian well (they should be soldiers, who have seen some service, intelligent and trustworthy men, one knowing Lithuania, the other Volhynia, Podolia, and the Ukraine), and a third who speaks German and has a good knowledge of Livonia and Courland. It will be the duty of these three officers to interview prisoners. They ought to be able to speak Polish,

Russian, and German like natives. They will have under their orders a dozen carefully selected agents, who will be paid for any reports they make. They too ought to be equally competent to give information as to the country through which the army is likely to pass.

I want Baron Bignon to set to work at once on this important organisation. As a first step, the three heads of the correspondence department ought to have agents on the roads from Petersburg to Vilna, Petersburg to Riga, and Riga to Memel; on the roads to Kiev; and on the three roads which run from Bucharest to Petersburg, Moscow, and Grodno; they ought to send other agents to Riga, Dinaburg, Pinsk in the marshes, and Grodno, with instructions to give daily information as to the state of the fortifications. If the reports are satisfactory I shall not mind spending 12,000 francs a month on this. During the war rewards of various kinds will be given to those who furnish information of occasional value. There are Poles who know the fortifications well, and who can tell us, at these various places, in what condition they are.

[CORRESP., xxiii, 18350. Napoleon had determined on war with Russia some months before the presentation of the Russian ultimatum on April 27, 1812.]


# 238

# IMPERIAL PORCELAIN

## TO M. DE CHAMPAGNY, DUKE OF CADORE, INTENDANT-GENERAL OF THE CROWN

PARIS, *DECEMBER* 31, 1811.

I have just seen the set of porcelain sent to the Empress as a present for New Year's Day. It is very ugly. See that it is prettier another year. Have a breakfast set made, in which every cup has portraits of the Empress and of the six princesses – my sisters and sisters-in-law. Make another set with portraits of the Empress's ladies-in-waiting.

[CORRESP., xxiii, 18405.]

## 239

# SOUP-KITCHENS

## NOTE DICTATED AT A MINISTERIAL COUNCIL

PARIS, *MARCH* 11, 1812.

His Majesty is informed that an opportunity is given for helping the indigent classes, by the use of Rumford soup. He notices that Rumford soup requires no flour. There is an undeniable shortage of flour in France. It would be advisable to order the Prefects and local authorities to set up plenty of Rumford soup-kitchens everywhere, not merely for the free distribution, but also for the sale of soup. They ought to start first in the Paris Communes and suburbs, notably at Saint-Denis. The Ministers of Home Affairs and of Trade must see to the carrying out of these arrangements. The Home Minister will write to all the Prefects, and inform them that the Emperor has been sorry to see how, in districts where bread is very dear, and where there is a shortage of food, they have taken no steps to establish Rumford soup-kitchens under the control of contractors who could sell to the public. He must give figures showing that this soup is as cheap and as nutritious as the same amount of bread; so that, in times of poverty, it affords the people as good a means of nourishment as bread at the same price. He is to issue instructions as to the best method of building and managing soup-kitchens.

Later the soup could be sold at half-price. At Saint-Denis and in the Paris suburbs it would be best for the Prefect to have the soup-kitchens managed by contractors, and to advertise them; and in Paris the plan for selling soup could be introduced quite independently of free distribution. A workman who is pretty well off might be ashamed to accept it as charity, and yet might be very glad to buy it cheap for the benefit of his family. It is better for the general public that it should be sold than that it should be given away; for there must be a limit to free distribution, whereas in districts where corn is dear there would be plenty of scope for cheap selling.

The Government might go further, and help towards setting up the kitchens, and seeing that the soup is as good and cheap as possible.

The Emperor adds to these observations the following questions:

How can we raise 10 millions to meet the needs of the poor – that is, at the rate of 2 millions a month from April to August? The only available source seems to be the revenue of the Communes. . ..

Once money is found, how can it be best employed, so that it may not become a source of abuse, and do more harm than good? These 10 millions ought to be employed for the relief of the poor, to compensate them for the rise in the price of corn. We must therefore find out in which Departments the price is highest, and where there is most suffering, and then settle the division of the money among the Departments and the procedure for distributing it.

We had best follow the precedent set by Paris, where they have distributed 30,000 lbs of bread, and 40,000 bowls of Rumford soup. We may fairly boast nowadays that not a single inhabitant of Paris suffers from lack of food. . . .

[CORRESP., xxiii, 18568. For Rumford, *v*. No. 69.]

# 240

# PUBLIC SCHOOL SYSTEM

## TO THE DUKE OF FELTRE

SAINT-CLOUD, *APRIL* 3, 1812.

I hear all kinds of complaints about the school at Saint-Germain. They have had the bad effect of preventing rich families sending their children there. I am assured that the boys are given bad bread, and not enough to eat; that they are worked too hard, and are taught nothing, except military training. Report to me on the way this school is conducted. The bread ought to be the best obtainable, there should be plenty of food, and the education ought to be better than that at La Flèche, with a homely atmosphere, and a wide curriculum. The boys ought to learn drawing, mathematics, history, geography, and literature. This school is not fulfilling my expectations. It is meant to receive the children of the richest families in France: instead, it is driving them away. It has a thoroughly bad reputation.

[CHUQUET, ii, 574. Saint-Germain was one of the schools set up as a result of Chaptal's Report: *v*. No. 60.]

## 241

# ABDUCTING THE POPE

## TO PRINCE BORGHESE, GOVERNOR-GENERAL OF THE TRANS-ALPINE DEPARTMENTS

DRESDEN, *MAY* 21, 1812.

. . . I have just heard that there are English vessels off Savona, and I think that the Pope must be put in a safe place. You are therefore to order the Prefect and the officer in command of the *gendarmerie* to send the Pope and his people away in two good carriages. The Pope will have his doctor in the carriage with him. Precautions must be taken to see that he passes through Turin by night, that he only stops at Mont Cenis, that he goes through Chambéry and Lyon by night, and that he is taken in this way to Fontainebleau, where orders have been given for his reception. I rely in this matter upon your prudence, and that of the officer commanding the *gendarmes*. Make sure that the Pope has a good carriage, and that all proper precautions are taken. The Pope must not travel dressed as a bishop, but only as a priest, so that he may not be recognised anywhere *en route,* except at Mont Cenis. Unless something unforeseen occurs, this matter is not so urgent that you might not send for the Prefect of Montenotte, and arrange the Pope's departure with him beforehand.

Send on the enclosed letter to the Duke of Lodi. I am writing to tell him to send the Archbishop of Edessa to meet you at Turin. When he arrives there, inform him on my behalf that you have an errand for him; and as soon as you hear that the Pope is one stage on the road beyond Turin, send the Archbishop to join him. He is to get into the Pope's carriage, and to accompany him the rest of the way. Explain to this prelate that the European situation, and the presence of the English off Savona, made the Pope's residence there dangerous; that he must be placed in the centre of the Empire; that he will be received at Fontainebleau by the bishops of the deputation; that he will occupy the same rooms there as he had before; that he will see the French cardinals, etc.

You must collaborate with the Minister of Police in carrying out these measures. I wish the greatest secrecy to be observed.

[CORRESP., xxiii, 18710. Napoleon was afraid that, during his absence on

the Russian campaign, the English might try to abduct the Pope from Savona.
Pius nearly died on the journey.]

## 242

# NURSERY NEWS

### TO THE COUNTESS DE MONTESQUIOU,
### GOVERNESS OF THE CHILDREN OF FRANCE

KÖNIGSBERG, *JUNE* 16, 1812.

I have received your letter of June 6th. I can assure you of
my satisfaction at the care you take of the King. I hope to hear
from you soon that he has cut his last four teeth. I have arranged
to pay the nurse all you asked: you can inform her of this.

[CORRESP., xxiii, 18802.]

## 243

# PUTTING RUSSIA IN THE WRONG

### TO ALEXANDER, EMPEROR OF RUSSIA

VILNA, *JULY* 1, 1812.

I have received Your Majesty's letter. The war which set
our states at issue was brought to an end by the treaty of Tilsit.
I attended the conference on the Niemen resolved not to make
peace until I had secured all the advantages offered by my situation. Accordingly I refused to meet the King of Prussia there.
Your Majesty said to me, 'I will act as second in your duel with
England.' This remark altered everything: its corollary was the
treaty of Tilsit. At a later date Your Majesty desired that certain
modifications should be made in the treaty: you wished to keep
Moldavia and Wallachia, and to extend your frontier to the
Danube. You negotiated; and this important modification of the
treaty of Tilsit, with all the advantages it carried for Your
Majesty, followed from the Convention of Erfurt. Apparently,
about the middle of 1810, Your Majesty wished for fresh modifications in the treaty of Tilsit. There were two ways of arriving at this result – negotiation or war. Negotiation had succeeded at Erfurt: why did Your Majesty this time adopt a different

method? You armed on a large scale, you refused to negotiate, and you seemed disinclined to press for modifications of the treaty of Tilsit, unless surrounded by your armies. The relations established between our two powers, after so many incidents and so much bloodshed, were broken off; and war became imminent. I also armed, but 6 months after Your Majesty had done so. I have not raised a single battalion, or drawn one million out of my Treasury for war expenses, without giving notice of the fact to Your Majesty and Your Majesty's ambassadors. I have missed no opportunity of explaining my intentions. Your Majesty issued to all Europe a kind of manifesto that the powers generally do not make unless they are about to fight, and have nothing more to expect from negotiation. I made no reply. Your Majesty was the first to mobilise your armies, and to threaten my frontiers. Your Majesty was the first to start for the front. Your Majesty, after 18 months' constant refusal to explain your intentions, finally forwarded, through your minister, a demand for the evacuation of Prussia, as a previous condition of such an explanation. A few days later this minister repeated your demand three times, and asked for his passports. From that moment, Your Majesty and I were at war. . . . I realised then that the lot was cast, and that this affair, like so many others, had been decided by that invisible Providence, whose rights and overruling power I never deny. I marched on the Niemen, profoundly convinced that I had done all I could to spare mankind these fresh misfortunes, whilst satisfying my own reputation, the honour of my people, and the sanctity of treaties.

There, Sire, is an account of my conduct. Doubtless Your Majesty will have much to say; but you should remind yourself that for 18 months you refused to give any explanation of your proceedings; that you subsequently refused to assent to any agreement unless I first evacuated territory belonging to my allies; by which means you hoped to deprive Prussia of the independence you were apparently guaranteeing , whilst at the same time you reminded me of the Caudine Forks. I deplored the ill-will of those who could give Your Majesty such advice. Never before, under any circumstances, had Russia been allowed to use such language to France: it is the sort of language the Empress Catherine might have used to the last kings of Poland.

We are at war, then. God himself cannot undo what has been done. But my ears will ever be open to negotiations for peace; and as soon as Your Majesty is willing to free yourself from men who are enemies of your family, your honour, and your Empire, you will find in me the same feelings of sincere friendship as before. The day will come when Your Majesty will admit that, if you had not changed your policy at the end of 1810, and if you had loyally negotiated for modifications in the treaty of Tilsit – a course which would have involved no change, your reign would have been one of the most famous in Russian history. Following a period of reiterated and resounding disasters, Your Majesty had by wise statesmanship healed the wounds of your state, and added to your Empire such huge provinces as Finland and the delta of the Danube. I too should have gained much. The Spanish business would have ended in 1811, and England would probably have made peace at the same time. Your Majesty has shown a lack of perseverance, of trustfulness, and (if I may say so) of sincerity. You have spoilt all your prospects. . . .

If Your Majesty wishes to end hostilities, you will find me ready to do so. If Your Majesty is determined to carry on, and would like to draw up an agreement on liberal lines, such as that men in hospital shall not be regarded as prisoners (then neither side need evacuate in a hurry – always a cause of heavy losses), or such as a fortnightly exchange of prisoners, rank for rank, according to a rota of exchange, or any other stipulations that the rules of war commonly allow between civilised nations; then Your Majesty will find me ready for anything. Even if, in spite of hostilities having broken out, Your Majesty wishes to keep up direct communications with me, that also could be provided for, and regulated in the agreement.

It only remains for me to end by begging Your Majesty to believe that, in spite of my pain at the turn you have given to your policy, with its lamentable results upon our lives and those of our peoples, my private feelings towards you remain unaffected by these events, and that, if fortune once more favours my arms, you will find me as I was at Tilsit and Erfurt, full of friendliness and esteem for your good and great qualities, and anxious only to prove it.

[CORRESP., xxiv, 18878. Napoleon had crossed the Niemen on June 24, and entered Vilna on the 28th. Here he met General Balashov, the Tsar's aide-de-camp, who had been sent to discover his intentions, and to say that Alexander would not parley so long as French troops were on Russian soil. This letter was Napoleon's reply. The 'Caudine Forks': *Furculae Caudinae*, a

narrow pass on the road from Capua to Beneventum, where a Roman army
surrendered to the Samnites in 321 B.C.]

# 244

# OPENING MOVES

## TO JÉRÔME NAPOLÉON

VILNA, *JULY* 14, 1812.

The messenger you sent from Grodno yesterday at 4 p.m.
has arrived. I was looking forward to his coming with pleasur-
able anticipation, thinking you would have sent the Major-General news of Bagration's army, of the direction taken by Poniatowski in his pursuit, and of movements in Volhynia. Imagine
my astonishment on hearing that he had received nothing but a
complaint about a general! I can only express my displeasure at
the scanty information you send me. I know neither the number
of Bagration's divisions, nor their names, nor the position he
occupied, nor the particulars of your captures at Grodno, nor
what you are now doing. I have five or six columns on the move
to cut off Bagration's retreat. I assume that you cannot so far
have neglected your duty as not to have been pursuing him
since yesterday. I hope, at any rate, that Prince Poniatowski has
pursued him with the whole of the fifth corps. My operations
are held up for lack of information from Grodno. I have had no
news since the 30th. Not a word from your Chief of Staff. Not
a word from Poniatowski. It is impossible to carry on war in
this fashion. You think and talk of nothing but trifles. I am distressed to see how paltry all your interests are. If General Vandamme has been guilty of embezzlement, you were quite right
to send him to the rear; but the matter is of such minor importance at the moment that I am sorry you did not send me, by
your messenger, information which would have been useful to
me, and particulars as to your position.

I don't know why Prince Poniatowski doesn't write to the
Major-General twice a day. I told him to.

P.S. – You are compromising the whole success of the campaign on the right flank. It is impossible to carry on war in this
fashion.

[LECESTRE, ii, 932. Napoleon's opening move was designed to isolate

Bagration's army on the Russian left, and defeat it in detail: but Jerome, in command of the French right (including 35,000 Poles under Poniatowski, and some 15,000 Hessians and Westphalians under Vandamme) moved so slowly that Bagration had time to retreat, and rejoin the main Russian army.]

# 245

# SMOLENSK

## TO M. MARET, DUKE OF BASSANO,
## MINISTER FOR FOREIGN AFFAIRS

SMOLENSK, *August* 18, 1812.

I have this moment come in. The heat is intense, and there is a lot of dust, which we find rather trying. The enemy's whole army was here: it was under orders to fight, but dared not. We have captured Smolensk without the loss of a man. It is a very big town, with walls, and pretty good fortifications. We killed 3 or 4,000 of the enemy, wounded thrice as many, and found plenty of guns here. According to all accounts, a number of their divisional generals were killed. The Russian army is marching towards Moscow, in a very discouraged and discontented state. Schwarzenberg and Reynier have won a joint victory over the Russians.

*Note*: – His Majesty went to bed directly after dictating this letter, and as the messenger was starting at once, it was sent to the Duke of Bassano unsigned.

[CORRESP., xxiv, 19098. Napoleon's first attack on Smolensk (August 16) failed; a second, the following day, was successful. 'Without the loss of a man' – actually the French lost 8 – 9,000 men to the Russians' 6,000.]

# 246

# FORAGING

## TO THE PRINCE OF NEUCHÂTEL AND WAGRAM,
## MAJOR-GENERAL IN THE GRAND ARMY

GHJATSK, *September* 3, 1812.

Write to the generals in command of the army corps, and tell them that we are losing numbers of men every day, owing to the disorderly way in which foraging is conducted; that it is

a matter of urgency that they should concert measures with the
various corps commanders for ending a state of things which
threatens to be fatal to the army; that the enemy is taking several hundred prisoners a day; that the soldiers must be forbidden, under the severest penalties, to leave the line of march, and
that food must be procured in accordance with the army regulations about foraging – that is, by army corps when the whole
army is together, and by divisions when it is subdivided; that a
general or officer of high rank must be in command of the foraging, and that there must be a sufficient force to protect the
foraging parties against the peasants and Cossacks; that, so far
as possible, when foragers come across inhabitants, they are to
requisition whatever they can provide, but not to do any more
harm to the country; and finally that this matter is so important
that I count on the zeal of the generals and corps commanders
in my service to take any measures that will end the disorders
in question. You must write to the King of Naples, who is in
command of the cavalry, that it is indispensable for the cavalry
to give adequate protection to foragers, and to secure the
detachments on this duty from the attacks of Cossacks and
enemy cavalry. You will advise the Prince of Eckmühl not to
advance more than two leagues ahead of the column of march:
make him realise that this is an important safeguard against foraging too near the enemy. Finally you must inform the Duke of
Elchingen that he is losing more men a day than if a battle were
in progress; that foraging must therefore be better regulated,
and less straggling allowed.

[CORRESP., xxiv, 19176. Four days before the battle of Borodino.]


247

BORODINO

TO FRANCIS I, EMPEROR OF AUSTRIA

MOJAISK, *September* 9, 1812.

I hasten to announce to Your Imperial Majesty the happy
issue of the battle of the Moskova, which took place on September 7, at the village of Borodino. Knowing the personal
interest that Your Majesty is good enough to take in me, I
thought I ought to announce this memorable event to you by my
own hand, and to tell you that I am in good health. I reckon the

enemy's losses at 40 – 50,000 men: he had between 120 and
130,000 men engaged. I lost from 8 to 10,000 killed or wounded.
I took 60 guns, and a great number of prisoners. My advance
guard is 6 leagues beyond the battlefield. . . .

[CORRESP., xxiv, 19183. Napoleon's losses are believed to have been
28,000.]

# 248

# MOSCOW

## TO ALEXANDER I, EMPEROR OF RUSSIA

MOSCOW, *SEPTEMBER* 20, 1812.

. . . The proud and beautiful city of Moscow is no more.
Rostoptchine has had it burnt. Four hundred incendiaries were
arrested in the very act: they all declared that they set fire to the
place by order of the Governor and the Director of Police. They
have been shot. Three houses out of every four have been burnt
down: only a quarter remain. Such a deed is as useless as it is
atrocious. Was it intended to deprive us of provisions? They
were in cellars that the fire could not reach. Besides, what a trifling object for which to destroy the work of centuries, and one
of the most lovely cities in the world! It is a plan which has
been pursued ever since Smolensk, and which has reduced
600,000 families to beggary. The fire-pumps in the city had
been broken, or taken away, and some of the arms in the arsenal
given to criminals, so that we had to fire several rounds of shot at
the Kremlin to dislodge them. Humanity, as well as the interests
of Your Majesty and of this great city, required that it should be
put under my care, when it was abandoned by the Russian
army: the administrative staff, magistrates, and civil guards
should have been left behind. Such was the course followed at
Vienna on two occasions, at Berlin, and at Madrid. We did the
same when Souvarof entered Milan. Fires are an incentive to
looting, by which the soldiery hope to save something from the
flames. If I supposed such things could have been done by Your
Majesty's orders, I should not be writing this letter; but I cannot possibly believe that, with your principles, your feelings,
and your ideas of what is right, you can have authorised excesses
so unworthy of a great sovereign and a great nation. . . .

I made war on Your Majesty without any hostile feelings. A single letter from you, before or after the last battle, would have stopped my advance, and I would willingly have surrendered the advantage of occupying Moscow. If Your Majesty still retains some part of your old feelings for me, you will take this letter in good part. In any case you cannot but agree that I was right in reporting what is happening at Moscow.

[CORRESP., xxiv, 19213. 'Souvarof entered *Madrid*' in the text, but *Milan* (in June, 1799) must have been intended. There is good reason to believe that some of the fires that destroyed Moscow, if not all, were due to French and Polish soldiers looting the city.]


# 249

# RETREAT

## TO M. MARET, DUKE OF BASSANO, MINISTER FOR FOREIGN AFFAIRS

DOUBROVNA, *NOVEMBER* 18, 1812.

I haven't had a courier for 5 days. I understand that the enemy were at Minsk on the 16th. Where was Prince Schwartzenberg that day? I have no information on the point. The Duke of Belluno had still made no move on the 16th.

Since my last despatch, our position has grown worse. Almost all our horses – 30,000 of them – have perished as the result of the cold – 16 degrees of frost. We have had to burn more than 300 guns, and a huge number of ammunition wagons. The cold weather has greatly increased the number of stragglers. The Cossacks have taken advantage of our complete lack of cavalry, and almost complete lack of artillery, to harass us, and to cut our communications, so that I am anxious about Marshal Ney, who stayed behind, with 3,000 men, to blow up Smolensk. Otherwise, given a few days' rest, some good food, (above all) horses, and a supply of artillery, we shall still make good. The enemy have one thing we lack – they are accustomed to moving on ice; and in winter this gives them an immense advantage over us. A gun or an ammunition-wagon that we cannot drag out of an insignificant ravine without losing 12 or 15 horses, and 12 or 15 hours, they can haul up, by using sledges and other apparatus made for the purpose, as rapidly as though there were no ice at all.

Publish news of us in Paris. See what artillery we can procure at Kovno and Vilna, and write to Dantzig, telling them to
fit out whatever artillery-wagons and transport material may be
there, and to send them to us. See what there is at Modlin, too,
and in the forts of the Grand Duchy.

[LECESTRE, ii, 935 . This was just a month after leaving Moscow.]

250

## THE BERESINA

### TO M. MARET, DUKE OF BASSANO,
### MINISTER FOR FOREIGN AFFAIRS

ZANIVKI, RIGHT BANK OF THE BERESINA,
NEAR ZEMBINE,
*NOVEMBER* 29, 1812.

I have received your letter of November 25. You say nothing about France, and give me no news from Spain, though it is
a fortnight since I received any information, or any messages,
and I am completely in the dark.

I am marching on Vilekia. It would be as well for Wrede
and others to concentrate there, in order to make sure of the old
bridges, and to construct a new one: have the necessary tools
and materials ready.

We had a very hot action yesterday with Admiral
Tchitchakof and Wittgenstein. We beat the former, who
attacked us along the right bank on the Borisof road, and
checked the latter, who was trying to seize the bridges over the
Beresina. We took 6,000 prisoners: but we are much distressed
at the loss of a brigade 3,000 strong under General Par-
touneaux, which took the wrong road, lost its way, and has
apparently been captured. We have had no news of it for two
days. The Duke of Reggio and a number of generals have been
wounded.

The army is strong in numbers, but terribly disorganised. It
would take a fortnight to reconstitute the regiments, and where
is a fortnight to come from? The disorganisation is due to cold
and privations. We shall soon be at Vilna: shall we be able to

hold out there? Yes, if we can do so for a week; but if we are attacked during the first week, it is doubtful whether we could stay there. Food, food, food! Without it, there is no limit to the horrors this undisciplined mass of men may bring upon the town. Perhaps the army will not rally until it is behind the Niemen. Things being in this pass, I may think it necessary for France, the Empire, and even the army, that I should be in Paris. Give me your advice.

There must have been a number of messengers captured. If you haven't had news of me since the 11th, write to Paris.

I am particularly anxious that there should be no foreign agents at Vilna. The army is not for exhibition purposes at the moment. Get rid of any who are there: for instance, you might tell them that you are going, and that I am going, to Warsaw, and direct them to follow us there, naming a day for their departure.

[CORRESP., xxiv, 19362. On November 26 – 9, Napoleon crossed the Beresina by extemporised bridges (the bridge on the Borisof road having been destroyed), but at the cost of some 30,000 men, largely wounded and stragglers. On December 5 he left the remnant of his army behind, and returned post-haste to Paris, which he reached on the 18th.]

# 251

# A NEW WAY WITH THE POPE

## TO POPE PIUS VII

PARIS, *DECEMBER* 29, 1812.

Most Holy Father: I hasten to send Your Holiness an officer of my Household to express my satisfaction at what I have heard from the Bishop of Nantes as to the good state of your health; for I was very much alarmed for a moment, this summer, by the news that you were seriously indisposed. The fact that Your Holiness is now staying at Fontainebleau will give us an opportunity of meeting; and I am most anxious to assure you that, in spite of all that has happened, my personal regard for you is unchanged. Perhaps we shall arrive at the goal we so much desire, and put an end to all the issues between State and Church. For my own part, I am strongly inclined to do so, and the matter will entirely depend upon Your Holiness. In any case I beg you to believe that the feelings of high esteem and perfect consideration that I have towards you are independent both of circumstances and of events.

I pray God, Most Holy Father, that he will preserve you for many years, so that you may have the glory of re-establishing the government of the Church, and may for long enjoy and reap the benefit of your work.

[CORRESP., xxiv, 19402. Written ten days after Napoleon's return from Moscow.]

# 252

# RUSSIA: OFFICIAL

## TO FREDERICK VI, KING OF DENMARK AND NORWAY

PARIS, *JANUARY* 5, 1813.

A letter from my minister, dated December 22, informs me that Your Majesty never received my reply to the letter you wrote me, which I received at Moscow, and answered two days later. My minister has sent me a number of Russian bulletins. I must tell Your Majesty that they are entirely untrue. The enemy was consistently defeated, and never captured a single flag or a single gun. On November 7 the cold became unusually severe, and all the roads were impassable: between the 7th and the 16th, we lost 30,000 horses. Part of our baggage-train and artillery broke down, and had to be abandoned. Our soldiers, unaccustomed to protect themselves against such cold, could not endure from 18 to 27 degrees of frost. They deserted their ranks to find shelter for the night, and, as there was no cavalry left to protect them, many thousands in course of time fell into the hands of the enemy's light troops. General Sanson, who was not Chief of Staff, but head of the topographical department at Headquarters, was captured by some Cossacks as he was retiring from a position. The same thing happened to other officers, but it was when they were isolated from the army. My losses are real, but the enemy can take no credit for them. My army has suffered much, and is still suffering: the disaster will end when the cold ends.

I have raised horses from every available source, in addition to those which, thanks to Your Majesty, have just arrived from Holstein and Jutland. I shall march in the spring with an army considerably larger than the Grand Army was at the opening of the last campaign. I am giving Your Majesty these details to save you from the false reports which are being so cunningly disseminated . . . .

[CORRESP., xxiv, 19424. 'Of some 600,000 who had marched into Russia, hardly more than 100,000 came back.... According to Russian reports, after the enemy had been driven out, the various provinces buried or burnt 430,707 men and 230,677 animals. . . The numbers include both sides.' – Kircheisen, *Napoleon*, p.587.]

# 253

# MURAT

## TO JOACHIM NAPOLEON, KING OF THE TWO SICILIES

FONTAINEBLEAU, *JANUARY* 26, 1813.

I am not going to tell you how displeased I am with your conduct, which has been diametrically opposed to your duties. It is due to your weak character, as usual. You are a good soldier on the battlefield, but off it you have no energy, and no character. Take warning by an act of treachery, which I attribute to fear, and give your best wits to my service. I am counting upon you – upon your remorse and your promises of amendment. If it were not so, you would be sorry for it. I don't imagine you are one of those who think the lion is dead. If you did, you would be badly out in your reckoning. Since you left Vilna, you have done me all the harm you could – but we will say no more about that. The title of King has turned your head: if you want to keep it, behave yourself, and be careful what you say.

[BROTONNE, i, 1033. Murat, left in charge of the army when Napoleon returned to Paris, himself deserted it, and came home.]

# 254

# ECONOMY

## NOTE DICTATED TO THE GRAND
## MARSHAL OF THE PALACE

PARIS, *FEBRUARY* 23, 1813.

I intend to adopt a totally different plan as regards my

baggage-train from that which I followed in the last campaign. I wish to have a much smaller suite, a reduced kitchen staff, and less plate – the bare necessities; not merely to save trouble, but also to set a good example. Both at the front, and on the march, the meals, including my own, will consist of soup, boiled beef, a roast, and vegetables, without any dessert. In the big towns they can do as they like.

Give me a list of what I had on the last campaign, and of what is proposed for this.

I don't want to take any pages: they are no use to me; though I might perhaps take those belonging to the hunt who are over 24, and sufficiently accustomed to fatigue to be useful.

Cut down the number of canteens to the same scale: have 2 beds in place of 4, 2 tents instead of 4, and furniture to correspond.

[CORRESP., xxiv, 19608.]

# 255

# BAD OFFICERS

## TO GENERAL CLARKE, DUKE OF FELTRE,
## MINISTER OF WAR

ERFURT, APRIL 27, 1813.

I have just been inspecting the 37th Light Infantry. It would be impossible to see a finer body of men – or a worse set of officers. If your department had deliberately set itself to appoint the most incompetent officers in France, it could not have succeeded better: their men laugh at them. In point of fact they have all been drafted from the colonial battalions, the Dutch service, or the National Guard of the Pyrenees and the Scheldt; and most of the captains have never seen a shot fired. Every day makes me more discontented with the work of your committee in what is the most important part of the service-organisation. I had rather you wasted none of your time on police matters: devote it all to organising the army. I shall have to dismiss all these officers, and send them home.

You are also sending me young people straight from school, who have never been to Saint-Cyr, and consequently know nothing; and you are actually posting them to new regi-

ments. It's impossible to do things worse than this committee of
yours does. I ordered you to put a responsible general officer at
its head. I regard its work as the most important in your ministry, and you give it the least attention.

I also gave you orders, before I left, to send on to Mayence
the 88 officers from Spain; but you have done nothing of the
sort, nor have you even sent a list of them to the Prince of
Neuchâtel, the Duke of Valmy, or myself. I badly need these
officers: there is a big gap without them: it would not have been
much trouble to send me the list. I don't know where these men
were sent, or where they are now, or what they are doing.

[CORRESP., XXV, 19915. Napoleon spent the winter of 1812 – 13 reor-
ganising his forces. By the end of April he had mobilised a new army of some
225,000 men. It was mainly French, but of poorer quality than ever before.]

## 256

## PUNISHING HAMBURG

### TO THE PRINCE OF NEUCHÂTEL,
### MAJOR-GENERAL OF THE GRAND ARMY

WALDHEIM, MAY 7, 1813.

. . .The Prince of Eckmühl must move at once on Hamburg,
occupy the town, and order General Vandamme into Mecklen-
burg. Here are his instructions.

He is to arrest summarily all citizens of Hamburg who have
served as 'Senators of Hamburg.' He is to court-martial the five
chief culprits among them, and have them shot. The rest he will
send to France, under strong escort, in order that they may be
incarcerated in a state prison. He must sequestrate their property,
and declare it confiscated: their houses, landed property, and so
forth will fall into the crown domains. He is to disarm the whole
town, shoot the officers of the Hanseatic Legion, and dispatch
to France all who have enlisted in that regiment, in order that
they may be sent to the galleys. As soon as the troops arrive at
Schwerin, and without any warning, he must try to seize the
Prince and his family, and send them to France for state imprisonment; for these dukes have been traitors to the Confederation.
Their ministers will be treated in the same way. . . .

He is to draw up a list of 500 persons for proscription out

of the 32nd military division, choosing the richest and worst-behaved. He will arrest them, and sequestrate their property, which will pass into the crown domains. This step is particularly necessary at Oldenburg.

He is to impose an indemnity of 50 millions on the towns of Hamburg and Lübeck, and to take steps for the assessment and prompt payment of this sum.

Everywhere he must disarm the countryside, arrest the gendarmes, artillerymen, coastguards, officers, soldiers, and officials: all have served against us, and therefore all are traitors. Their property is to be confiscated. Above all, he must not forget the Hamburg families who have behaved badly, and who are ill-disposed. The properties must be alienated: otherwise one can never be sure of the country.

Hamburg must be put in a state of defence, the gates be provided with draw-bridges, cannon placed on the ramparts, the parapets heightened, and a citadel established on the Hamburg side, so that 4 – 5,000 men may be safe there from any attack by the people within or the enemy without. . . . All these measures are obligatory. The Governor may not modify them in any particular. He is to declare that they are enforced by my express order, and to carry them out with such prudence as time and place require. Every individual known to have taken a leading part in the revolt must be shot or sent to the galleys. . . .

[LECESTRE, ii, 1001. A Russian army under Tettenborn had entered Hamburg on March 18. On June 1 the place was retaken with Franco-Danish forces by Vandamme, under orders from Davout (the Prince of Eckmühl), and the latter carried out some of the punitive measures here described.]

# 257

# APPEAL TO AUSTRIA

## TO FRANCIS I, EMPEROR OF AUSTRIA

DRESDEN, *MAY* 17, 1813.

I am deeply touched by what Your Majesty says in your letter about your interest in me. I deserve it only for my very sincere feelings about yourself. If Your Majesty is at all concerned for my happiness, you will help me to preserve my honour. I have made up my mind to die, if need be, at the head of all honourable Frenchmen, rather than become the laughing-stock of

the English, or allow my enemies to triumph over me. Let Your
Majesty think of the future. Do not throw away the fruit of three
years' friendship, or renew the intrigues of the past, which
plunged Europe into wars and convulsions whose issue might
have no end. Do not sacrifice for meagre motives the happiness
of our generation, and of your own life; do not sacrifice the real
interest of your subjects, and (why should I not say it?) of a
member of your family who is sincerely attached to you. For
Your Majesty must never doubt my affection.

[CORRESP., XXV, 20018. Written the day before Napoleon left Dresden to
fight and win the battle of Wurschen or Bautzen on the 20th – 21st. On the
15th and 16th he had had long conversations with General Bubna, who had
stated, on behalf of Metternich, the Austrian terms for non-intervention.]


# 258

# ARMISTICE

## TO EUGÈNE NAPOLÉON, VICEROY OF ITALY

NEUMARKT, *June* 2, 1813.

I sent you a special messenger yesterday; I am sending a
second today, and I will send a third as soon as the armistice is
signed. I do not mind telling you that what has induced me to
arrest my victorious course is the arming of Austria, and the
desire to gain time for your army to encamp at Laybach, whilst
I have two armies, one camped on the Regnitz and the other at
Pirna. There is no end to the insolence of Austria. In honeyed,
almost sentimental phrases, she proposes to deprive me of Dalmatia, Istria, and perhaps even more territory, right up to the
Isonzo. She would like to break up the Bavarian frontier, recover the left bank of the Inn, and take back the part of Galicia
which she gave up by the peace of Vienna. These people are
mad, and hopelessly out in their reckoning. No court could be
more treacherous. If one were to give them what they ask now,
they would soon be wanting Italy and Germany. Assuredly they
will get nothing from me.

After the armistice is signed, I shall move my headquarters
to Glogau, and immediately afterwards take up my personal
residence near Dresden, so as to be within closer touch with my
states of Italy and France. It will then be as well to establish
messengers between Milan and Dresden viâ Verona, so that you

can communicate with me, and receive my orders as promptly as possible. I expect the armistice to last till August 1st, and I hope that early in July you will be able to encamp at Laybach with 50,000 men and 100 guns. It is necessary that you should do so, in order to influence the negotiations, if indeed (which I rather doubt) any good comes of them; certainly nothing will, unless through the threat of your army advancing on Vienna, together with the position of the Mayence army on the Regnitz and at the camp at Pirna, which I mean to reconnoitre for myself. When Austria sees these three armies ready to attack her, she will begin to realise the ridiculous folly of her demands.

[CORRESP., XXV, 20071. On June 4, after several days' negotiations, an armistice was arranged between Napoleon and the Allies, to last till July 20.]

# 259

# THANKSGIVING SERVICES

## TO PRINCE CAMBACÉRÈS
## ARCH-CHANCELLOR OF THE EMPIRE

HAYNAU, *JUNE* 7, 1813.

I disapprove of the Empress going to Nôtre Dame. Unless these great functions are rare, they become cheap. If the Empress were to attend the thanksgiving for the victory of Wurschen, she would have to do the same for every other victory. Just as it was a good move to do so for the victory of Lützen, which was unexpected, and changed our whole position, so in the present case it would be useless. It requires uncommon tact to deal with people like the Parisians.

Neither do I approve of the failure to sing the *Te Deum,* because it was Whitsun Day. I wish the *Te Deum* to be sung as a general rule on the Sunday next following the reception of the news of a victory. To postpone it is extremely inconvenient. War is full of uncertainty. It would be absurd to sing the *Te Deum* for a victory, if, meanwhile, news had come of a defeat.

[CORRESP., XXV, 20094. On May 20 – 1 Napoleon won an expensive victory at Wurschen or Bautzen.]

## 260

## PROPRIETY

### TO MARIE-LOUISE, EMPRESS QUEEN AND REGENT

HAYNAU, *June* 7, 1813.

Madame and darling; I have got the letter in which you tell me that you received the Arch-Chancellor while you were in bed. It is my intention that you shall not, under any circumstances, or on any pretext, receive anyone while you are in bed. It is improper until over the age of thirty.

[CORRESP., xxv, 20093.]

## 261

## PLAY-ACTING

### TO PRINCE CAMBACÉRÈS, ARCH-CHANCELLOR OF THE EMPIRE

BUNZLAU, *June* 8, 1813.

The Groom of the Royal Household ought to have written to Count Rémusat, asking for some actors for Dresden. I want this matter to be well advertised in Paris: it is bound to have a good effect in London and in Spain, if it makes them believe that we are amusing ourselves at Dresden. It is not a good time of year for theatre-going; so don't send more than six or seven actors at most: but they should be carefully chosen, and capable of playing six or seven pieces. Arrange for them to travel without publicity, and without causing trouble *en route*. But that is no reason why you should not have inquiries made at Paris on the assumption that the whole company is starting off; and allow plenty of gossip on the subject. The actors will be chosen either by Rémusat, or by the Comédie Française, or by Feydeau. If we can't get good actors, the whole idea had better be dropped.

[CORRESP., xxv, 20105.]

## 262

# THE PEACE-LOVER

### TO PRINCE CAMBACÉRÈS,
### ARCH-CHANCELLOR OF THE EMPIRE

DRESDEN, *JUNE* 18, 1813.

In his 'Police Notes' (which are generally most satisfactory, thanks to the details they contain, and the evidence of his zeal that they afford) the Minister of Police seems to be trying to make me out a peace-lover. This can lead to nothing; and it does me harm, because it might suggest that I am not really what he claims. I do want peace; but not a dishonourable peace, not one which will force me within three months to take up arms again. I know better than the Minister my financial situation, and the state of the Empire: there is nothing he can tell me under those heads. Make him understand the impropriety of his remarks. 1 am not given to boasting. I don't make war my business in life. No one is fonder of peace than I am. But I regard the conclusion of peace as a serious undertaking; I want it to be lasting; and I must consider the situation of my Empire as a whole. Nothing else will influence my deliberations.

[LECESTRE, ii, 1020.]

## 263

# OBITUARY

### TO COUNT BIGOT DE PRÉAMENEU,
### MINISTER OF PUBLIC WORSHIP

DRESDEN, *JULY* 17, 1813.

The Bishop of Nantes was the most enlightened priest in the Empire, and the most distinguished doctor at the Sorbonne: he bears comparison with any of those bishops who are the chief pride of the Gallican church. No one was more imbued with the true spirit of the Gospel. No one knew better how to respect the prerogatives of the crown, and to distinguish the rights of the Church from the monstrous abuses and the foolish and insane teachings of the Roman curia – teachings which are merely ridiculous nowadays, but which in the ages of ignorance

caused so much schism and bloodshed. If all bishops and the-
ologians had understood the spirit of religion as well as he did,
and had possessed as much enlightenment and good faith,
Luther, Calvin, and Henry VIII would never have been schis-
matics, and the whole world would still be Catholic. I desire
that a monument be put up to the memory of this worthy prelate
in Nantes cathedral, the cost to be defrayed by Our Imperial
Treasury.

[CORRESP., xxv, 20278. Duvoisin, the bishop of Nantes, was Marie-
Louise's confessor. Napoleon at St. Helena described him as the best and most
learned churchman he had known – the only one who might have converted
him – 'but I knew too much history for that.']

# 264

# THE END IN SPAIN

## TO GENERAL SAVARY, DUKE OF ROVIGO,
## MINISTER OF POLICE

DRESDEN, *JULY* 20, 1813.

I think I told you that I am quite determined that the King
of Spain shall not come to Paris, or anywhere near it. He must
stop at Morfontaine. If he were to come to Paris or to Saint-
Cloud, you would have to take steps to arrest him – he must be
under no illusion on this point. My intention is that he shall be
seen by no member of my household, or high official, or minister, or sectional president of the State Council or Senate. In
short, he is to preserve a complete incognito till my arrival. He
is to receive no one except his wife, Madame, his family, a few
of his Spanish friends, and Roederer; and in any case without
calling special attention to the fact. Our misfortunes in Spain, as
you will have seen from the English papers, are all the more
serious because they are absurd: that is how the English themselves look at it. They are no dishonour to the army. The army
in Spain had no general, and a supernumerary King. Ultimate-
ly (I admit) I am myself to blame. If I had sent the Duke of Dalmatia to Valladolid to take over the command there – the idea
did occur to me just as I was leaving Paris – this would never
have happened. . . .

[LECESTRE, ii, 1056. On June 21 Wellington defeated the French at Vittoria. Napoleon deprived Joseph and Jourdan of their commands, and sent
Soult (the Duke of Dalmatia) to take charge. For the sequel, cp. No. 272.]

## 265

# EMPIRE DAY

### TO THE PRINCE OF NEUCHÂTEL,
### MAJOR-GENERAL OF THE GRAND ARMY

MAYENCE, *July* 31, 1813.

Inform the Marshals, the Commanders-in-chief, the Governors of Dresden and Magdeburg, the Commandant of Würtzburg, etc., that, under the special circumstances, the Emperor's Day will be kept on August 10. To this end I order that a bonus of 20 sous be given to every N.C.O and man in the ranks. The Marshals are to take steps to have this bonus paid on the 9th. It will go towards the cost of a dinner to celebrate the day: – the troops will be allowed double rations of bread, rice, brandy, and meat.

I wish the Marshals to order each divisional general to entertain separately all the officers of his division: where a Marshal is attached to a division he will do so himself. To meet this, I am allowing, over and above the double rations, six francs a head. This sum will be paid *en bloc* to the Marshal, who will distribute it to the divisional generals.

I also wish the *Te Deum* to be sung in every camp; and in the evening there are to be grand illuminations, and a display of fireworks. In fact, I want each Marshal to do everything appropriate to celebrate a day that Frenchmen hold so dear, both to encourage the men, and to impress our allies. The allied troops will receive the same bonus as the rest.

It will look best if the officers dine in the open air, and at the same time as the men. Each toast will be followed by a salvo of 100 guns. In the allied countries invitations are to be sent to the local authorities and leading residents Even in enemy countries the authorities are to be invited, and those of the principal inhabitants whose conduct has been satisfactory. Wherever possible, the generals will give a ball.

At Dresden the Imperial Guard will give a dance for the whole town. In the evening there will be manoeuvres, and instead of blank cartridges, the troops will let off fireworks, which will be more effective. . . .

[LECESTRE, ii, 1065.]

## 266

# JUNOT

### TO GENERAL SAVARY

DRESDEN, *AUGUST* 7, 1813.

I have received your letter of August 2. It really pains me to read what you say about poor Junot. I lost my good opinion of him during the last campaign; but never my attachment to him. Now I can respect him again, for I see that his timidity was a result of illness. I approve of all you propose. See the Arch-chancellor – I am writing to him. There should be no difficulty in getting the girls into Écouen – though you don't tell me how old they are.

Speak to the Arch-chancellor about the Duchess of Istria also, and see what ought to be done to put her affairs in order. I want to help her too.

[LECESTRE, ii, 1090. Junot had been sent home in disgrace after the failure at Smolensk in August, 1812, and had gone out of his mind. The Duchess of Istria had been left a widow by the death of Marshal Bessières at Lützen on May 1.]

## 267

# JUVENILIA

### TO THE COUNTESS DE MONTESQUIOU

DRESDEN, *AUGUST* 14, 1813.

I have received your letter and the King's of the 9th. I think that the King writes poetry very well, and that it expresses sound sentiments. I rely upon the Empress to see that he is given some toys.

[X 181. The King of Rome was 2 years 5 months old.]

## 268

# CONSCRIPTION

### NOTE FOR THE MINISTER FOR WAR

DRESDEN, *September* 27, 1813.

The Minister of War will make a report to introduce the proposed *sénatus-consulte* on conscription.

He will say that we are asking for 200,000 men merely to impress Europe, and that the conscription for 1815 will not really be enforced until the following year. As regards the 120,000 men from the older classes, they are scarcely one-seventh of those still available, of whom there are more than 900,000: 120,000 are enough for the moment; but if more were needed later on, the number would have to be doubled; even so, the rest of the 900,000 who have not been called up must hold themselves in readiness to join up, if circumstances require it.

The Minister will say:

That the Emperor has given Austria no cause for complaint, as indeed is shown by the Austrian manifesto; that he refused to negotiate at Prague, because war was already determined; that the choice between peace and war did not turn upon one province more or less, but upon the powers of Europe, who, in their jealousy of France, saw and seized what they thought was a good opportunity to show their resentment; that the enemies of French renown listened to nothing but the inner voice of hatred; and that, whilst there are doubtless some sensible men amongst them who condemn the war, there are just as many who talk of nothing but the devastation of our lands.

That England, as Europe is aware, has rejected every proposal of peace, and that she will not listen to anything until she is in a position to dictate the secret terms she wishes to impose upon us, to close the mouth of the Scheldt, and to forbid our having more than 30 men-of-war. What Frenchman would purchase peace at such a price?

That Russia has shown herself an implacable foe; that she has used her influence to stop all negotiations; and that, having brought upon herself, in a war that she provoked, the misfortunes which have befallen her provinces, and having, by her own admission, kindled the fires of Moscow with her own hand, she now hopes to avenge evils which were of her own making, and to carry the incendiary's torch into the cities of the

Empire, and perhaps, if she is blind enough to conceive such a hope, to Paris itself.

That the allies never intended peace at the Congress of Prague, and that they did not risk presenting an ultimatum, because their claims were so extravagant that they dared not acknowledge them.

That the question of peace or war did not depend on the cession of the Duchy of Warsaw, or of the Illyrian provinces, or of any part of our territory, the loss of which would not be fatal to the power of our Empire, but upon the jealousy of the powers, the hatred of the secret societies, and the passions fomented by English cunning.

That, in order to defeat designs conceived by foreign jealousy and hatred, there is need of sacrifices – sacrifices of men and of money; that when a power with a population of 5 millions has put 200,000 men in the field, an empire of 60 millions should be capable of the sacrifices demanded of it; that these sacrifices are a sure means of keeping the war far from our own frontiers, of preserving the integrity of the Empire, and of making our enemies regret their rash designs; that it is the only way (why should I not say it?) in which the country can show itself worthy of a sovereign who acknowledges neither fatigue nor danger, if he can secure the welfare of his subjects, and the honour of his Empire; that it is a great opportunity, challenging the French people to display the whole range of their finest feelings; and that the Senate, the highest body in the state, will set them an example.

That no one can fail to see that the sacrifices required by such a crisis are a small matter compared to those that would be necessary, if a failure to respond now meant that in the long run we should have to provide for the needs of a war in the heart of the Empire.

That this war, which is arming almost the whole of the present generation, is the work of England; that, were this power once to renounce its implacable jealousy, it would end; and that the Emperor is ready to make any concessions, and has publicly announced his willingness to do so, in order to obtain that peace at sea, and freedom of commerce, without which France could not exist – without which, indeed, France would have to forgo her independence, and submit to any restrictions England might choose to place upon her navigation, or any commercial treaty she might care to impose; in a word, to become tributary to

England, and to work for her like the Hindus.

That, since so many enemies are united against us by passions of jealousy and hatred, every Frenchman must feel the need to resort to arms in order to defend our allies, to save our territory from war, and to give fresh proofs of his love of his Emperor, his country, and his honour.

That the subjects of the Kingdom of Italy will be no less forward than those of France, and that our enemies' designs will be overthrown by the devotion of 60 million men.

[CORRESP., xxvi, 20645.]

# 269
# FLAGS

## TO GENERAL CLARKE, DUKE OF FELTRE, MINISTER OF WAR

MAYENCE, *November* 3, 1813.

I am ordering the Major-General to send you 16 flags taken at the battles of Wachau, Leipzig, and Hanau. I enclose a letter to the Empress on this subject. My intention is that you should carry these flags through the streets of Paris, and present them to the Empress, sitting in the Throne Room, according to etiquette, in the proper place for the Regent, and surrounded by the Senate and other authorities. You will read her my letter, and add a few complimentary remarks to the effect that these flags are evidence of the courage of the French troops, and of the successes they have won in three battles. I believe that there are only 16 flags; the other 4 were lost.

When the Empress has replied to your speech, you will have the flags taken to the Invalides. On this occasion I want you also to carry about 100 flags, 6 of them English, which were captured in Spain. They are to be carried without special ceremony; but you will give orders that the 6 English flags taken at Albuera are to be ceremonially restored to the Invalides. As for the 16 flags, you must put up a marble tablet in the Invalides with this inscription: 'Flags captured at the battles of Wachau, Leipzig, and Hanau,' and add my letter to the Empress. The 40 flags I captured at the battle of Dresden were unluckily left behind in that town.

You have known for a long time what I think of these military functions; but at the present moment I fancy they will be useful. I needn't tell you that each flag must be carried by an officer on horse-back, and that the procession must be in full parade order. As I have no time to write to the Arch-chancellor, show him my letter, and arrange with him to make this ceremony as magnificent as possible.

[CORRESP., xxvi, 20854. The battle of Dresden was in August; the affair at Wachau preceded the 'Battle of the Nations' at Leipzig in October; the fighting at Hanau was during the retreat to the Rhine.]

# 270

# LOUIS AGAIN

## TO MADAME MÈRE

MAYENCE, NOVEMBER 6, 1813.

Madame, and dearest Mother; I hear by telegraph that Louis has arrived at your house. I send you a copy of his letter to me.

If he has come as a French prince, to stand by the throne, I am ready to welcome him, and to forget the past. I taught him when he was a child; I overwhelmed him with kindnesses: he has repaid me by libelling me in every Court in Europe. But I will forgive him once more; as you know, I am not accustomed to nurse grievances. If, on the other hand – and his letter makes me fear this – he has come to ask for the restoration of Holland, he will force me to the painful necessity (1) of taking proceedings against him, and (2) of doing so irretrievably; for I shall be obliged to summon him through the Arch-chancellor, and in the presence of the Vice-Grand Elector, the President of the Senate, the Grand Judge, and the Family Secretary; and if he refuses to recognise the laws of the Empire, he will find himself declared a rebel.

It is ungenerous on his part to cause me fresh embarrassment, and to oblige me to proceed against him, at a moment when I have so much on hand, and when my heart needs consolation rather than fresh causes of anxiety. Holland is French, and will remain so. It has become so by a constitutional law, and no power on earth can take it away again. So if Louis still has that bee in his bonnet, I appeal to you to spare me the pain of having to arrest him as a rebel. Get him to leave Paris. Let him go and live quietly and unostentatiously in some out-of-the-way place in Italy. He used to be in Switzerland: why did he ever leave it?

In spite of the evidence he has given me of his hatred, I can't believe he is so bad a man, and so unkind a parent, as to wish to force on me the additional unpleasantness of prosecuting him at a moment when all Europe has risen against me, and my heart is bruised by so many anxieties.

I end by repeating that, if (after all) he has come simply as a French prince to support the throne at its moment of peril, and to defend the interests of his country, his family, and his children, then I forgive his past offences, and shall not speak of them again; and I shall welcome him, in the memory, not of his conduct during the last ten years, but of the affection I had for him when he was a child.

[LECESTRE, ii, 1097. 'Telegraph' means semaphore.]


# 271

# TOWARDS TERMS

## TO GENERAL CAULAINCOURT, DUKE OF VICENZA, MINISTER FOR FOREIGN AFFAIRS

PARIS, JANUARY 4, 1814.

. . .I think it is doubtful whether the Allies are honest, or whether England desires peace. I desire peace, but it must be substantial and honourable. A France without her natural frontiers, without Ostend, and without Antwerp, would lose touch with the other states of Europe. The natural frontiers were recognised by England and all the powers at Frankfort. The French conquests up to the Rhine and the Alps do not balance all the territory that Austria, Russia, and Prussia have acquired in Poland and Finland, and that England has overrun in Asia. Austria will be influenced by English policy, and by the resentment of the Russian Emperor. I accepted the principles proposed at Frankfort; but it is unlikely that they represented the Allies' real ideas; they were only a mask. Once negotiations are allowed to be influenced by changes in the military situation, a system is admitted whose results cannot be foreseen.

You must keep your eyes and ears open. It is not certain that you will be received at Headquarters; for the Russians and English would like to exclude beforehand every opportunity of explanation or conciliation with the Emperor of Austria. You must try to find out what the Allies' views are, and give me daily reports of what you discover, so as to make it possible for me to give you instructions: at present I should not know on what to base them. Do they want to reduce France to her ancient frontiers? It would be an insult. They are vastly mistaken if they suppose the misfortunes of war reconcile us to such a peace as that. In six months' time there would not be a man in France who failed to feel the indignity of such terms, or to reproach a government which had been so cowardly as to accept them.

Italy is intact, and the Viceroy has a fine army. Before the week is out, I shall have mobilised forces enough to fight any number of battles, even without waiting for the arrival of my troops from Spain. The damage done by the Cossacks will drive the countryside to arms, and double our forces. If the nation stands by me, the enemy is marching to his destruction. If fortune betrays me, I have made up my mind what to do. I am not wedded to the throne. I will not dishonour my nation or myself by signing a shameful peace.

You must find out what Metternich wants. It is not in Austria's interest to push matters to extremes. One more step, and she will lose her leadership.

In the present state of affairs I cannot give you any orders. Confine yourself for the moment to keeping your ears open, and telling me what you hear. I am just off to the front. We shall be so near each other that your first reports will not be too late to act upon. Send me frequent messengers.

[CORRESP., xxvii, 21062. The Allies had paid no attention to Napoleon's proposals for peace during the battle of Leipzig, October 17, but on November 9, at Frankfort, on Metternich's suggestion, they offered terms which would give France her 'natural frontiers' of the Rhine, the Alps, and the Pyrenees, and leave her in possession of Savoy, Nice, and Belgium; and Napoleon after a long delay replied that he was willing to negotiate. But by that time the Allies had changed their minds, and both sides prepared for a fresh campaign. On December 1 the Allies decided to cross the Rhine, and on January 25 Napoleon left Paris to meet them in the field.]

## 272

# JOSEPH'S CHOICE

### TO KING JOSEPH

PARIS, *JANUARY* 7, 1814.

I have received your letter. It is too clever for my present situation. The point can be put in a nut-shell. France is invaded. All Europe is in arms against her, but more particularly against me. You are no longer King of Spain. But your abdication is of no use to me. I don't want the Spanish throne myself. I don't want to give it to anyone else. I will have nothing more to do with the affairs of that country, beyond keeping the peace there, and freeing my army for other ends.

What are your intentions? Will you, as a French prince, come and stand by the throne? You may then count on my friendship, and on your appanage; and you will be my subject, ranking as a prince of the blood. In that case you must do as I do; declare yourself openly, write me a short letter for publication, be at home to all my ministers, show that you are devoted to me and to the King of Rome, and favour the proposed Regency of the Empress.

Perhaps you can't do this. Perhaps you haven't enough good sense. In that case you must retire 40 leagues from Paris, to some house in the provinces, as inconspicuously as you can. If my life is spared, you will live there undisturbed. If I die, you will be arrested, perhaps put to death. You will be useless to myself, to my family, to your daughters, and to France: but you will be doing me no harm, and you will be out of my way. Choose quickly, and decide which you will do. All questions of sentiment at such a moment are idle and dangerous.

[LECESTRE, ii, 1123. After Vittoria (*v.* No. 264) Joseph fled on horseback to St. Jean de Luz. He answered this appeal, came to Paris, and was adviser to Marie Louise as Regent during the summer of 1814.]

## 273

# INVASION

### TO GENERAL CAULAINCOURT, DUKE OF
### VICENZA, THE EMPEROR'S PLENIPOTENTIARY AT THE
### CONGRESS OF CHÂTILLON

PINEY, *FEBRUARY* 2, 1814.

. . . The enemy's troops are behaving abominably. All the inhabitants are taking refuge in the woods. There are no peasantry to be found in the villages. The enemy eat up everything, seize all the horses and cattle, and all the clothes they can find, even the poor rags of the peasants; they beat everyone, women as well as men, and commit rapes galore. I have seen this state of things with my own eyes. You can readily understand how anxious I am to rescue my subjects as promptly as possible from this really horrible state of misery and suffering. It ought also to give our enemies something to think about: for the French are not a patient people; they are naturally courageous; and I soon expect to see them organising themselves for guerilla warfare. You must draw a vigorous picture of the enemy's excesses. Towns like Brienne, with 2,000 inhabitants, haven't a soul left in them!

[CORRESP., xxvii, 21168. After receiving Napoleon's letter of January 4th (*v.* No. 271) Caulaincourt wrote to the Allies complaining that no Peace Congress had been summoned to carry out the intentions expressed at Frankfort. It was then agreed that negotiations should be begun at Châtillon, where, on February 7, the Allies stated their terms, viz., that France should give up Belgium, Savoy, and Nice, and retire from the Rhine to the frontier of 1791. Meanwhile the invasion of France went on.]

## 274

# PARIS IN WAR-TIME

### TO PRINCE CAMBACÉRÈS,
### ARCH-CHANCELLOR OF THE EMPIRE

NOGENT, *FEBRUARY* 7, 1814.

I have received your letter of the 6th. I see that, instead of keeping up the Empress's spirits, you are discouraging her. Why do you lose your head so? What is the meaning of these *Miserere's*, these Forty Hours' intercessions in the Chapel

Royal? Is all Paris going mad? The Minister of Police, instead of informing himself as to the enemy's movements, talks and acts like a fool. I don't understand why he hasn't got agents all over France, to keep him properly informed, by messengers, as to what is going on. Speak to him about it. It is much more worth his attention.

[CORRESP., xxvii, 21197.]

# 275

# DESERTERS

## TO GENERAL SAVARY, DUKE OF ROVIGO, MINISTER OF POLICE

LES GRÉS, *February* 7, 1814, MORNING.

It seems necessary to take steps to prevent soldiers deserting from the army, and becoming marauders. The gendarmes, National Guards, and civil agents ought to be employed on this job. I have announced in an Army Order that every tenth deserter will be shot. The police have been useless to me in this connexion. They might have done a lot for us during the past year. Since we crossed the Rhine more than 40,000 men have deserted, and nothing has been done about it.

[BROTONNE, i, 1317.]

# 276

# COMMISSARIAT

## TO M. DAURE, QUARTERMASTER-COMMISSIONER

NOGENT, FEBRUAY 8, 1814.

The army is dying of hunger: all your reports that it is being properly fed are pure moonshine. Twelve men have been starved to death, though every place on the road has been given over to fire and sword to extract food. And yet, if I am to believe your reports, the army is being properly fed. The Duke of Belluno has no provisions; General Gérard has none; the cavalry of the Guard are dying of hunger. It's twice as bad – though there's no remedy for it  – when you hoodwink the authorities, and fancy all is well. It would have been easy enough to give every man a pound of rice at Troyes, with meat to follow. There is no way of putting a stop to the scandal, since those responsible for the business deceive themselves, as well as the Headquarters Staff. Let me have returns of the amount of rice in the different army Corps, and let me know the situation this evening; but let it be an accurate report – don't double the figures of the stock in hand. Let me know how much can be expected from the depots. If bread fails, we shall have to distribute flour to the troops.

Send General Gérard, who is acting as rear-guard, a convoy of carts loaded with hay and flour: he will be able to bake bread at Pont-sur-Seine and the neighbouring villages, and feed his troops.

[CORRESP., xxvii, 21214.]

# 277

## ATROCITIES

### TO COUNT DE MONTALIVET,
### MINISTER FOR HOME AFFAIRS

TROYES, *FEBRUARY* 16, 1814.

I could not be more displeased than I am at the feeble efforts made to rouse the patriotic feelings of the country. It cannot be done by verses and odes: it needs facts – plain and true details. It's a perfectly simple matter. I don't mean articles written in Paris, or anything to deceive the public; but merely that everyone should be able to read what the enemy is doing. Such articles are as effective at Amiens, or Lille, or Arras, or anywhere in the Empire, as they are in Paris. The Minister of Public Worship ought to be asking for letters from the Bishops, Canons, and parish clergy; the Home Minister, from the Prefects and Mayors; the Finance Minister, from those of his Staff who have remained at their posts during the foreign Occupation; the Postmaster-general, from his directors and postmasters; the Lord Chief Justice, from Emperor's Counsel, Judges, J.P.'s, notaries public, and so on. They should be asked what they have seen and heard. We don't want any fanciful pictures; these letters should be printed just as they come in. Towns occupied by the enemy ought to send deputations to Paris to describe what they have seen and heard, and what has happened in their own locality; and reporters must be present to take down what they say. Usually full names should be given. The total effect of all these narratives will be to produce anger and indignation; and then each individual will feel himself bound to take steps to defend himself, rather than see his wife or his daughter violated, or find himself beaten, robbed, looted, and heaped with every sort of outrage. But my orders are no longer obeyed. You are all cleverer than I am. You are for ever opposing me, with your 'buts', and 'ifs,' and 'fors.' And so the time for action has almost gone by: these articles ought to have been published at the very moment the things happened. We ought to give all the names indiscriminately. We ought to specify the Prince of Württemberg, if he has behaved badly. They should all be unmasked. Even royal remarks should be quoted. I can't write to all my ministers; have this letter circulated among them. But for the timidity of ministers, who are always afraid of calling attention to the administration, the whole of France would by this time be under arms. They ought to collect quantities of letters every day – letters from every part of France, letters written by middle-class citizens, landed gentry, and men of business: they ought to have them printed, names and all, and let the public know everything.

[CORRESP., xxvii, 21375.]

# 278

# FORLORN HOPE

## TO JOSEPH

NANGIS, *FEBRUARY* 18, 1814.

The Prince of Schwartzemberg has at last given signs of life; he has just sent an envoy asking for a suspension of arms. Could anything be more cowardly! Time after time he has refused, in most insulting terms, to grant any kind of armistice or suspension of arms, Or even to receive my envoys – after the capitulation of Dantzig, for instance, and of Dresden; an outrage almost unparalleled in history. And now, at the first setback, these wretches fall on their knees! Luckily the Prince of Schwartzemberg's officer was refused admission. I have only received his letter, which I shall answer at my leisure. I shall never grant an armistice until they have cleared out of my territory.

Judging from what I hear, the Allies' position is entirely altered. A few days ago the Emperor of Russia broke off negotiations, because he wished to impose on France worse conditions than the old frontiers. Now he wants to reopen them; and I have hopes that I shall soon secure a peace on the lines of the Frankfort proposals – the minimum that I can honourably accept. Before the beginning of my campaign, *I offered to sign terms on the basis of the old frontiers, provided that the Allies held up their advance at once.* This proposal was made by the Duke of Vicenza on the 8th. They replied in the negative, saying that they would not stop hostilities at the signing of the preliminaries, but only when all the articles of peace were signed. They have been punished for this incredible answer; and yesterday, the 17th, they themselves demanded an armistice!

As you can imagine, when I saw myself on the eve of a battle, in which I had made up. my mind to conquer or to perish, and in which retreat would have meant the capture of my capital, I was ready to consent to anything to avoid so great a risk. It was only right to sacrifice my pride to my family and to my people. But now that the Allies have refused this, now that the opportunity for a decisive battle has passed, and everything turns once more upon ordinary warfare, in which Paris is no longer threatened, and in which the conditions are all in my favour, it is due to the interests of the Empire and to my own prestige to negotiate for a genuine peace. If I had signed on the basis of the old frontiers, I should have gone to war again within 2 years, and should have told the nation that it was not a peace that I had signed, but a capitulation. I couldn't say that, as things are now; for fortune has turned again in my favour, and I can dictate my own terms. The enemy is in a very different position to what he was at the time of the Frankfort proposals: it is pretty certain that he will get very few of his men back across the frontiers. His cavalry is thoroughly exhausted and discouraged; his infantry is tired of marching and counter-marching: in a word, he is utterly disheartened. I hope, therefore, to be able to make such a peace as any reasonable man could wish; *and the Frankfort proposals are the limit of my desires.*

Give it out that the enemy is in difficulties, and has asked for an armistice, or a suspension of arms; and that this is absurd, because it would deprive me of the advantages my manoeuvres have won. Add that this only shows how completely the enemy is demoralised. Don't print this, but see that everyone talks about it.

[JOSEPH, x, 133. The negotiations at Châtillon (*v.* No. 273) were resumed on February 18. When both sides were at the point of agreeing to the 'limits of 1791,' a temporary success of Napoleon at Montereau, and the Allies' request for an armistice, led him to stand out for the 'natural frontiers.']

# 279

# PUBLICITY

## TO M. DE CHAMPAGNY, DUKE OF CADORE

SURVILLE, *FEBRUARY* 19, 1814.

The Empress has sent me a very interesting portrait of the King of Rome in Polish costume, saying his prayers. If only he were wearing the uniform of the National Guard, I should like to have the picture engraved, under the title, 'I pray to God for my father and for France.' We might have another edition printed in Polish dress. If this little engraving could be produced within 48 hours, and put on sale, it would have an excellent effect. . .

[BROTONNE, ii, 2264.]

# 280

# NAPOLEON OF NAVARRE

## TO MARSHAL AUGEREAU, DUKE OF CASTIGLIONE, IN COMMAND OF THE ARMY AT LYON

NOGENT, *FEBRUARY* 21, 1814.

The Minister of War has shown me the letter you wrote to him on the 16th. It has pained me bitterly. What! You were not yet on the march, six hours after receiving the first troops from Spain! Six hours' rest was plenty for them. I won the fight at Nangis with a brigade of dragoons from Spain which had not unsaddled since it left Bayonne. The six battalions of the Nîmes division, you say, are short of uniforms and equipment, and are untrained: that is a poor reason for Augereau to give! I have annihilated 80,000 of the enemy with conscript battalions which had no cartridge-pouches, and uniforms in rags! The National Guardsmen, you say, are pitiable. I have 4,000 here, from Angers and Brittany, with civilian hats, no cartridge-pouches, and wooden shoes; but they have good muskets, and I have drafted a fair proportion into the army. You go on to say that you have no money: and where, pray, do you expect to get any? You can't have any, until we have recaptured our own receipts from the enemy. You are short of transport-animals? Commandeer them from any source you like. You have no food-depots? That is really too ridiculous. I order you to start within 12 hours of the receipt of this letter, so as to take part in the campaign. If you are still Augereau of Castiglione, you may keep the command: if your 60 years lie heavy on you, give it up, and hand it over to your senior General Officer. The country is threatened, and in danger. It can be saved – but only by daring and devotion, not by idle temporising. You must have got a nucleus of over 6,000 picked troops. That is more than I have; yet I have destroyed 3 armies, taken 40,000 prisoners, captured 200 guns, and thrice saved Paris. The enemy is in flight all round me towards Troyes. Be the first on the field. It is no question, now, of the kind of conduct which has served during the last few years: you will want your old boots, and the resolution that carried you to victory in '93. When Frenchmen see your plume leading the line, and yourself the first to face musket-fire, you will be able to do with them what you will! . . .

[CORRESP., xxvii, 21343. For a discussion of Augereau's exploits at Castiglione (July 30 – August 5, 1796) v. Rose, *Life of Napoleon*, I, 108 f.]


# 281

# APPEAL TO AUSTRIA

## TO FRANCIS I, EMPEROR OF AUSTRIA

HEADQUARTERS, NOGENT-SUR-SEINE, *FEBRUARY* 21, 1814.
I did all I could to avoid the battle which has taken place. Fortune favoured me: I destroyed the Russo-Prussian army under General Blücher, and subsequently the Prussian army under General Kleist. The present state of things, whatever preconceived ideas your Headquarters may have about it, is this: – my army has more infantry, cavalry, and artillery than your

Majesty's; and if the certainty of this fact were necessary to make up Your Majesty's mind I should have no difficulty in demonstrating it to any man of sound judgment, such as Prince Schwarzenberg, Count Bubna, or Prince Metternich. I think it my duty to write to Your Majesty, because this struggle between a French army and one that is predominantly Austrian seems to me as contrary to your interests as it is to mine. If fortune betrays my hopes, Your Majesty's position will be even more embarrassing. If I defeat your army, how will you retreat from France, whose population is exasperated to excess by the crimes of all kinds committed by the Cossacks and Russians?

Things being so, I propose to Your Majesty that peace should be signed, without delay, upon the principles laid down by yourself at Frankfort, and adopted by myself and the French people as the utmost we can concede. I will go further, and say that these principles alone can re-establish the equilibrium of Europe. If any other conditions could have been imposed upon France, peace would not have lasted long.

The Allied plenipotentiaries at Châtillon presented a note whose contents, were they known in France, would excite a fever of indignation. It was the realisation of Burke's dream, who wished to erase France from the map of Europe. There is not a Frenchman alive who would not rather die than submit to terms that would make us slaves of England, and strike France off the list of the powers. Such terms can be no part of Your Majesty's intentions: certainly they are not in the interests of your monarchy. England may wish to destroy Antwerp, and to place a permanent obstacle in the way of any restoration of the French navy. But you, Sire – what interest have you in the anni-hilation of the French navy? By the principles laid down at Frankfort, Your Majesty also becomes a maritime power. Do you wish your flag to be violated and outraged by England, as has constantly happened before? What could Your Majesty stand to gain by putting the Belgians under the yoke of a Protes-tant prince, whose son is destined to mount the English throne?

In any case such hopes and designs are beyond the powers of the coalition. Even were I to lose the forthcoming battle against Your Majesty's troops, I have the means to fight two more before you are at Paris; and were Paris taken, the rest of France would never support the yoke prepared for her in a treaty dictated, apparently, by English politicians. The nation's death-agony would double its energy and power.

I will never give up Antwerp and Belgium. A peace on the lines of Frankfort can be honestly enforced, and will enable France to turn all her attention to rebuilding her fleet, and re-establishing her commerce. Nothing else can. If Your Majesty persists in sacrificing your own interests to the selfish policy of England, or the resentment of Russia; if you will not lay down arms except upon the frightful conditions proposed at the Congress; then Providence and the genius of France will be on our side.

The Emperor Alexander has no reason for thirsting for revenge. Before I entered Moscow, I offered to make peace; at Moscow I did all I could to extinguish a conflagration that his own orders had kindled.

Finally, there are 200,000 men under arms in Paris; they have learnt from Russian deeds the value of Russian promises, and they know the fate that is in store for them.

I beg Your Majesty to avoid the hazard of a battle. I beg you to make peace – to make it at once, and to base it on the proclamation published by Prince Schwarzenberg, the declaration of the Allied Powers dated December 1st, and inserted in the *Journal de Francfort,* and the terms offered by Prince Metternich, Count Nesselrode, and Lord Aberdeen to Baron Saint-Aignan – terms which I accepted then and accept still, though the Allies' position is very different from what it was, and though, impartially considered, the chances are now on my side.

May I be allowed to say that, in spite of all that Your Majesty has done against me since the invasion of my territory, and in spite of your forgetfulness of the ties that unite us, and of the relations of common interest that should subsist between our states, I preserve the same feeling towards you, and cannot view with indifference the personal unhappiness and the international disasters which would ensue, were you to refuse these overtures; whereas by a single word you could stop the whole war, end the whole quarrel, and restore to the world, especially the world of Europe, a durable peace? Had I been coward enough to accept the terms proposed by the Russian and English ministers, Your Majesty should have dissuaded me; for you knew that no peace can be durable which dishonours and degrades 30 million men.

One word from Your Majesty would end the war, secure the happiness of Austria and of Europe, safeguard you against the fickleness of fortune, and put an end to the miseries of a people which is the victim of no ordinary ills, but of the crimes of desert Tartars, scarcely deserving the name of men.

Your Majesty will hardly ask why I address myself to you. I cannot turn to the English, whose aim is the destruction of my navy, nor to the Emperor Alexander, whose only feelings about me are those of vengeance and passion. I can only address myself to Your Majesty – you, who were once my ally, who, both for the size of your army and for the grandeur of your Empire, are considered the predominant power in the Coalition, and who, after all, whatever the sentiments of the moment, have French blood in your veins.

[CORRESP., xxvii, 21344. For the circumstances cf. No. 278. Napoleon takes advantage of the Allies' discouragement to press Austria to make a separate peace. On the 27th the Emperor refused to do so.]

# 282

# SOVEREIGNTY

## TO JOSEPH

REIMS, *MARCH* 14, 1814.

I have received your letter of March 12. I am sorry you told the Duke of Conegliano what I wrote to you. I don't like all this tittle-tattle. If it were part of my plan to put the Duke elsewhere, all the prattlers in Paris would not prevent my doing so. The National Guard in Paris is part of the French people, and I will be master *everywhere* in France, as long as I have a breath in my body. Your character is quite different from mine. You like flattering people, and falling in with their ideas: I like people to please me, and to fall in with mine. I am master today, every bit as much as at Austerlitz. Don't let anyone flatter the National Guard. Refuse to allow Regnaud, or anyone else, to become its advocate. I suppose they *do* admit that there is a difference between the times of Lafayette, when the people was sovereign, and the present moment, when I am? I have decreed that 12 battalions of the mass levy are to be raised in Paris. This measure must not be held up on any pretext whatsoever. I am writing to the Ministers of Home Affairs and Police to the same effect. If the people once see us doing what they like, instead of what is good for them, they will obviously imagine that they are the sovereign, and will have a very poor opinion of those who govern them.

[JOSEPH, x, 198. General Moncey (the Duke of Conegliano) commanded the National Guard in the defence of Paris against the Allies on March 29 – 30.]

# 283

# EXILE

## TO GENERAL COUNT DALESME,
## COMMANDANT OF THE ISLAND OF ELBA

FRÉJUS, *APRIL* 27, 1814.

Circumstances having led me to renounce the French throne, sacrificing my rights to the welfare and interests of my country, I have reserved for myself the sovereignty and proprietorship of the island of Elba, with the fortresses of Porto-Ferrajo and Porto-Longone; and the powers have agreed to this arrangement. I am therefore sending General Drouot, so that you may make over the island to him without delay, with its stores of food and ammunition, and all the properties belonging to my Imperial Domain. Announce this new order of things to the inhabitants, and tell them that I have chosen the island for my residence because I know the kindness of their character and the excellence of their climate. They will always be an object of liveliest interest to me.

[CORRESP., xxvii, 21563. By the treaty concluded at Fontainebleau on April 11, Napoleon was given the island of Elba during his lifetime as sovereign principality. He left Paris on the 20th, and reached Elba on May 3.]

# 284

# ELBAN NAVY

## (1) NOTE FOR GENERAL DROUOT

ELBA, *MAY* 28, 1814.

The fleet must be organised on the lines I laid down. No dining allowances will be given. The brig 'Inconstant' will have the same crew as the schooner. M. Taillade will be in command of this vessel, but without any increase of pay.

The 18 marines of My Guard who are here will be counted on the strength of the Navy. As we no longer have the 'Light Woman,' M. Rich will be put in command of one of the feluccas belonging to the mine. The command of the other will be given to M. Carnavali, the chief coxswain. He will therefore be included on the strength, filling one of the posts already created. Representations must be made as to the forwarding of the mine vessels here as soon as possible. Their crews can continue to serve them. I need these two vessels at once. They will be named the 'Fly' and the 'Bee.'

## (2) TO GRAND MARSHAL BERTRAND

ELBA, *JUNE* 14, 1814.

The naval Budget should include a heading for 'Upkeep of vessels.' The provisional grant under this head will be 600 francs, assigned as follows: –

| | |
|---|---|
| For a copper compass for My cutter | 50 francs |
| For cushions, tapestry, curtains, etc. | 450 francs |
| For greasing the 'Caroline,' painting the cutters, and other necessary expenses. . | 100 francs |

Give orders that My cutter has all the necessary work done on it before the end of the week.

## (3) TO GENERAL DROUOT

LONGONE, *SEPTEMBER* 9, 1814.

Give orders that when the sailors of My Guard go on board

My cutters, they are always to take with them their sabres, muskets, and two clips of cartridges in their cartridge-cases. Racks must be fitted in the cutters to hold these weapons.

[PÉLISSIER, pp. 1, 9, 110.]

## 285

# ELBAN BUDGET

### TO GRAND MARSHAL BERTRAND

ELBA, *OCTOBER* 15, 1814.

I have received your report on Supplementary Expenditure for the month of September.

*Gardens.* Reprimand the gardener for employing three men all the month on a garden the size of my hand, and 11 grenadiers for loading up a few cartfuls of earth. I disapprove of the proposed expenditure on turf during October: I would rather have grass seed. The gardener must bargain with the grenadiers to load earth at so much a cubic metre, and use just enough carts to keep them constantly employed. I don't think this ought to cost more than 80 francs. Similarly the O.C. Engineers must bargain with the grenadiers for the excavation of the gardens. I estimate the cost at 400 francs. I therefore allow 480 francs for the Supplementary Estimates for the gardens during October.

*Stables.* I can't allow more than 600 francs a month. It's impossible to do things on the same scale in this country as in Paris. Chauvin and the deputy-chamberlain must agree, and arrange matters accordingly. They can have the shoeing done on account, and it certainly won't cost more than 200 francs a month. They can treat the other expenses in the same way, provided they keep within the limit of 600 francs. I can't give more than 150 francs for the side-saddle.

*Stores.* This account is in a great muddle. The ordinary expenditure should suffice for a watchman (whom I don't see put down), 2 or 3 women in permanent employment, and a valet who can also do upholstering. I should like this last, if possible, to be the man who came with Madame. Conti, who supplied the furniture, ought not to be employed any more in the Stores. Have a separate account made for all the items under the head of 'carriage of Princess Pauline's things'. I refuse to pay the 280 francs demanded by the Stores department for petty cash. I can only allow 40 francs. Have an estimate made out for the ordinary expenditure of the Stores during October, as well as one for Supplementary Expenditure. As Saint-Martin and the Princess's apartment are being furnished, the Supplementary Estimates for October are likely to be higher than in other months: my provisional estimate is 800 francs. Make out a list of the proper charges for carriage from the fleet at Longone to the citadel at Merciana and to La Madone, and from the fleet to the palace of Porto-Ferrajo. The Stores department will conform to this tariff; but it must be strictly forbidden to employ the carrier for any transport work that can be done by our own vehicles.

[PÉLUSSIER, p. 159.]

# 286

# THE LAST OF ELBA

## TO GENERAL COUNT BERTRAND,
## GRAND MARSHAL OF THE PALACE

PARIS, *MARCH* 23, 1815.

Send Bernotti post-haste to the Isle of Elba. Entrust him with news for the island. He must sail from Toulon. Write to Lapi telling him to run up the tricolour.

Recover from Elba any of my things that are worth sending. I am anxious to have my Corsican horse, if it is not ill, and can be sent back. The canary travelling-carriage, the big carriage, and two of the state coaches, are worth the trouble of returning, as well as my underwear. I am presenting my library to the town, along with my house: the house will do for a casino, but the library must be left in it.

[CORRESP., xxviii, 21696. Napoleon left Elba on February 26, landed in France on March 1, and reached Paris on the 20th. Lapi was a native of Elba whom he appointed Governor of the island in his absence.]

# 287

## PAPER WAR
### TO GENERAL CAULAINCOURT, DUKE OF
### VICENZA, MINISTER FOR FOREIGN AFFAIRS

PARIS, *MARCH* 28, 1815.

I want you to instruct Bignon to write a history of the Congress of Vienna. One could print in an Appendix all the documents, with appropriate extracts from Talleyrand's despatches. Such a work would be useful, as showing foreign greed and injustice. But until it is written we can't really tell whether it is suitable for publication.

I also think it very important to have a history written of all the treaties during my reign, such as those of Campoformio, Lunéville, Amiens, Pressburg, Tilsit, and Vienna, as well as the whole Bayonne affair, with the original documents, my letters, and the sovereigns' replies. This work seems to me to be of essential importance for the history of the nation, and for its glory and mine, since these events need to be presented in their proper light. . . .

Find me a competent man, who could be entrusted with this work.

It is necessary that you should send daily articles to the *Moniteur*, dated from different countries, to let people know what is happening; for instance, the dispute between Sweden and Denmark over Pomerania; the differences between Saxony, Bavaria, and the Prince of Orange, who refuses to give up his family estates in Germany; and so on. Public curiosity can thus be fed upon articles edited from a proper point of view, so as to bring to light the greediness of the powers.

[CORRESP., xxviii, 21739.]

# 288

## DA CAPO

### TO JOACHIM NAPOLÉON, KING OF NAPLES

PARIS, *MARCH* 29, 1815.

. . .It is my sincere desire, as you can imagine, to keep the peace, especially as Your Majesty's future depends upon it. But if we were forced to take up arms again, I should reckon myself perfectly ready from that moment to face whatever may happen; for the unanimity with which Frenchmen are gathering round me convinces me that the whole nation is prepared to give me its energetic support. France is ready to make any sacrifice in order to reject once for all the hateful and degrading regime from which it has just been delivered; and all parties agree in desiring a government which can give them powerful protection. I can thus face the future without alarm. My confidence is increased by Your Majesty's support. If your attachment to me has not changed, it will be a pleasure to me to give you fresh proofs that you can always count on my friendship.

[BROTONNE, i, 1379. In May, 1814, after unsuccessful hostilities against the Austrians in S. Italy, Murat had fled to Corsica. In 1815 he tried to regain Naples, but was captured and shot (October 13).]

## 289

## CIRCULAR LETTER

### TO THE SOVEREIGNS OF EUROPE

PARIS, *APRIL* 4, 1815.

Monsieur, my Brother,

You will have learnt, during the course of the last month, of my landing again in France, of my entry into Paris, and of the departure of the Bourbon family. Your Majesty must by now be aware of the real nature of these events. They are the work of an irresistible power, of the unanimous will of a great nation conscious of its duties and of its rights. A dynasty forcibly reimposed upon the French people was no longer suitable for it: the Bourbons refused to associate themselves with the national feelings or the national customs; and France was forced to abandon them. The popular voice called for a liberator. The expectation which had decided me to make the supreme sacrifice was in vain. I returned; and from the place where my foot first touched the shore I was carried by the affection of my subjects into the bosom of my capital.

My first and heartfelt anxiety is to repay so much affection by the maintenance of an honourable peace. The re-establishment of the Imperial throne was necessary for the happiness of Frenchmen: my dearest hope is that it may also secure repose for the whole of Europe. Each national flag in turn has had its gleam of glory: often enough, by some turn of fortune, great victories have been followed by great defeats. Today a finer arena offers itself to the sovereigns of Europe, and I am the first to descend into it. I have provided the world in the past with a programme of great contests: it will please me better in future to acknowledge no rivalry but that of the advocates of peace, and no combat but a crusade for the felicity of mankind. It is France's pleasure to make a frank avowal of this noble ideal. Jealous of her independence, she will always base her policy upon an unqualified respect for the independence of other peoples.

If Your Majesty's personal sentiments – as I confidently trust – are the same, there is assurance of a widespread and long continued repose; and justice, seated on the confines of the various states, will be competent to guard their frontiers. I eagerly embrace this opportunity to repeat the sentiments of sincere esteem and perfect friendship with which I remain,

*Monsieur* my Brother,
Your good Brother,
NAPOLÉON.

[CORRESP., xxviii, 21769.]

# 290

# AFTER WATERLOO

## TO KING JOSEPH

PHILIPPEVILLE, *JUNE* 19, 1815.

. . . All is not lost. I suppose that, when I reassemble my forces, I shall have 150,000 men. The *fédérés* and national guards (such as are fit to fight) will provide 100,000 men, and the regimental depots another 50,000. I shall thus have 300,000 soldiers ready at once to bring against the enemy. I will use carriage-horses to drag the guns; raise 100,000 men by conscription; arm them with muskets taken from royalists, and from national guards unfit for service; organise a mass levy in Dauphiné, the Lyon district, Burgundy, Lorraine, Champagne; and overwhelm the foe. But people must help me, and not deafen me with advice. I am just off to Laon. I am sure to find somebody there. I have heard nothing of Grouchy. If he has not been captured, as I rather fear, that will give me 50,000 men within 3 days – plenty to keep the enemy occupied, and to give Paris and France time to do their duty. The Austrians are slow marchers: the Prussians are afraid of the peasantry, and dare not advance too far. There is still time to retrieve the situation. Write and tell me how the Chamber has been affected by this disastrous skirmish. I trust the deputies will realise that it is their duty at this crisis to stand by me, and to help me to save France. Prepare them to give me worthy support. Above all, steadfastness and courage!

[LECESTRE, ii, 1225. Written during the retreat, the day after Waterloo. Napoleon reached Paris on the 21st.]

# 291

# THE NEXT PHASE?

## TO M. BARBIER, THE EMPEROR'S LIBRARIAN

PARIS, *JUNE* 25, 1815.

The Grand Marshal begs M. Barbier to be so good as to bring to La Malmaison tomorrow:

(1) The list of 10,000 books and engravings, such as those of Denon's travels and the Egyptian Commission, of which the Emperor had several thousand copies;

(2) Some works on America;

(3) A detailed bibliography of everything that has been printed about the Emperor during his various campaigns.

The Emperor's travelling library must be brought up to date. It ought to include the books carried on each campaign, and to be supplemented by a number of works on the United States.

The Grand Library must contain a complete set of the *Moniteur,* the best encyclopaedia there is, and the best dictionaries.

This library should be consigned to some American house, which will forward it viâ Havre to America.

[CORRESP., xxviii, 22064. Two fast frigates were at Rochefort, ready to take Napoleon to America. On the 29th he left Paris, and was at Rochefort on July 3. But instead of accompanying Joseph, who reached America, he waited till the 15th, and then rowed out to the *Bellerophon*, and 'put himself under the protection of British law.']


# 292

# THEMISTOCLES

## TO THE PRINCE REGENT OF ENGLAND

ILE D'AIX, *JULY* 14, 1815.

Your Royal Highness: victimised by the factions which divide my country, and by the hostility of the European powers, I have ended my political career; and I come, as Themistocles did, to claim a seat by the hearth of the British people. I put myself under the protection of British law – a protection which I claim from Your Royal Highness, as the strongest, the stubbornest, and the most generous of my foes.

NAPOLÉON.

[CORRESP., xxviii, 22066. Themistocles, ostracised from Athens in 472 B.C., and pursued from Corcyra to Epirus, obtained the protection of Admetus, King of the Molossians.]

# INDEX

Other books in this series are listed below. Copies should be available from your local bookshop but in the case of difficulty can be purchased direct from the publisher.

Prion Books Limited, Unit L, 32-34 Gordon House Road, London NW5 ILP

**The Atrocities of the Pirates**
by Aaron Smith                          £8.99 ........copies
**The Marquis of Montrose**
by John Buchan                          £8.99.........copies
**Napoleon and his Marshals**
by A.G. Macdonell                       £8.99.........copies
**The River War**
by Winston S. Churchill                 £9.99..........copies
**Napoleon's Letters**
by J.M.Thompson                         £10.00........copies
**Disraeli**
by Robert Blake                         £16.00........copies


Payments can be made by cheque or postal order (payable to Prion Books Limited).

Unfortunately we cannot accept credit cards.

Do not send cash or currency. UK customers and B.F.P.O. please allow £1.00 for postage and packing for the first book, plus 50p for each additional book.

Overseas customers including Ireland, please allow £2.00 for the first book plus £1.00 for the second book. **Orders for three or more books placed at the same time are supplied post free**.

NAME (Block Letters)

ADDRESS



I enclose my remittance for £